ADDICTED
TO DANGER

ADDICTED TO DANGER

— A Memoir —

Jim Wickwire and Dorothy Bullitt

POCKET BOOKS

New York   London   Toronto   Sydney   Tokyo   Singapore

POCKET BOOKS, a division of Simon & Schuster Inc.
1230 Avenue of the Americas, New York, NY 10020

Chapter 8, "Uemura," is a revised and expanded version of
"Unforgettable Naomi Uemura," which appeared in *Reader's Digest*
(Japanese Edition, August 1985).

ISBN: 0-671-01990-2

First Pocket Books hardcover printing June 1998

10 9 8 7 6 5 4 3 2 1

POCKET and colophon are registered trademarks of Simon & Schuster Inc.

Printed in the U.S.A.

Endpapers: K2 viewed from Concordia, the meeting place of several glaciers.

To Mary Lou
and
Anne, Cathy, Susie, Bob, and David

A man who has been in danger,
when he comes out of it forgets his fears,
and sometimes forgets his promises.

— *Euripides*

CONTENTS

INTRODUCTION

Over the years many have encouraged me to write my memoirs. Since my twenties I have kept extensive, detailed diaries, not only about climbing but my professional and family life as well. Although they provided a rich source of raw material, I'd always known their transformation into publishable form would be a demanding task. I was deterred by a busy law practice and concerned that, if I did write a memoir, it would be just another climbing book.

Two things combined to change my mind—the passage of time and the intervention of a friend. At fifty-six, I at last felt ready to look back on my life with a degree of detachment. I was prepared to discuss the tragedies I had experienced, my successes and failures, and how I had changed as a result. When my friend Dorothy Bullitt offered to help me tell my story, I realized the right collaborator was just what I had been missing.

Dorothy knows me well, I trust her, and her drive and intensity resemble my own. As a nonclimber (but the daughter of one), she naturally focused on those aspects of my diaries most likely to interest the general audience I hoped to reach. What I did not understand or expect was how thoroughly she would force me to analyze my motivations and reflect upon my choices. She insisted I deal with issues I had never before faced, let alone published. At times, I resisted and lashed out. There were times when I awoke in the middle of the night, seriously tempted to abandon the project.

Yet I realized, for this book to be more than a simple account of my adventures, I had to be prepared to examine my weaknesses as well as my strengths; the costs I imposed as well as the costs I incurred. I needed to understand why I made certain choices, and what values and beliefs lay behind my actions. In many ways, writing about my life proved as challenging as climbing any mountain.

The title, *Addicted to Danger,* came to me early in this process. As I recalled my repeated promises to stop climbing and my inability to follow through—despite small children at home and the deaths of several companions—I recognized that I climbed not only for the solitude, beauty, physical exertion, or bonds of friendship I found in the mountains, but also because of an attraction to danger. This has been a sobering insight. I selected the title not to explain why others climb, but to cast light on my own motivation.

Although I have enjoyed a generally stable, satisfying family life and legal career, I believe it has been my response to tragedy and failure—both in and out of the mountains—that has shaped the man I've become and defined what I most care about. In writing this book, I revisited many difficult experiences. As I reviewed my voluminous diaries, sorted through photographs, and discussed what had occurred and why, I took stock of my conduct. Whenever I concluded I had been selfish or unfair, I attempted to reach out, make amends, or talk things over. This book generated conversations with my wife and children about matters we had never previously discussed.

Facing up to my past has helped me see what I value most in the present.

Jim Wickwire
Seattle, 1998

one

CREVASSE

W e moved down the Peters Glacier slowly, a sled between us loaded heavy with supplies. Twenty feet of rope linked us— too close, we knew, but required by the rough, undulating surface beneath our feet. A glacier is not a fixed, solid thing. It flows like a river, with currents, some parts smooth, others rough. Where it changes direction, or where the angle of its slope steepens, the surface will split, creating cracks as deep as a hundred feet. A thin layer of snow can make them invisible.

Chris walked in front. I walked behind, righting the sled each time it flipped. The afternoon sun beat down on us, softening the snow, casting long shadows. Moments after we had decided to head toward smoother ground, Chris broke through the crust and plunged headfirst into a crevasse. I was concentrating on the sled and did not see him fall. Just as I sensed trouble, the rope yanked me into the air, then down into an icy void. "This is it," I thought, "I'm about to die."

In an instant, the sled and I slammed on top of Chris. Stunned but still conscious after the impact, I checked myself for injuries. My left shoulder felt numb and I could not raise my arm. (I later learned my shoulder had broken.) Suppressing an urge to panic, I glanced around

1

and considered what I should do. Balanced awkwardly with one foot on the sled, the other against a slight bulge in the ice, I tried my best to reassure Chris as I took off my pack and squeezed it into an eighteen-inch space between the walls. Then, using my pack for support, I shoved the sled off Chris into an area just below us, where it lodged.

All I could see of my companion were his legs, still in snowshoes, dangling behind his large black pack, which had compressed to half its normal width between the crevasse walls. Suspended facedown, parallel to the crevasse bottom far below, he yelled, "I can't move, Wick, you've got to get me out!" Trapped under the pack, Chris's entire upper body was immobilized. When I noticed his left hand, twisted back, caught between his pack and the wall, I grabbed it and asked if he could feel the pressure. "No," he barked, "I can't feel anything! You've got to get me out, Wick!" I assured him, "I will, Chris, I promise." I tried lifting him by his pack, but hard as I pulled, he would not budge. Within a few minutes I realized I could do nothing more for him until I got myself out of the crevasse.

The tapered walls were as slick as a skating rink. The distant slit of daylight looked a hundred feet away. To make it to the surface, I needed to put on my crampons—steel spikes attached to each boot to prevent slipping. Luckily, they were on the back of my pack. In a space so tight I could maneuver only by facing the wall, I awkwardly pulled off my snowshoes and strapped the crampons on. Then I retied our rope to the back of Chris's pack, clipped a three-foot aluminum picket and a pair of jumars—mechanical devices to move up and down a rope—to my waist sling, and prepared to climb out. When I tried kicking the front two points of a crampon into the wall, they bounced off. I tried using my ice hammer, but without room to swing my arm, I barely made a scratch. How could I get out if I couldn't penetrate the ice? I began to panic. "Calm down," I told myself, "think of something that will work."

I tried chipping out a little indentation, narrower than a finger width, and placed the front points of my crampon on the tiny ledge. I edged myself up, placing my back against the opposite wall as a counterforce. The front points held my weight. Using my good arm to wield the hammer, I slowly worked my way up the cold, glassy walls, chiseling a ladder of little ledges as I went. Three chips and a step up, again and again. I concentrated harder than I ever had before. The whole time Chris kept yelling from beneath his pack, "You've got to get me out, Wick! You've got to get me out!" Between puffs and grunts I continued to reassure him, "It'll be okay, I'll get you out." And I felt sure I could.

Despite my impatience to reach the surface, I never let the distance between indentations exceed six inches. I knew that if I fell back down, I would probably get wedged, like Chris, between the walls or be hurt worse than I already was. This was my only chance. Near the top, where the shaft widened to about three feet, I twisted my upper torso, drove the ice hammer into the lip of the crevasse at my back, and pressed my feet against the opposite wall. With one rapid movement, I levered my body over the lip and onto the surface of the glacier. It had taken an hour to ascend what turned out to be a twenty-five-foot shaft.

Nearly exhausted, relieved to be alive, I lay on the snow and gasped for breath. Raising my head to look around, I was startled by the quiet and the brightness of the sun on the broad, tilted glacier. Though tempted to rest a little longer, a sense of urgency made me struggle to my feet. I knew I must work fast. If I didn't get Chris out before nightfall, he would die from the cold.

From the crevasse edge, I took up the slack in the rope and pulled with all my might. He did not budge. I tried again—nothing. And again—still no movement. I would need to go back down. I tied the rope to the picket, which I pounded into the hard snow. Then I attached the rope to the jumars (with nylon slings for my feet), which allowed me to descend swiftly but safely into the crevasse.

It took me about five minutes to return to Chris. Hanging a few inches above him, I tried to hoist his pack with my hands and one good arm, but nothing budged. In the hope that changing the rope's position would make a difference, I tied it to each of the pack's accessible cross straps and pulled. But still the pack did not move. I tried

*Peters Glacier from accident site with low mountains to north;
flank of McKinley's Wickersham Wall at right.*

to reassure Chris, but when I drove my ice hammer into the pack, all
I did was move the top a few inches; then it settled back into place. I
attempted to use the power of my legs to lift the pack by stepping
upward in the slings. Nothing was working.

I thought that if I could open Chris's pack and empty its contents, enough pressure would be released to let him move, but when I tried tearing its tough fabric open with my ice hammer I could only make ineffectual punctures. The pack, like a block of wood in a vise, was simply too compressed. Lacking equipment with which to construct a pulley system, I could not dislodge Chris. So, after two hours of continuous effort, I stopped. "Sorry, this isn't working," I conceded.

"I'm going back up to try to get someone, *anyone* on the radio."

After hauling up my pack, I retraced our tracks to a nearby knoll, where I desperately radioed for help: "This is an emergency. Can anyone hear me? If you can, I need your help." I repeated the message again and again, but no one answered; I never really expected a reply. In this valley, so far away from anyone who might have come, our line-of-sight radio was useless. We had set out to climb Mt. McKinley by a remote, untraveled route, and this was the price we paid. No one would come to help. We were alone.

I went back down with little hope of freeing my friend and repeated the rescue maneuvers I feared would fail. Chris's incessant pleas subsided as he gradually realized I could *not* get him out. Having planned to climb Mt. Everest with me the following year, he said, "Climb it for me, Wick. Remember me when you're on the summit." A classical trumpeter, Chris asked me to take his mouthpiece there. "I don't know about me," I replied, "but someone will. I promise." We spoke of his imminent death, but I could not believe that so young and vibrant a man was actually about to die right in front of me.

After asking me to relay messages to his family and closest friends, Chris entreated me to help him die with dignity. However, I could think of no way to ease his suffering or speed his death. I asked him whether he wanted his body left in the crevasse or brought out. He said his father could decide. At about nine-thirty, six hours after we fell into the crevasse, Chris conceded, "There's nothing more you can do, Wick. You should go up." I told him I loved him and said a tearful good-bye. As I began my ascent, Chris said simply, "Take care of yourself, Jim."

Back on the surface, physically spent, emotionally exhausted, and racked with guilt, I pulled on a parka and collapsed into my half-sleeping-bag and bivouac sack—an uninsulated nylon bag used in emergencies for protection against the wind. Lying at the edge of the crevasse, I listened to my friend grow delirious from the searing cold. He talked to himself, moaned, and, at around eleven, sang what

Chris Kerrebrock the night before the accident.

sounded like a school song. At 2 A.M. I heard him for the last time. Chris Kerrebrock was twenty-five. I was forty.

The next morning I wrote in my diary,

> *I feel indescribable guilt and failure for not getting him out and for leaving him to die alone. I don't know how I got myself out with my injured arm. I had to if I would see my precious wife and children again. I can't write more because of sobbing.*

Chris and I had arrived on Mt. McKinley the week before, eager to undertake a challenging route up the mountain's Wickersham Wall. No one had climbed it since 1963, eighteen years before, when first a group of Canadians and then the Harvard Mountaineering Club established the only routes up its treacherous face. Its reputation as an avalanche trap kept climbers away. We planned to take a new line up the massive wall between the two existing routes. Although I felt confident about our prospects, I left my wife, Mary Lou, with more than the usual trepidation. Why, I was not sure.

After a spectacular flight over Kahiltna Pass to check out our route, Doug Geeting, the bush pilot I'd used on several expeditions to Mt. McKinley, dropped us at the mountain's main landing site. He said he would pick us up in about three weeks. In the interim he promised to fly over and check on us at least once. From the air, Wickersham Wall looked huge, but not particularly steep. While concerned about its ice cliffs and the prospect of avalanches, we saw nothing to deter us. Dangerous in places, yes, but climbable. Barring bad weather, we believed we could reach the summit.

Storms confined us to a camp close to the landing site. For the next three days, we ate bacon, eggs, steak, and fresh fruit as we planned our climb and became friends. Reading the Harvard Mountaineering Club's expedition summary reinforced our decision to climb by an entirely new route. Since we had elected to climb the mountain in a single push, with just four ice screws and two pickets between us, we could not take their more technical route.

Chris's easy company and good humor made me look forward to the next three weeks. A year earlier Chris had entered graduate school in philosophy at Columbia University, after earning a degree in classical music at Oberlin, and a reputation for exceptional strength and speed at Mt. Rainier, where he had worked as a summer guide for Rainier Mountaineering, Inc. (RMI). Through his father's contacts with Chinese government officials, he had managed to obtain a coveted permit to climb Mt. Everest from Tibet, then asked Lou Whittaker, one of RMI's owners, to organize and lead an expedition the following spring. During the months spent planning that climb, Chris and I came to know and like each other. Although we had never climbed together, we suspected we would be a compatible team.

We each approached Lou and asked him what he thought. He encouraged me to climb with Chris, describing him as one of the strongest members of the Everest expedition. While characterizing me as an expert climber, Lou cautioned Chris to go to McKinley prepared to look out for himself since I was not a trained guide.

Just as Chris and I finished the last of our fresh food, the weather cleared and other climbing parties began passing our camp on their way to more popular routes. On Tuesday, May 5, 1981, we set out, taking turns in the lead. To make it up Wickersham Wall, we would need to be a fast, strong, and well-coordinated team.

On Wednesday, I wrote,

> *Chris and I are getting along marvelously. Our personalities seem to mesh and thus far there isn't the slightest semblance of getting on each other's nerves. We make a good team and if this expedition is the trial run for Everest, we should do well there together.*

The next day we left a route crowded with climbers and proceeded alone. We crossed over the pass separating the usual West Buttress climbing route on McKinley from the remote north side of

Aerial view of Wickersham Wall.

the mountain where few, if any, climbers go each year. Descending 2,000 feet to the Peters Glacier, our route to the base of Wickersham Wall, we negotiated a tricky series of crevasses, ice cliffs, and a bergschrund—a large crevasse at the head of the glacier. There we discovered the most beautiful campsite either of us had ever seen. Surrounded on three sides by a ridge curved like an amphitheater, we were protected from the wind and restored by the silence. As the soft afternoon light swept gently over the cirque, we felt safe and at peace.

I could see that Chris, having come through the rigors of the day in excellent spirits, possessed not only the requisite energy and strength for this climb, but the good temper and patience to wait out the storms that would inevitably slow our progress. Refreshed, euphoric, and eager to set off the next morning for the base of Wickersham Wall, we talked late into the evening. Though we had not known each other long, we related remarkably well. In addition to shared interests in classical music, philosophy, and mountaineering, we laughed a lot, thanks mostly to Chris's warm, infectious wit. The force of Chris's personality and the gleam in his eyes moved me to photograph his face, made rosy by the fading northern light. As night fell, Chris commented philosophically, "When your number's up, it's up," to which I remarked, "I plan to do all I can to stay alive since I want to grow old with Mary Lou." I told myself that as a climber I might risk my life, but I would never consciously court death. Just where that line falls is a matter of opinion.

On Friday, May 8, we spent a leisurely morning enjoying the glacier's quiet beauty and reveling in our solitude. We talked about the National Park Service's policy against landings and airdrops in the area. Chris pointed out, "If the prohibition were lifted, masses of climbers and their attendant garbage would desecrate this wonderful place. How satisfying to know it can only be reached on foot."

Saturday, May 9

Chris is dead. I am injured. My only hope is Doug Geeting.
I pray he does a "flyby" before the next big storm.

I spent the day in my bivouac sack consumed with grief and guilt, impatient for Geeting to come. My mini–weather radio predicted cold air from the northwest. Did that mean a storm, I wondered, or just colder weather? I kept imagining the sound of an airplane, but all I really heard was an occasional rock or chunk of ice falling in the distance. A setting that once seemed benign became ominous. As I gazed up at the huge ice cliffs that towered above me, I hoped I could escape an avalanche. In the distance, low hills completed the valley, blocking my radio signal.

Although Doug had said he would fly by to check on us, I realized he might not come for several days. With just a few pieces of beef jerky, a bottle of water, and a half-empty thermos of lukewarm soup, I knew I must conserve. Intense pain in my shoulders, upper arms, and chest made shifting position in my bivouac sack difficult. The adrenaline I had produced after the fall and in my frantic attempts to rescue Chris must have blocked the pain, but now I began to feel the full force of my injuries. I would need sleeping pills to get through the night.

All day long I tried to think of how I could have freed Chris. From where I lay I could see the hole we had made when we broke through the snow roof and plunged into the crevasse. On each side of the hole I saw a telltale dip we should have noticed. I kept asking myself, "He noticed all the others, why not this one? Why didn't I tell him to slow down?" I despaired that Chris, a young man with such a promising, adventurous future before him, had lost his life because of a single misstep. I hated being the only one who knew he was dead.

As I reeled from Chris's death and my own close call, thoughts of my wife overwhelmed me. From now on I planned to stay closer to home; I committed to quitting serious climbing. I promised myself that, if I survived, I would withdraw from the Everest expedition.

It snowed all night, but by Sunday morning the sky had cleared. Then a cloud descended, blotting out the surrounding valley, and I knew that if Geeting waited much longer, storms would keep him away for several days. I prayed he would remember to check on us, not wait for us to call him from the summit.

When I had left Chris as he was dying, it did not occur to me to dig through our sled for supplies. Now I needed them, but I could not face the prospect of going back down. In the two days since the accident I had eaten just two sticks of beef jerky, a cup of soup, and a few sips of water. I felt light-headed from dehydration. Without my stove (tucked deep inside the sled) I knew melting snow would be difficult. To keep my bottle as full as possible, I started adding snow to the water and slowly melted it with the heat of my body. Though I grew desperately thirsty, I could never afford to drink enough.

I thought back to the hour before the accident when I told Chris I had lost a buckle from the waist belt of my pack. We dropped our gear and retraced our steps a quarter mile before I realized I hadn't lost my buckle after all. Returning to retrieve the sled, we discussed whether to change positions. We didn't. Chris remained in the lead, pulling while I braked. If we had switched positions, I would be the one dead in the crevasse. What wedged Chris between the walls was the weight of his body and pack plunging into the crevasse, compounded by the weight of the eighty-five-pound sled, me, and my fifty-pound pack.

Although I knew second-guessing would not bring Chris back or lessen my anguish, thoughts of the accident continued to haunt me. I kept thinking, "Why couldn't I free him?" I didn't, I simply didn't. I tried everything I could but it wasn't enough. The way Chris died seemed so much worse than if he had died instantly, as in a fall. It was not a particularly difficult part of the climb that got us but a crevasse on easy terrain, just like so many others we had encountered and crossed without mishap. Some people would say we were careless. Perhaps we were.

Why had I survived the accident? Doubting divine intervention, I wondered, "Could it be my amulets?" Since first attempting K2 in 1975, I had always carried a Zuni owl for protection. Some sixth sense had led me to bring a second amulet on this climb. A year after I left a plastic, pink match case on the summit of K2, Reinhold Messner—the first person to climb all fourteen of the world's highest mountains—found it, protruding from where I'd buried it on the windswept, snowcapped peak. Ever since he returned it to me, I had kept it as a good-luck charm.

I had survived bivouacs on K2 and Mt. Rainier, and now this. Why? Convinced there must be some reason, some higher purpose for me, I resolved to hold out until someone found me. I told myself, "I *will not* die here." Our tent, stove, pots, and most of our food remained in the crevasse. I wondered how far I would be able to stretch twelve sticks of beef jerky. Rationing one a day, my supply would last twelve days. I couldn't imagine Doug Geeting waiting any longer than that, but I steeled myself for the worst. As much as I wanted to get up and walk out of there, I knew my best hope was to sit tight and wait.

Thoughts of my wife both upset and sustained me. I longed to be with her, to hold her and cry. But it sickened me to realize that had I died in the crevasse, she and our five children would never have known what happened to me. I resolved never again to take so great a risk. For twenty-one years I had pursued mountain climbing with an intensity greater than I had devoted to either my family or my career. This was my tenth expedition in nine years. There was still time for me to become a better husband, a better father, a better son to my aging parents. I wrote:

> Something good must come from this tragic expedition. I think of a photograph of an old Patagonian couple whose faces radiate serenity; after lives lived together in love. I don't want to drift apart from Mary Lou in our middle and later years, as so many couples do. I want us to grow closer, to become like the couple in the picture.

I told myself to heed the words of Maurice Herzog from his mountaineering classic, *Annapurna:* "There are other Annapurnas in the lives of men; a new life begins." It was time for me to stop serious mountain climbing and begin a new kind of life. From now on I would live differently, my priorities would change—I owed it to those I loved.

Sleeping pills let me get through the freezing night so I was only vaguely aware of the snow and wind bombarding my bivouac sack. I awoke to a brilliantly clear morning—a perfect time for Geeting to fly by. As I dried my soaked parka and half-bag, I heard the sound of aircraft engines. But they were only my imagination. "Please remember to check on us, Doug. You must remember." In my gut, I knew he would not come.

When I stood up for the first time since the accident three days before, I felt light-headed and my legs felt weak. I looked at the ice cliffs towering above me and wondered if they would crash down in the next storm. Should I move up the hill? Concerned about traveling alone over such dangerous terrain, I resolved to wait, at least until I felt stronger.

All day I tried to figure out how I could have rescued Chris and thought about the people who would suggest they could have freed him. Uphill where we encountered so many crevasses, Chris had led cautiously, detecting the slightest depressions where the snow sagged over them. Once we had passed through what seemed the most dangerous terrain, we mistakenly relaxed and picked up our pace. Had we approached the crevasse from more of an angle—instead of nearly parallel—Chris's momentum would have carried him across, but he hit the opening in such a way that he was propelled down the shaft.

Desperate for a temporary respite from my predicament, I read *The Snow Leopard* by Peter Matthiessen and was struck by his comment that "in high mountains, there is small room for mistake." After *The Snow Leopard,* I began *Pnin,* a short novel by my favorite author, Vladimir Nabokov. Nabokov's recurrent theme of deep marital love consoled me, but it also made my heart ache for home. Lying in my bivouac sack for hours, looking out over the lonely white landscape, I began to search my soul. When I returned to Seattle, I intended to visit one of the few priests I felt I could talk to. Perhaps he could help make sense of this tragedy.

Tuesday morning I dozed, waking briefly when two planes (the first I'd seen since before the accident) flew over around ten. Both were quite high and headed southwest, and I could reach neither on my radio. The wait seemed endless. Though the weather remained clear and cold, another storm would surely wipe out our tracks. Would Geeting find me without them? Perhaps he would wait until May 23, the day we planned to fly out. Could I survive eleven more days? When I left Chris for the last time, he warned, "Sit tight, Wick; don't try walking out alone. The risk of falling into another crevasse is too great." I knew he was right. Besides, I felt too hungry and weak.

All afternoon, I thought about the challenge and satisfaction Chris and I would have had climbing the Wickersham Wall and felt depressed. I had refused to contemplate going back into the crevasse, but now hunger convinced me to reconsider. To survive another eleven days I'd need more than beef jerky. I reassured myself that Chris would not mind, that he would want me to survive. Though the prospect of confronting his corpse scared me, and

Hole into crevasse five days after accident.

my left arm and shoulder still caused me considerable pain, I realized I must go back down.

Early Wednesday morning I returned to the crevasse with my stomach in a knot. On the Friday before, the ice had echoed with Chris's pleas; now there was an eerie quiet. His legs, once shaking with agitation, stuck out stiff from beneath his snow-encrusted pack. Hanging in the slings, I could reach only one end of the sled and felt lucky to find pilot bread, margarine, honey, and raspberry jam. Stretching to retrieve the food, I accidentally touched Chris's body. I had dreaded going so close, but since the frozen corpse was no longer my friend, touching it did not upset me. I did not linger but grabbed what food I could quickly find and left. As I made my way up the crevasse walls, I looked down at Chris's pack and realized there was no way I could have freed him.

I ascended slowly and paused frequently to rest. With one arm useless, the other strained by my exertions, and my strength diminished by a week's starvation, I relied mainly on willpower to get myself out. After I got back to my bivouac sack, I prepared a meal of pilot crackers smeared with jam and honey. The taste was indescribable.

Even though an afternoon snowfall drenched everything, I felt reasonably warm in my bivouac sack where I lay, listening for airplanes. None came, but the noises the mountain made often sounded like aircraft engines and raised my hopes. "Where is Geeting?" I lamented. "Why doesn't he come?" I wondered if I should retrace our steps and try heading out. I owed it to Chris to deliver his messages, but trying to walk out, only to fall into a crevasse and die myself, would mean failing him yet again.

Six days since the accident and Geeting still hadn't come. At moments I felt angry. "A plane could fly in this weather," I grumbled to myself. "Where is he!" In another week we would be overdue. In that case surely someone would undertake a search. But maybe they would conclude we died in an avalanche on Wickersham Wall. Maybe they wouldn't even look. I did not want to contemplate that alternative. I kept hearing planes, but they always sounded far away or around the other side of the mountain. They were probably my imagination.

On the seventh day, the mountain cleared and my spirits rose. Perhaps someone would fly over, notice a minute speck on the huge glacier, and rescue me. As a storm approached, my hope faded. Reluctant to get drenched again, I created a sort of lean-to by propping up two snowshoes, laced together with rope on which I rested my pack. This kept some of the wet snow off my head, but I still got cold enough to begin worrying about frostbite.

Nearby avalanches triggered by the storm increased my fears, so on Friday, May 15, I got up and moved with my equipment to a safer site higher on the hill. Before I left, I wrote a note, which I wrapped in a piece of cloth and attached to a rope on the picket two feet from the crevasse: *In the event I do not make it out, Chris Kerrebrock and I fell into this crevasse at 3:00 P.M. on Friday, May 8, 1981. He died early Saturday morning. God have mercy on his soul.* After signing the note, I stood at the edge of the crevasse and prayed for us both. I thanked God for letting me survive and asked for help in getting safely home. With that, I turned and walked away.

My arms hurt so much I barely got my pack on. Weak from hunger, legs unsteady from lying in my bivouac sack for six days, I trudged uphill, stopping frequently. Once I lost my balance and fell over backward. By retracing our faint tracks I reached the crest of the hill—high enough to be out of the avalanche path. After testing the ground with my ice ax, I decided to stop. As I removed my snowshoes, I kicked through the crust of a crevasse. Spinning to one side, I quickly caught myself and managed to keep from falling in. Shaken, I stumbled a few feet away from the hole where, crawling into my bivouac sack, I felt safe. Farther up the glacier our tracks had disappeared; to continue without them as a guide would be too dangerous. I must stay put.

*Self-photo of Jim
seven days after accident.*

That afternoon the weather deteriorated, though I could glimpse the upper mountain through the clouds and falling snow. Despite my foray into the crevasse, my food supplies looked meager. I wondered how I could make them last if I had to survive another week. I decided to take each moment as it came. If I thought of everything that might interfere with my rescue, I feared I would go crazy. At times I turned to talk to someone, sensing I was not alone. Was it part of my personality disengaging from itself? Or Chris's spirit? Or was it just my fear and loneliness? Other times I got depressed, but most of the time I believed everything would work out. Doug Geeting would show up eventually.

After a crystal-clear morning, clouds came. Eight days and still no Geeting. Perhaps reading another selection from *The Portable Nabokov* would keep me from feeling so frustrated. Just as I settled down to read, an avalanche from high on McKinley's northwest wall crashed down above me with a deafening roar. I watched its cloud blast roll toward me with the speed of a hurricane. Afraid of being hit by heavy ice debris, I grabbed the top of my bivouac sack and hunched down. Luckily, a large crevasse between me and the slope above consumed most of the debris. Only a small storm of ice pellets made it far enough to pepper the back of my head and shoulders.

The absence of planes overhead made me think it might be difficult for small craft to get around to the mountain's north side. Despite the risk of falling into another crevasse, I decided that to survive I must move to a place where my radio could reach a pilot flying overhead—somewhere far from the threat of avalanches. With just an ice ax and an ice hammer, I carefully negotiated my way through a honeycomb of crevasses, most less than a foot wide. Crawling on all fours, punching my ice ax into the crust in front of me each time I moved, I avoided the few large crevasses and crossed the small ones. After I reached an isolated knoll, I returned to retrieve my pack and bivouac sack and moved on to my second temporary campsite.

I planned to probe my way across what remained of the most treacherous terrain. Then, if all seemed safe, I would move my camp again. By proceeding slowly and cautiously, I decided to try to make it to the other side of the mountain where there would be climbers who could help me. In spite of my sore arms and weakened body, I believed I would get there, eventually. That evening, I wrote in my diary,

> It's Saturday evening in Seattle. Susie must be performing in her school play right about now. I wonder if the entire family is there? I wish I were home.

The next morning I traversed the worst part of the basin. Through my binoculars I spotted two crevasses higher on the glacier that I would need to cross on Monday. After that—assuming all went well—I could speed up. On the way to my next campsite I managed to spill honey all over my meager food supply. Though I generally abhor sugary meats, I discovered that starvation made honey-coated beef jerky taste *delicious*. It took restraint to resist eating everything I had, and my will was weakening. After my tiny lunch I settled down to read Nabokov. Resting in the sunshine, I felt cautiously hopeful, and looking over at the ice cliffs that had produced Saturday's avalanche, I was glad I had moved.

My resolution to stop climbing, made in the wake of Chris's death, began to weaken. I no longer wanted to give up climbing completely. But the thought of going to Everest on an expedition Chris had conceived still bothered me. I decided to wait a few years, then do something smaller, maybe a joint Pakistani-American climb.

In the late afternoon, I realized that while making my way to the new campsite, my ice hammer had dropped off my pack. Relieved to find it just thirty feet away, I decided to stamp out an SOS before crawling back into the bivouac sack. As I did, I dropped my guard and kicked through the crust, nearly falling into another crevasse—I lunged to the side just in time. Early morning was obviously the only safe time to walk around on this treacherous terrain. The sun might feel good, but it was melting the glacier's crust.

Alone, so far from all the climbers on the other side of the mountain, I realized I might never be rescued. But barring another bad storm, I should reach the main trail by late the next morning. Just a few more hours of danger, just a few more crevasses to cross. I left early Monday, and walking straight up the glacier, sometimes staggering drunkenly from weakness, I made it past the last of the crevasses. As I approached the two-thousand-foot slope I would need to climb to reach the other side of the mountain, the wind increased. I decided to stop and wait out what was fast becoming a ground blizzard.

With my food supply depleted, all I could afford to eat was one stick of beef jerky and three-quarters of a pilot cracker smeared with jam and margarine. Delicious, but not enough to keep me going long. My stomach ached, but I willed myself not to think of the food I craved: fresh fruit and vegetables, hot soup and meat, cocoa, hot tea, and bread. The hungrier I got, the lonelier I felt; I yearned to talk to someone about the accident. The storm raged on all day and through the night, freezing my feet. Hoping to forestall frostbite a little longer, I managed to clear a huge pile of snow pinning me down and changed my inner socks. I feared the violent storm might tear my bivouac sack; without it intact I knew I would die of hypothermia.

I began to dread the prospect of confronting the media back home. Although I planned to recommend leaving Chris's body where it was when the National Park Service asked me to prepare a report, the Kerrebrocks might feel the need to see his remains. Removing the frozen corpse would be difficult, but not impossible with enough people and equipment. I wondered what I would decide had Chris been my son.

With only a little food left, I began thinking more and more about the people on the other side of the pass. Perhaps one of the parties Chris and I had encountered before heading off toward Wickersham Wall would offer me something hot to drink. Oh, how I wanted a hot drink, more than almost anything else I wanted a hot drink. Increasingly discouraged, I wrote,

> *I'm so frustrated and so lonely. Why choose to put myself in this kind of danger? It makes no sense. I promise to change.*

When I awoke Tuesday morning, I felt warmer and once again comforted by the sense I was not alone, that someone was there with me. The storm continued to rage. Drifting snow, hard-packed during the night, nearly covered my bivouac sack. My left arm and shoulder hurt so much I could hardly write in my diary—the main outlet for my anxiety and loneliness. Chris once said he relished our isolation but would never want to be here alone. My solitude had become almost unbearable. I wanted to be out of the sack, off the glacier, away from Mt. McKinley, Now! But I knew I must be patient and stay calm—not waste the little energy I had left.

On the third day of the storm, the twelfth since the accident, I stayed huddled in my bivouac sack daydreaming about various projects I should do around the house. Maybe I would install some new bookshelves in the study, maybe a new fence in the backyard. In the afternoon, during a lull in the wind, I heard a large bird swoop by. Did I look like something to eat? Or was it simply investigating a strange blue and red object in the middle of nowhere?

I worried that when I finally climbed the last two thousand feet to the main route, all the new snow might trigger an avalanche. I prayed that once there, someone would make me a meal and a hot drink. Hot chocolate, chicken soup, hot tea, maybe even steak and bacon brought in by a recent arrival to the mountain. Craving food did nothing but distress me. I had to force myself to think of something else.

My mini–weather radio estimated subzero temperatures and winds as high as seventy-five miles per hour. Throughout the storm, I had kept out the snow and wind by drawing together the top of my bivouac sack, then tying it with cord. Buffeted by wind, squeezed by mounting snow, I prayed the sack would not tear. At times I felt like an astronaut confined in a capsule without a smidgen of extra space. A benefit of my starvation diet was that my bowel movements had ceased—not a bad thing when one is living in a small nylon sack in the midst of a blizzard. And what would I have done without my pee bottle?

Bivouac sack on Peters Glacier following four-day storm.

This experience convinced me that I must start reaching out to others, first and foremost to my family. I wanted to be more than simply "one of the first Americans to climb K2" or "the mountain climber." I was determined climbing must no longer dominate my life. As a climber I had remained in a kind of perpetual adolescence, often neglecting my primary responsibilities. It was time for me to reset my priorities and grow up.

Making up for a sleepless night, I dozed most of the morning. Other than for my sore arm and shoulder I felt pretty good, especially when the sky began to clear. My weather radio predicted sunny skies and my spirits soared. At four-thirty Thursday afternoon, thirteen days after the accident, I heard an airplane and flipped on my line-of-sight radio just in time to hear Doug Geeting notify someone of his plans to rescue an injured climber on the other side of the mountain. "A storm's coming," he explained. "I need to move fast." Though I frantically tried to break into the conversation, he did not hear me. Despite my disappointment, the sound of Doug's voice filled me with fresh energy and optimism. I was almost home.

Early the next morning, I once again heard the sound of a plane. Quickly turning on the radio, I called Doug and this time he answered, "Chris. Jim. Where are you? Are you on the summit?" "No," I replied, "Chris is dead. I'm here, on the upper glacier. Can you see me? I'm just below the pass." "I see you, Jim!" he exclaimed, and began circling his plane in search of a safe place to land. As I moved to pick up my pack, my foot punched through yet another crevasse. There weren't supposed to be any more crevasses. I lunged forward and rolled to safety. Then, scared and relieved, I sat on the snow and wept.

I watched Doug's plane approach me, a silver speck growing ever larger until it skidded to a stop thirty feet away. When Geeting opened the door and helped me in, I weighed twenty-five pounds less than when he had dropped me off three weeks before. All my frustration about why he had not come sooner disappeared. Emotion and gratitude overwhelmed me, and as we flew over the crevasse where Chris had died, I told Doug what had happened. Beyond the base of the mountain we flew over green trees; returning to all those things we take for granted, I felt profoundly grateful to be alive.

When I called Mary Lou, her compassion made me break down and cry. Although I did appreciate *receiving* phone calls—Lou Whittaker was particularly understanding—I found them difficult to make. Mary Lou knew this and took the burden on herself. When she called my parents, Dad told her he couldn't understand why Chris and I ever chose to go somewhere so isolated in the first place. She called her mother, who mentioned having had a troubling premonition about the expedition. Mary Lou reported that, while relieved I had survived, our relatives all expressed frustration that I continued to

Doug Geeting.

risk my life for reasons they could not understand. Yet, even as I affirmed my commitment to stop serious climbing, I could feel my resolve begin to fade.

A park ranger called Chris's father, Jack Kerrebrock. Hoping to notify Chris's brother and sister before they heard about his death on the news, Dr. Kerrebrock asked the ranger to wait a day before releasing his son's name to the media. He promised, but the *Anchorage Daily News* got hold of the story anyway, and the phone rang off the hook. Fortunately, the Kerrebrocks reached Chris's siblings in time.

Later, Dr. Kerrebrock asked the Park Service if they would assess the feasibility of retrieving Chris's remains. So on the morning before I returned to Seattle, two climbing rangers and I boarded a helicopter and headed for the crevasse. When dense clouds forced us back short of the Peters Glacier, the others promised they would go back.

Flying home, I felt a deep sense of loss. Facing danger with another person creates a strong bond, transcending the limits of time and place—perhaps even death. I suspect that is one of the reasons I climb. My friendships are deeper in the mountains than in the city, where I tend to be more of a loner. In the mountains, awed by nature's beauty, thrilled by the risk and the physical challenge, my heart opens.

On May 24 three climbing rangers and a pilot flew to the accident site and for three hours chipped away the ice from around Chris's body. Once it was loose, they used a Z-pulley to remove his remains from the crevasse. In his report, the chief climbing ranger wrote:

> *If Wickwire and Kerrebrock had each been travelling with a lighter sled rather than the one heavy sled between them, then they could have travelled further apart and Wickwire might not have been pulled into the crevasse when Kerrebrock fell.*
>
> *But given the fact that both fell into the crevasse and that Wickwire injured his shoulder in the fall, I do not think that Wickwire could have done anything differently. Kerrebrock's body was tightly wedged by a bulge in the wall of the crevasse, and it was only with three hours of chopping with a small hatchet that we were able to remove enough ice to free the body. With Wickwire's injured shoulder and without having a small hatchet*

(even a small ice ax or ice hammer was too big to maneuver in the narrow crevasse), I do not think that Wickwire could have chipped enough ice away to free Kerrebrock from the crevasse. I also do not feel that even a well-constructed Z-pulley system with minimal friction and one healthy person pulling could have extricated Kerrebrock from his wedged position until sufficient ice was chipped away. Given the circumstances of the incident, the injury that Wickwire received, and the equipment that was available to him, I feel that Wickwire attempted everything possible.

Mary Lou and Jim at home after return from Mt. McKinley.

The ranger's words eased my guilt but not my grief. Although they confirmed my own estimate of what steps were possible once the accident had happened, they have not stopped the second guessing. Why didn't I notice where Chris was headed? Why didn't I tell him to slow down? Why didn't we keep more rope between us? Why didn't I spot the sag of the hidden crevasse? Seventeen years later, what happened to Chris remains my greatest regret.

I will never stop wishing I could have saved him.

FIRST STEPS

hris's death made me keenly aware of my mortality. For the previous forty years I had felt invulnerable.

Born in 1940, on the eve of World War II, I was the oldest of seven, six boys and a girl. We grew up in Ephrata, a small town in eastern Washington. My father's name was James Frederick Wickwire; I'm James Francis, named for him but not a junior. My most vivid recollection of early childhood was his absence.

I remember the train ride from Seattle to Oakland in 1944. Mom and I slept together on the lower berth, Dad slept with my brother Bob on the upper. In San Francisco we watched as my uniformed father, standing on the step of a streetcar, went away to serve on an aircraft carrier in the Pacific—the last I saw of him for nearly a year.

A private man of integrity, my father was a lawyer, judge, civic leader, and my role model. We got along fine but rarely talked about anything except sports. I may have asked him questions about practicing law, but I don't recall his encouraging me to follow in his footsteps. My decision to become a lawyer was gradual. When I finally announced my plans to Dad, he hardly

Jim's parents, James and Dorothy Wickwire.

reacted, but I think he approved. He was the kind of father who generally signaled his encouragement and admiration without words. However, when I played halfback on my high school's football team—I was all-state two years in a row—Dad told me how much *that* pleased him.

Growing up, I admired my father but vowed to risk more in my life than he had in his. With his mind I thought he could have achieved great things, and I was silently critical of him for burying himself in a small town. It took me most of a lifetime to realize my error.

My mother, Dorothy, instilled in me a love of classical music as well as a wanderlust and yearning for adventure. Constrained by the small-town atmosphere, haunted by memories of a harsh, motherless childhood, Mom eventually started to drink. My father's Wednesday afternoons and weekends on the golf course only compounded her sense of isolation. Her dreams of travel and adventure thwarted, then discarded, my mother drank more and more. It always amazed me how, though maudlin after a couple of stiff drinks of bourbon, she could rise the next morning bright-eyed and cheerful. Her good humor seemed particularly remarkable in light of a series of ailments she endured throughout her adult life: broken toes, elbow, and collarbone, the loss of her gallbladder, femoral-artery surgery, and on and on.

But despite her drinking and chronic ill health, Mom was my inspiration and the one to whom I confided everything that mattered, well into my teens. She always made me feel that by taking risks, achieving goals, and really experiencing life I fulfilled some of her own ambitions and lessened her disappointment. As my parents' firstborn child, I have strived to live a life melding their values and aspirations, avoiding their regrets.

My brother Bob, just ten months my junior, was my constant companion and impetus to achieve. A superb athlete, he always made me feel clumsy by comparison. When we threw baseballs back and forth, I nearly always missed his mitt; when we climbed trees I was the cautious one. Trying to compete, I drove myself extra hard, eventually becoming a passable, then good, athlete—spurred on by my younger brother's superior natural talents. Bob became the athletic standard against which I measured myself.

Between the ages of twenty and twenty-three I made three decisions that have defined my life. I began mountain climbing, I entered law school, and I married Mary Lou.

My climbing did not begin as a physical activity. First it came to me through books. As a teenager, I read several accounts of expeditions to Mt. Everest and K2, the world's two highest mountains. I even wrote a high school term paper on the climbing history of Everest.

But it was Maurice Herzog's book, *Annapurna*, an account of the French expedition in 1950 to the 26,493-foot mountain of that name, that most stirred my interest in climbing. With his companion, Louis Lachenal, Herzog was the first to climb an eight-thousand-meter peak—one above 26,200 feet, of which there are only fourteen in the world.

Herzog and Lachenal were caught in a sudden storm on their way down from the summit and forced to spend the night in a crevasse with two companions who came up to meet them. They all eventually made it down to safety, but at great cost to Herzog and Lachenal. Both suffered horrible frostbite injuries. I would never forget the images of Herzog as he was carried out from the mountain on a litter with the flesh literally hanging from his fingers.

The last sentence of Herzog's book, beginning "There are other Annapurnas in the lives of men," became almost a sacred text for me. I read the word *Annapurna* to refer not to other mountains, but rather to other challenges that we face in life. Herzog had been through a terrible ordeal, but now he could face anything. There would be times in the years ahead when I would try to heed Herzog's words and turn away from climbing to other pursuits. I would be only partially successful.

Not long after the start of my sophomore year at Gonzaga University, I was sitting on the library steps one afternoon when I observed a cluster of older girls escorting a striking, dark-haired young woman with deep, hazel eyes. They were making her skip along backward and sing "Mary Had a Little Lamb." Neither frightened nor flustered, she calmly defended herself with pointed barbs directed at her friendly tormentors. Who was this remarkable woman? I wondered. An eighteen-year-old freshman, Mary Lou Custer had grown up in Portland, Oregon, the eldest of twelve girls and a boy. She had come to Gonzaga on scholarship after finishing second in her high school class.

Mary Lou Custer.

Over the next several days I saw Mary Lou around the campus; I wanted to ask her out on a date, but it took the encouragement of a buddy, who accompanied me to her dorm, for me to finally work up the courage. Our first evening together we spent sitting on the floor of a crowded hotel room talking nonstop, oblivious to the party that swirled around us. From the start we confided in each other, mainly about our families and my new passion for mountain climbing. If there is such a thing as love at first sight, I experienced it with Mary Lou.

In those days of separate dorms for men and women, we found our own place to meet alone. Across the street, away from the stern eye of her dorm mother, Mary Lou and I embraced in the dark stairwell of an abandoned house. Although we weren't yet old enough to vote, we knew, within a matter of months, that we wanted to marry. For it to happen anytime soon, we concluded that Mary Lou must drop out of college, where she'd excelled, and go to work—the first of many sacrifices Mary Lou would make for our relationship.

She returned home to Portland and found a job at an insurance agency. I continued at Gonzaga, working summers in Ephrata, and for over a year we saw each other only occasionally. Since long-distance phone calls were expensive we wrote each other instead. It was difficult to be apart, but we adapted, as we would to other separations in the years to come. Since then, we have exchanged hundreds of letters, communicating with each other in a way we never could have in our child-filled home.

We got married on August 25, 1962, a happy occasion when both our large families met for the first time. For years afterward, we heard about all the fun they'd had together following our departure from the reception for a brief honeymoon on the Washington coast. On the long drive back to Gonzaga, I wanted to show Mary Lou the Talon, a hundred-foot-high rock spire that two friends and I had climbed and named the year before. Mary Lou had no problem hiking up the rocky fifteen-hundred-foot hillside, but when we began our descent, her legs got wobbly and she needed my assistance to

Mary Lou and Jim on their wedding day.

reach the car. Unnerved by the experience, she announced, "Jim, you can climb if you want to, but this is *my* last climb."

Not long after our honeymoon, we attended a party at an apartment complex where, with similar adolescent bluster, I dove from a second-floor balcony into a swimming pool twenty feet below.

Although not particularly impressed, Mary Lou humored me. A few months later I took her to watch me and several friends climb a high-angle rock wall alongside a highway. After she observed us inch our way up the four-hundred-foot face, Mary Lou remarked, "I'm struck by how carefully you climb, but it's so slow—and boring."

As a college student I often went rock climbing at Minnehaha, a hundred-foot-high granite cliff east of Spokane. In 1960, the year I started climbing, a friend and I attempted the central crack splitting Minnehaha's face but turned back at a difficult spot. Unwilling to accept defeat, I returned, this time alone. I quickly regained the high point from where we had retreated. Forcing myself to stretch farther than before, I grabbed the hold that had eluded me and got past the most difficult spot. As I reached the flat top of Minnehaha, I felt a tremendous rush of exhilaration and *knew* I wanted more.

Two and a half years later, on a warm February afternoon, I returned with a couple of friends. As I climbed the most exposed section of the wall, one of my friends belayed me from below. As a safeguard, I should have placed a piton—a metal spike—in the rock. Delicately balanced with my feet and right hand on tiny friction holds, I stretched my left arm above me, curling my fingers over the top of a large jug-handle hold. As I transferred my weight, a chunk of rock broke off in my hand. Without piton protection, the rope attaching me to my friend could not arrest my fall. Dropping feet first, face to the wall, I struck a small bulge and spun around ninety degrees. For the next fifty feet I windmilled my arms in an effort to slow down, until I slammed into something hard.

Entangled in bushes, I gradually regained consciousness. Except for my left wrist, which throbbed ominously, I felt numb. Looking at my hand, twisted like a pretzel, my stomach heaved. I gingerly moved my right arm, then my legs, and they seemed okay. So far, so good. To be really sure, I needed to get on my feet. So over my friend's protests, I struggled to rise. As I did, I noticed six uniformed police officers watching me silently. Although never unconscious, I must have gone into shock since I remembered nothing that had happened between the time I fell and their arrival.

I looked back where I had landed, then up at the slanting rock ledge I must have hit. Except for the moment my feet struck the rock bulge, I'd free-fallen sixty feet in less than three seconds. My left wrist and buttock took the full force of the fall. Had I hit the ground or the ledge at a different angle, I would have been killed or horribly injured. The officers escorted me to a parked ambulance. Declining an offer to ride in the back on a stretcher, I insisted on sitting in front. At the hospital, I called Mary Lou but did not explain what had happened, saying only, "I've had a little accident; I hurt myself but I'm okay."

It took two months for my broken wrist to heal. When it did, the

first thing I wanted to do was return to Minnehaha. At first I felt scared, but this time we used pitons, and protected all the way, I reached the top without incident.

Falling made me a more careful climber—most of the time. But it also left me with a heightened attraction to danger that would get me into trouble more often than I'd like to admit.

Jim climbing Minnehaha Rock.

I'm ashamed to confess that my admiration for Mary Lou did nothing to alter my assumptions about what it meant to be married. In the early sixties a husband was supposed to be the boss, his wife a sex object available to take care of his clothes, cook his meals, and care for his children. I approached our first few years of marriage with this attitude, and despite Mary Lou's obvious intelligence, drive, and strength of character, she went along, trained as she'd been in a fifties-era Catholic home.

When Mary Lou expressed herself in a group, I was often hyper-critical of what she had to say. I felt so superior I wouldn't even allow her name on our checks and instead doled out money to her as if she were a child. As Mary Lou made more and more decisions, I gradually abandoned my anachronistic views of marriage. Although she had sacrificed her college education for our marriage, once the kids were out of diapers, Mary Lou became a voracious reader who could more than hold her own in conversation. Since I traveled so much, she took over our finances, deciding where our money went—the charities we gave to and the expenses we incurred.

While I finished college, Mary Lou worked full-time for an insurance agency. Within two years I had completed my first year of law school and our daughter Anne was born. Mary Lou worked up until two weeks before Anne's birth, and when she was three months old, Mary Lou returned to work. Two months later she got pregnant again. When Cathy, our second child, came, Mary Lou switched to a part-time job. Susie arrived eighteen months later, just before I graduated from law school and headed to Seattle to study for the bar exam. Mary Lou quit her job and took the three kids to spend the summer with my parents in Ephrata—hard for someone who had grown up in a city. But she never complained; she seldom does.

That August I received a call from U.S. senator Henry "Scoop" Jackson asking me to come for an interview. (I had succeeded one of his aides as editor of the *Gonzaga Law Review*.) When I went to see the senator, he offered me a job on the spot, going so far as to call the Washington State attorney general on the phone and say, "I understand Jim Wickwire has agreed to work for you this autumn. Would you release him from his obligation so he can work for me?" The attorney general did, so Mary Lou and I drove across the country with our three little girls and settled outside Washington, D.C.

On June 6, 1968, the day Robert Kennedy died, our fourth child and first son was born—earlier than expected. I was away from home interviewing with a Seattle law firm and nearly missed his birth. Terribly upset by the assassination, I found it difficult to focus on the newest addition to our family. Sadness hung over me so heavily it took several days before I could be happy about our new baby. I suggested we name him Robert Francis in Kennedy's honor, and Mary Lou agreed. Our second son and final child, David, arrived a year later. In what had become a pattern, I left on a climb a few days after his birth. When I returned from an unsuccessful attempt of Canada's Mt. Robson, I discovered that in my absence Mary Lou had hemorrhaged and ended up back in the hospital. She was okay but I felt terrible.

A devout Catholic, Mary Lou has always gone to church. With a sense of religious duty and obligation instilled in her as a child, she draws strength from prayer and attending mass. We sent our kids to Catholic school, and they attended mass with her most Sundays. She never emphasized formal Catholic doctrine to the children, more a structure of "Christian" values by which she has always lived: courtesy, tolerance of differences, speaking well of others, and community service.

Though my father converted to Catholicism when he married my mother, Mom took responsibility for my religious education. Despite her efforts to raise a good Catholic, I gradually grew disenchanted with the Church. I stopped taking Communion when I was twenty-seven—to do otherwise seemed hypocritical. To support Mary Lou, I continued going to mass, off and on, for many years. But sitting in the pew while Mary Lou and the kids went up to take the sacraments, I remembered the men I had observed as a child, sitting alone waiting for their families to return to the pews, and felt awkward.

With five small children and only five years separating the oldest from youngest, Mary Lou and I often found ourselves fending off questions from well-meaning friends and acquaintances: "Aren't you worried about world population growth?" "Why don't you do something about having so many children?" Following the baptism of our fourth child, the officiating priest infuriated me when, unsolicited, he offered us advice about limiting the size of our family. "It's not a sin," he admonished. In time we did resort to birth control, but on our own terms. Both Mary Lou and I had enjoyed growing up within large families, and we consciously set out to raise our own.

Jim and Mary Lou with Anne (7), Bob (3), Susie (4), Cathy (6), and David (2).

As a young mother Mary Lou did not drive; instead she dragged a large red wagon to and from the supermarket with the children trailing behind her. When I left on my first expedition in 1972, she decided the time had come to get her driver's license, and at age thirty, with children ranging from three to eight, she found a degree of independence previously lacking in our marriage.

Mary Lou raised our children for a world different from the one we had entered. She encouraged our daughters to wait to marry until they were older than she had been, so they might have a chance to travel, work, explore the world, and experience more of life. Concerned our sons might feel pressured to become lawyers like my father and me, she told them, "It is perfectly okay to aspire to be a plumber or a carpenter—whatever fulfills you." She wanted our children to feel a sense of responsibility, but she also tried to instill a sense of self-worth. Always making a point to let the children know she admired their competence, Mary Lou encouraged them every step of the way.

My experience working for Senator Jackson unexpectedly set the course for my entire legal career, although I worked for him less than two years. I admired the senator and we kept in touch long after I left Washington, D.C. Whenever I returned from a difficult climb, particularly those in which a companion died, the senator would call and express his concern. In September 1983, he called to ask me to take his son up Mt. Rainier. I promised I would and for the first time in our relationship, called him by his nickname, Scoop. That evening he died suddenly of a heart attack.

In late 1968 my family and I moved to Seattle, where I joined Davis Wright, a large downtown law firm. When the firm began representing a group of Inupiat Eskimos pursuing their aboriginal land claims on Alaska's North Slope, the partner-in-charge summoned me, and another associate who had worked in the Senate, to his office. "You guys are the only ones we have with any experience in Congress," he explained. "For the next several months your assignment is to work with the Eskimos."

The legal career I thought I had embarked upon—representing banks and other corporate clients—took an abrupt turn, and I spent the next two and a half years advancing legislation that culminated in the passage of the Alaska Native Claims Settlement Act of 1971. Little did I realize I would devote the rest of my legal career to representing the Arctic Slope Regional Corporation (ASRC), the Inupiat Eskimo–owned entity established to manage the land and cash received in the historic settlement. My clients, particularly two men, Jake Adams and Oliver Leavitt, have stuck with me for more than twenty-five years, tolerating my frequent absences, worrying about my safety, and joking about my moments of notoriety.

In time, I grew restless working for a big firm, so two colleagues—Yale Lewis and Chuck Goldmark—and I left and, with John Dystel and Jon Schorr, created our own boutique firm. Wickwire, Lewis, Goldmark, Dystel & Schorr expanded and thrived until tragedy cut it short in the mideighties. After that, I moved to a large law firm where I stayed until I again broke off with some colleagues to create Wickwire, Greene, Crosby, Brewer & Seward, a smaller firm more to my liking. At that firm (like its predecessor, Wickwire, Lewis) my partners would indulge my compulsion to climb along with various other idiosyncrasies.

Despite satisfying work, I still had my mother's wanderlust. If my career was to be relatively staid and stable, I needed to look elsewhere for adventure. I would provide for my family, serve my clients, but I planned to *live.* And for me "to live" meant climbing mountains.

From the beginning of our relationship, Mary Lou has supported my climbing career, confident in my judgment, certain I would survive. People often asked her if being stuck at home with the kids during my long absences got her down. She always said no, that "when Jim takes off on business or climbing trips, I become a different person—more myself." If she had been dependent, unable to live without me there all the time, our marriage might not have survived. But she has thrived during my absences; enjoying the increased responsibility, the opportunity to make more decisions, the chance to catch up with her friends and relatives, and the time for community service.

When the children were small, Mary Lou volunteered at their schools. Later, she found additional ways to serve. For a few years, she assisted families of cancer patients who came to Seattle for bone-marrow transplants: picking the families up at the airport, taking them on errands, sitting with them at the hospital, and generally easing their suffering. More recently she has tutored adults just learning to read. Mary Lou's volunteerism is not confined to institutions. For example, once, during her morning jog, she noticed that the bushes bordering a nearby park needed tending so she took her shears and a bag for clippings and cut them back—as she has every August for the twelve years since. No one ever asked her to, nor has anyone ever thanked her; she simply does it because she sees that it needs doing.

At times, people have expressed something close to irritation with Mary Lou for not trying to stop me from climbing mountains. Her response has been, "Love lets go. It doesn't clutch. Climbing is a big part of who Jim is, and I get a lot out of my association with his climbing. I've had opportunities to travel to exotic places like Japan, Pakistan, and China, and by bringing all sorts of interesting people to our home, Jim opened the world to our children." Steeled to the prospect of an early widowhood, Mary Lou was also quick to note, "If anything ever happened to Jim, the kids and I knew we would be secure financially. That has made the risks he's taken easier to accept. The realization that Jim might not come back from an expedition has helped keep us from sweating the small stuff."

In the early years I climbed close to home, reluctant to leave my small children and fledgling law practice for more than a few days at a time. But my restlessness grew. The rock climbs of the kind I'd undertaken as a student were no longer enough. I wanted more challenge and found it on ice. Fighting the elements, meeting the threats of avalanches and blizzards, appealed to me. Each challenge I met on ice left me wanting more. And for twenty-five years, exhilarated by risk, I kept raising the stakes—at no small cost to my family and firm.

While I was climbing Mt. Rainier in May 1971, my grandmother died. The family postponed the funeral and waited for me to return. After five days without word from me, they decided to proceed in spite of their growing concern for my safety. Their worries were warranted, for I was engaged in a struggle for survival.

The trip began smoothly enough when I set out with my friend Ed Boulton, age forty-four, an insulation contractor and mountain-rescue volunteer. A short, stocky, man-who-built-America type of guy, Ed had an open sense of humor and lack of pretense I thoroughly enjoyed. Our objective was Willis Wall, a four-thousand-foot-high precipice on the mountain's north side that I had last climbed the year before, when

Mt. Rainier's Willis Wall from air. Liberty Cap to right; main summit to left.

Alex Bertulis and I made the first successful winter ascent. Climbed just four times by three different routes, Willis Wall had a well-deserved reputation for danger. Ice avalanches fall from the ribbon of ice cliffs near its summit, and once the sun strikes its slopes, rocks fall incessantly. Ed and I took a more difficult route than I'd taken in either of my two previous climbs, a steep rib of rock and ice right up the middle.

It took us a day and a half to hike to a campsite at the left edge of the wall, safely out of the path of avalanches and rockfalls. We started climbing at midnight when the loose rocks were still frozen into place. Our only equipment consisted of one bivouac sack, a few ice screws and rock pitons, a 150-foot rope, a gas stove, and a half-sleeping-bag, but no down parkas and only enough food and water for a couple of days. Relying on a forecast of excellent weather, we traveled light, expecting to climb up and down the mountain in a day.

Ed Boulton on approach to Willis Wall.

But once we climbed several hundred feet above the bergschrund, clouds drifted in from the southwest, and the stars disappeared—a bad sign. Then an ice avalanche roared down the gully alongside us, pelting us with small chunks of ice. Cut off from a safe retreat, we had no choice but to keep climbing. A cloud cap now shrouding the mountain, we felt our way up in a whiteout. It was easy to get disoriented in these conditions since our sense of scale and balance got upset. Objects that appeared far away kept turning out to be right in front of us.

Except for a few short sections, the ice was hard and slick, but not particularly steep. After several hours of steady upward progress, with most of the four-thousand-foot-high wall now below us, snow began to fall. We cursed the weathermen for their misleading forecast. Ominous rumbles and cracks from the ice cliffs above made us as nervous as cats. We were unable to see more than fifty feet in front of us. Startled by a sharp crack from above, I yelled to Ed to take cover, and we cowered alongside some rocks, hunched against an avalanche that did not come.

Still nervous about avalanches, we moved cautiously up the last three hundred feet of exposed ice to the base of a high-angle rock cliff on which the huge summit ice cliff perched. We could not see the ice hanging overhead, but nonetheless felt threatened by its presence. To reach our only means of escape—a narrow ledge—we needed to climb two hundred feet of rock. As I searched for the best available route, Ed and I got separated by a large rock bulge. A moment later I slipped. By driving the pick of my ice ax deep into the hard ice, I caught myself. When I turned to look for Ed, I slipped again and the exertion—and fear—briefly exhausted me. Still roped together, both Ed and I would have plunged down the wall had I failed to stop myself.

We climbed up a shallow gully on seventy-degree, snow-covered, iced-up rock. I led the first sixty feet, then Ed took over. He was fifty feet above me when I heard him yell, "I'm stuck!" I scrambled up to him, then over to a horn of rock—the only decent belay anchor I could find. Once we were both protected, Ed extricated himself and we climbed the remaining thirty feet of rock to the ice-laden ledge. To gain easier ground, Ed had to remove a blob of ice blocking our way. But the storm intensified, and blinded by wind-driven snow, we agreed we should stop.

We needed a place to spend the night protected from the storm and the avalanches it might trigger. Ed recalled seeing a rock overhang fifty feet back, so we reversed our tracks and there, beneath the overhang, we found a small opening. By excavating and leveling the interior we made a space roughly four feet wide, four feet high, and

Ed Boulton on Willis Wall's hard ice.

seven feet deep. After a supper of soup and hot lemonade we settled in for a long, uncomfortable night, sitting with our legs jammed together in our solitary bivouac sack. Over the next few hours, avalanches pounded the slope outside. I shivered throughout the night, dozing intermittently.

We rose early—the fourth day of our journey. Except for an occasional glimpse of the ice cliff looming overhead, the whiteout continued. Trudging through deep snow, we eventually reached the corner up which we had to climb to reach the wide snow ramp between Willis Wall's two largest ice cliffs. The new snow had not adhered to the steeper ice so, delicately front-pointing, I led 150 feet to rock directly beneath the highest ice cliff. When we reached the broad ramp we shook hands, relieved to be off the wall.

Less than a thousand feet remained to Liberty Cap, one of Mt. Rainier's three summits, most of it a traverse on thirty-degree slopes. It should have been an easy walk, but it wasn't. The storm had dumped such large quantities of snow that Ed had to plow through up to his knees, thighs, waist, sometimes even armpits. He said he could continue leading, but not with any speed. Waiting behind him, I got colder as the storm continued. If we were to reach Liberty Cap that day, we would have to move faster, so I took the lead. Each upward thrust required great effort. Each step meant clearing the top layer of snow away with my left hand before planting my upward foot. Inching upward at a turtle's pace, we finally reached the summit five and a half hours later, eleven hours after leaving our bivouac.

With wind and driving snow gusting to seventy-five miles per hour, we could not descend, so at about 5 P.M. we decided to dig in and wait for a break in the storm. After an hour of strenuous work, with us alternately overheating and shivering, a cave began to take shape. Then the roof collapsed and we had no choice but to begin again a few feet away. Using our ice axes, we removed inches, then feet of snow as hard as asphalt. An hour or two later we'd hacked out enough room to stretch out our bivouac sack, with just a foot above us in which to maneuver. After Ed managed to melt some water, I spilled it over myself as I tried to drink.

Ed propped up our packs to protect the entrance, but within a half an hour snow had blocked the opening. Although we were shivering and wet, I figured we were better off than we would be outside in the gale. Ed feared we would suffocate, so he kept poking his snow shovel through for ventilation. When he could stand it no longer, he declared, "We must get out of here right now!" And out he went into the wind.

In the time it took me to decide to follow him, enough snow blew in to make it difficult to extricate myself from the bivouac sack. Beginning to panic, I forced my way out. For a few minutes I stood with Ed in the raging storm before yelling, "We *have* to get back in the sack." We pushed it down into what was left of the snow cave and got in, one after the other. Lying across the entrance of the cave, I shivered violently and began to hyperventilate. As the snow piled over our calves, then our thighs, our hips, our torsos, and finally our shoulders, Ed complained of claustrophobia. Though I tried to calm him, I felt the same sense of imprisonment. After an hour or so, Ed announced, "We need to get out and clear off this snow."

As we attempted to rearrange the bivouac sack, it ripped in the wind, leaving us with no recourse but to wrap the remnants around us and huddle together. As I shivered in ever more violent spasms, new snow enveloped us. Each new blast of wind drove particles of snow deeper into our faces. No matter how we drew the bivouac cloth around us, we could not escape the storm; I thought we might die.

Just before dawn we glimpsed stars. Thinking the storm was about to blow itself out, we decided to head down. Weakened by hypothermia, I feebly tried to retrieve Ed's pack from the cave, but it had frozen solid in the ice. By the time I managed to dig out my own, we were socked in again. To descend in a whiteout would be foolhardy, so using my pack for a seat, we sat under the torn bivouac sack and waited for morning. Exhausted as I was by cold, hunger, and lack of sleep, my head kept nodding forward; by the next day my neck ached terribly.

The wind remained fierce, but by dawn the sky had finally cleared. Adamant we consume calories, Ed insisted, "We must eat to stay strong," though nearly all our food was buried in the snow cave—as were Ed's rucksack, stove, hardhat, fuel, cooking pots, half-bag, jumars, down vest, and water bottle, and my foam pad and bowl. Fortunately, my gear was still in my pack, but our only food was a frozen orange and a package of peanuts. As I began peeling the orange, Ed ordered me to eat it all. I ate a chunk, he fed me a peanut, he ate a bite of orange, and so on until we were done. Although at first I nearly threw up the peanuts, I managed to keep them down, and they gave me some strength.

Our next chore was to put on the crampons we'd retrieved from the cave. Back under the bivouac sack Ed put his on first. Struggling,

I got my right crampon on, but my numb fingers made me clumsy. I couldn't manipulate the left one, so Ed fixed the crampon to my boot. When he attempted to jerk our rope out of the snow, it did not budge. Frozen solid. During the time I took to stuff the torn bivouac sack into my pack, Ed traveled fifty yards down the ridge. When I stood up to follow him, I stumbled and fell. Back on my feet I staggered forward. As Ed turned around to check on me, I fell a second time and called him back. With our arms around each other's backs, we walked down past the saddle to the start of the glacier descent, but I kept slipping from his grasp. Our descent of the Emmons Glacier seemed to go on forever. I was so weak and exhausted that at moments I lost the will to continue. But each time I told Ed I could go no farther, he emphatically assured me that I could. Later he mentioned that, unable to see clearly (he had lost his glasses in the snow cave), he had used his boot to trigger small avalanches in order to spot the crevasses.

About a thousand feet above the Schurman Hut at 9,800 feet, I began to feel that I would make it after all. Emboldened, I forged ahead. Still staggering, I reached the hut five minutes ahead of Ed. The door had frozen shut, so we entered through the unlatched front window. Inside, alongside bunks blanketed by drifting snow we found a radio. After checking for batteries and adjusting the antenna we determined it could not transmit. But it did receive. After locating dry bunks away from the windows, Ed broke into a metal storage locker behind the hut and brought back a five-gallon tin full of food. The stove fired up immediately. Relieved to be dry, we waited out the rest of the storm in the hut.

Exhausted, I spent the fifth day of our journey resting on a bunk, wrapped up in a tent we had found folded in the hut. Ed cooked for me, but each swallow of warm liquid tore through my chest like a knife—I must have hurt my esophagus while hyperventilating. The storm continued the next day, our sixth. Still weak, I lay on the bunk reading most of the day. I'd had difficulty sleeping the previous night, plagued by my extreme chest pain and bitterly cold without a sleeping bag or pad. So the next night Ed and I wrapped ourselves together in the tent for warmth and managed to sleep a little.

On the seventh day the storm got worse—something we hadn't thought possible. But I felt much improved and eager to head down, so we decided to crampon up. For a rope we tied together several strands of quarter-inch cord we'd found in the hut. As we opened the door, gale-force winds nearly knocked us off our feet, so we scrambled back inside.

Just when it seemed as though the storm would last forever, the sky grew calm and bright. In the waning, soft light of early evening, we began to descend the glacier. Although the snow conditions were firmer than we'd expected, I still had trouble keeping up with Ed.

Five long hours later we reached the White River campground. Ed led all the way except for the last few hundred yards. We could go no farther and flopped down together on the front porch of the unoccupied ranger cabin where I wrapped my arms around Ed's middle, warming him so he could sleep. At 4 A.M. we hiked the last few miles to the highway where we flagged down a highway-department snowplow. The driver took us back to a maintenance shop where he served us hot coffee and I called Mary Lou. After telling me that several of our climbing companions from eastern Washington were on the mountain searching for us, she told me that my grandmother had died.

I never climbed with Ed again, but I remember what he did to get me off Mt. Rainier where, numbed by hypothermia, I could not move under my own power. Ed Boulton saved my life.

In spite of my close call on Mt. Rainier I longed to climb higher, more distant peaks. In 1972, on my first major expedition, some friends and I climbed a new route up the south face of Alaska's Mt. McKinley, at 20,320 feet the highest peak in North America. Our team was the first ever to use lightweight tactics. Climbing bottom to top in a single push, we took no tents, slept most nights in snow caves, and once, during a two-day storm, hid in a crevasse. After reaching the summit with relative ease, I felt terrific.

Before we left the mountain we started contemplating another, bigger challenge.

three

DISCORD ON K2

ountain-climbing expeditions can forge friendships, strengthen character, and foster heroism. They can as easily sour relationships, expose human weakness, and humble the arrogant. K2, the mountain that would one day represent my greatest success, was in 1975 the scene of my greatest failure. It was a failure not because someone died or suffered a serious injury, but because my obsession to reach the summit helped doom our expedition to disappointment, discord, and, for a time, disgrace.

With its perfect, conelike shape, K2 called to me as Everest never did. In high school, leafing through a history of Himalayan expeditions, I saw a photograph of the mountain, as steep and symmetrical as an Egyptian pyramid, and dreamed of one day climbing it.

Why the second-highest peak at 28,250 feet instead of Everest, nearly a thousand feet higher? Because in 1963 Americans had reached the summit of Mt. Everest, but despite four previous attempts, no American had so far climbed K2. Only one team, the Italians in 1954, had ever made the summit. Our team hoped to make the second ascent up the uncharted northwest ridge. It would have been easier to follow the Italian route up Abruzzi ridge, but we wanted the

The photograph of K2, which Jim first saw while in his teens.

challenge of, and recognition for, completing a new, untested route.

K2 presented risks much greater than those posed by McKinley or any other peak I'd climbed. On the five previous expeditions to K2, six men had died. Its nickname, the Savage Mountain, underscored the risk and increased the attraction. Despite the danger, my McKinley companions and I felt confident we could reach the summit and all return alive.

Located in the Karakoram range nine hundred miles northwest of Everest, the mountain had been closed to climbers for nearly fifteen years because of Cold War border tensions between China and Pakistan. We hoped the gradual thawing of relations between China and the United States resulting from President Nixon's historic visit to China in 1972 might convince Pakistan to open the border area.

Lacking the time and resources to organize a K2 expedition ourselves, we turned to Jim Whittaker, the first American to climb Mt. Everest, to take the lead. As president of Recreational Equipment Inc. (REI), Jim used his contacts in the outdoor-recreation industry to raise $200,000. To help us obtain the coveted climbing permit, he approached his friend Sen. Ted Kennedy. Jim's relationship with the Kennedys dated back to 1965, when he and Sen. Robert Kennedy climbed a remote Canadian mountain named for the late president. After Robert's assassination, Jim served as a pallbearer and remained close to the family. Senator Kennedy convinced the Pakistani government to allow us to attempt K2 in 1975—the first expedition since the border had closed.

Jim's role was never limited to being the expedition's leader. As a climber, he still possessed the enormous personal drive that had got him to the top of Everest twelve years before. When he walked into a room, everybody noticed. Charismatic and six feet five with an Olympian physique, Jim Whittaker seemed bigger than life. During the months we spent preparing for the expedition, I grew to like and respect him more and more. I sensed that, although a bit short on temper, Jim would be an ideal mountain companion.

Though most of our nine-person team had climbed together in

the Cascades, some on Mt. McKinley, only Jim had experience in the Himalayas. Three members of the team had been together on McKinley in 1972: myself, Rob Schaller, a Seattle surgeon, and Leif Patterson, a Norwegian math professor living in Canada.

I considered Rob something of an enigma. He assumed the heavy burden of assembling the medical supplies for the K2 expedition. Rob sacrificed more professionally than any of the rest of us to make the trip, and no one could question his drive, especially up high on a mountain. But his tendency to get depressed sometimes pulled down those around him. This caused me to have some reservations about how he would perform on K2, but if his problem knee held up, I believed Rob could reach the summit.

I harbored no reservations about Leif. A strong man with a gentle soul, I knew he would be good company and, barring illness or injury, would make the summit. My most vivid memory of Leif was stomping up the final seven hundred feet of Mt. McKinley, with him hard at my heels. A superb rock and ice climber, he always put the interests of others ahead of himself. His mountaineering judgment was the best of the lot.

With our support, Jim invited two close relatives to join the expedition: his wife, Dianne Roberts, and his identical twin brother, Lou. This decision would later present some serious problems though, in my opinion, each added value to the expedition. As an owner/manager of Mt. Rainier's guide service, Lou Whittaker climbed year-round. He had expected to go to Everest with Jim in 1963 but backed out because of business conflicts. Lou and I first climbed together in 1969 when we helped rescue an injured man high on Mt. Rainier. I considered Lou the expedition's strongest, most resourceful climber and expected we would pair up on K2. Like me, he was consumed with a desire to reach the summit. When I imagined standing there, it was always with Lou.

At the time Dianne joined the expedition as its photographer, she planned to go no farther than base camp. Gradually, her role changed. After she arranged to get an oxygen mask fitted, we realized she intended to climb high on the mountain. Her lack of climbing experience concerned several members of the team, particularly Lou, as well as some of our wives, who feared her inexperience would put the rest of us at risk. Dianne's declaration that the mountain did not frighten her and Jim's observation that she could go all the way to the summit contributed to their alarm. There was also a concern that Dianne would keep Jim from being "one of the boys," creating distance between him and the rest of us. Unlike most of my companions, I wasn't bothered by Dianne's presence. I suspected how high she went on the mountain would be a function of her strength, adaptation to altitude, and the difficulty of the route, making all the talk at sea level largely irrelevant.

Also invited were Fred Dunham and Fred Stanley, my old friends and climbing companions from eastern Washington, men who had come to search for Ed Boulton and me on Mt. Rainier. I considered Fred Dunham, a friend since we were four, my equal (if not superior) on rock and ice, but seriously questioned his drive to reach the summit. Stanley was invited to replace architect Alex Bertulis—an emigrant from Soviet-controlled Lithuania—with whom Rob, Leif, and I had climbed McKinley. It was Alex who first asked Jim Whittaker to organize the K2 expedition. But we dropped Alex from the team when conflicts developed between him and several members of the group. We did not handle Alex's expulsion well and he left bitter. I regretted losing his friendship but did not regret our decision nor dispute its correctness.

Though Stanley had been my climbing companion back in the early sixties, he was not my first choice to replace Alex. Though able and amicable, I feared his natural caution might make him say "Let's stay in camp" when, to reach the summit, "Let's go for it" was the only choice.

To round out the team we invited cinematographer Steve Marts and the highly acclaimed climber/photographer Galen Rowell. Steve came to make a documentary of the expedition. Galen came prepared to write a book. Once a brilliant rock climber, Steve quit serious climbing for several years following a scare on a vertical wall. I doubted he had the drive to get up high, but in his role as filmmaker that wouldn't really matter. As for Galen, other than for a romp up Mt. Rainier training for K2, we had never climbed together. Although Galen was undeniably strong, with an extraordinary climbing record, he lacked experience above fourteen-thousand feet. How he would perform on K2 remained open to question, but from what I knew, I expected he would do well. Despite some reservations about specific climbers, I believed our team possessed the experience, resolve, and stamina necessary to reach the summit of K2.

1975 K2 expedition team. From left: Leif Patterson, Rob Schaller, Fred Dunham, Jim Whittaker, Dianne Roberts, Lou Whittaker, Jim, Fred Stanley, and Galen Rowell.

Responsibility for raising funds for this and later expeditions fell primarily to the Whittakers. To finance this expedition, Jim Whittaker and Dianne Roberts called on contacts in the recreational clothing and equipment industry and publishers of magazines and books such as National Geographic and Sierra Club Books. I made a commercial for Alaska Airlines, "No one knows Alaska like Jim Wickwire knows Alaska," to raise some money for the trip. Some of us gave slide presentations about previous expeditions to groups that helped cover a bit of the cost. The book contract helped as well.

Years later, after a rash of publicity about my climbing, an acquaintance called to say he had overheard an interesting conversation. Sitting in a coffee shop in a small mountain town, he had eavesdropped on a couple of men. One asked the other, "How do you suppose Wickwire can afford to go on all these expeditions?" "Obvious—he must be dealing drugs," replied the other with utter seriousness. The fund-raising involved in big expeditions is awkward, slow, and arduous—but not illegal. After doing it myself for later, smaller expeditions, I give the Whittakers great credit for all they did.

Team members supported by our families and legions of friends organized the massive supplies required for the long, complex expedition. After our houses overflowed, we rented a warehouse where we could spread out the food and equipment. Mary Lou prepared enormous quantities of granola and other durable foodstuffs. Anne, Cathy, Susie, Bob, and David stuffed candy and other small items into hundreds of plastic bags. Several weeks before our scheduled departure the team met at the warehouse and loaded ten tons of gear into a container for ocean shipment to Pakistan.

Wickwire kids helping pack supplies for K2 expedition. Bob (6) in foreground. Cathy (9) and Susie (8) to left with Anne (10) in background.

My wife, children, and parents all came to the airport to see me off. As I walked to the plane, my nine-year-old daughter, Cathy, whispered in my ear, "Daddy, don't get killed!" In Mary Lou's first letter, she told me that she and my mom had shed a few tears when the plane lifted off, but "more from the excitement" of seeing me leaving on my big adventure "than sadness at being parted." After the family got home, she said six-year-old Bob "went up to his bed, hid his face under the pillow, and cried. He was brave at the airport but couldn't hold back once he got home."

On the plane to Pakistan I asked myself why my desire to climb K2 was so strong. I thought about the business I'd neglect and the birthdays I'd miss. Anne would celebrate her eleventh birthday—the sixth in a row without me there. Bob would turn seven. Mary Lou would have a birthday, and so would I.

I figured I climbed mostly for the challenge. Novelist and climbing historian James Ramsey Ullman observed, "Challenge is the core and mainspring of all human activity. If there's an ocean, we cross it; if there's a disease, we cure it; if there's a wrong, we right it; if there's a record, we break it; and, finally, if there's a mountain, we climb it." I wondered what it would mean to reach the summit of K2. If we succeeded, there would undoubtedly be a lot of media publicity. But that was not a motivation. What was? The inner satisfaction of having faced and overcome the most difficult physical and psychological challenge of my life. And though I did not long for media attention, I did want the recognition of other climbers.

On the flight into Skardu, where we would begin our trek to K2, our pilot flew close by the summit. My heart soared. Through a window, Lou Whittaker and I thought we saw a feasible route past a series of jagged pinnacles near twenty-two thousand feet on the mountain's northwest ridge. Other than that brief aerial view, all we had to go on was an old photograph of the ridge taken in 1909 by the first Italian expedition into the area. We learned later that it is one thing to make judgments about a mountain's difficulty from a photograph or an airplane, quite another when one is climbing it.

To reach the base of K2, we had to walk over a hundred miles, passing through villages in the Braldu River valley, lush and fragrant with orchards. The river flowed with such force it hurled boulders. Most of the time we traveled high above its banks, but sometimes we had no choice but to cross on precarious rope bridges. Gradually the green of the valley faded into the gray and white of the massive Baltoro Glacier.

Dianne Roberts and Jim Whittaker
in hot spring on approach to K2 base camp.

Because of the food and equipment necessary to support a three-month expedition, we hired several hundred local porters. Manzoor Hussain, the Pakistani government's handsome, compact young liaison officer, bore principal responsibility for coordinating them. A major in the Pakistani army long captivated by K2, Manzoor had asked the government for the opportunity to accompany our expedition and convinced them to let him travel to the United States to help organize the food and equipment for shipment to Karachi.

Throughout the approach to base camp, Rob treated more than a hundred porters and their relatives seeking care for various serious, previously untreated ailments such as intestinal parasites and eye damage from cooking smoke. Leif, who aspired to go to medical school, assisted him, taking notes on every case. Rob's competence as a physician impressed me.

With several weeks and fourteen thousand feet to go, Jim Whittaker told Lou and me that we ought to have first shot at the summit. As things presently stood, he expected he and Leif would go second. Although I felt flattered by Jim's confidence, I realized it was far too early to decide the composition of the summit teams, and I wondered how democratic our expedition was going to be. Would selection of the summit team be Jim's alone? Would other members of the expedition help make the decision? As much as I wanted to be on that first summit team, I expected the mountain would ultimately decide. Though neither Lou nor I talked to the others about Jim's comments, they sensed we would be first to attempt the summit. I recall Fred Dunham saying he knew we were supermotivated to get there, but hoped we would be careful when we tried. I could tell he didn't expect to go for the summit, assuming instead he'd be hauling supplies for those of us who did.

No climbing expedition had approached K2 in fifteen years, and the poorly clad porters, many lacking boots, were clearly intimidated by the harsh and unfamiliar mountain environment. Fred Stanley and Fred Dunham criticized Manzoor for his failure to control the porters and the Whittakers and me for nearly every decision we'd made, however small, particularly those involving equipment.

Just as we started alienating other members of the team, our frustrations with them began to grow. Jim expressed concern about Fred Dunham's propensity to get depressed, and Rob and Galen were getting on my nerves. Galen seemed to analyze every issue to death, and Rob was so morose I found it difficult to be around him. To me, life has so much good in it, why focus on the negative? Climbing a mountain requires action, not endless talk.

One morning Rob and Galen became greatly alarmed. Their ski poles had been "stolen" in the night by those "untrustworthy porters." Rob threatened to cut off all medical treatment unless the stolen poles were produced. Galen made similar dire threats. Upon breaking camp, we discovered the poles: Rob's by his tent, Galen's with ours. Exasperated, I told them this would never have happened had they marked and kept track of their poles. Despite my own occasional frustrations with the porters, I felt drawn to them and their intriguing culture. Watching them pray to Mecca every evening, I envied the personal connection they seemed to have with God.

From the beginning, Galen took a lot of verbal abuse from the Whittakers. He particularly irritated Lou. For instance, Galen once asked what he should say in his book about Lou's climbing record. Critical of climbers who wrote books about their expeditions, Lou exploded, "I've been a mountaineer since I was sixteen—I'm a climber, and that's that." Once, after several days of overhearing them second-guess his decisions, Jim blew up. If Rob, Steve, and Galen had gripes, they ought to lay them out on the table in a group meeting. "We never have meetings," came the chorus from their tent. So we had one, hoping to clear the air.

Before we ever reached the mountain, fears of going to the far end of the glacier made half the porters decide to return to their villages. In an effort to keep the rest from leaving, we threatened not to pay them. To underscore our threat we burned some Pakistani currency—much to Manzoor's horror. The eighty porters who remained refused to proceed until we paid them their wages. We paid, and they continued toward base camp. But time was slipping away.

That evening Galen received a letter from his wife, Carol, telling him his father had died. Mary Lou had written me on Carol's behalf asking if I would relay the news to Galen, sparing him the pain of learning about it in a letter. But by the time I spoke to him, he'd already read his wife's letter. Still, he appreciated my sympathy and gave me a brief hug as we walked to the cook tent. That seemed to break the ice, and our relationship began gradually to improve. Walking back to my tent, I wished I'd hugged my own dad good-bye.

Five weeks after leaving home, already three weeks behind schedule, we saw K2's magnificent pyramid emerge from behind a ridge. Soon after that, we arrived at our seventeen-thousand-foot base camp, where we stayed several weeks to adjust gradually to the altitude. On our last trip to haul supplies to the camp, Jim pitched forward into a hidden crevasse. He kept himself from falling all the way in by bracing his upper body against the walls with one foot hooked over the lip of the crevasse. Lou grabbed Jim's heel in the nick of time, and he, Leif, and I, working together, managed to pull him out.

K2 viewed from Concordia, the meeting place of several glaciers.

Unlike our rapid ascent of McKinley, on K2 we established a series of camps, each separated by a few thousand vertical feet.

Several high-altitude porters helped us transport necessary food, rope, oxygen, and other supplies to nineteen thousand feet, where we placed our first camp two thousand feet below a saddle straddling the China-Pakistan border. The ice was so steep the porters could go no farther, so we resorted to winching loads up the last several hundred feet.

From Camp 2, on the saddle, we took periodic forays up a steep slope, searching for a route past the pinnacles between us and the upper northwest ridge. Just as our hopes began to rise, a series of unusually severe storms—with sixty-mile winds and subzero temperatures—imprisoned us in our tents for several days.

I began having a recurring dream in which we came to Pakistan to climb K2 but, for some inexplicable reason, went back to the United States before we had a chance to try. I clamored to return in time to make the climb, but never did. When I awoke, I always felt immense relief to be on the mountain. My dream mystified me at the time, but by mid-June I began to anticipate failure.

Everything now depended on getting around or over the pinnacled ridge to the upper mountain. If we couldn't, then our try for the top of K2 would be aborted—a disaster in more ways than one. Aside from keen personal disappointment and an undercurrent of "I told you so's" from climbing-world pundits, we'd be deep in debt. To be forced back at twenty-two thousand feet would not help sell Galen's book. Steve's film might do slightly better, but not much. Our expedition could end up as much as $50,000 in debt with only minimal prospects of bailing ourselves out through lectures and endorsements.

In spite of the prospect of failure, we continued to discuss summit strategy and hoped for a major breakthrough. Jim, Lou, and I identified climbers we considered strong enough to make the necessary push. After a bout of pneumonia, Leif seemed too weak. But he was improving fast. Rob, so far consigned to base camp and a few carries to Camp 1, appeared full of energy and eager to try. Galen had bronchitis, Fred Dunham a cough, Fred Stanley a sore throat.

The bleaker our prospects for success, the more people complained. Dianne and I discussed the tension within the team. She said she felt unwelcome and ostracized. "They are wrong to assume I have ambitions for the summit," she complained. "All I want is to make this expedition a success." Both Freds felt they had had little involvement in expedition decision-making, and that their suggestions were routinely ignored by Jim. That night after dinner, Dunham told Steve and Galen that my lack of warmth and Jim Whittaker's constant put-downs deeply depressed him. I could hear them talking in subdued voices far into the night. The next morning, Galen reported the Freds might leave the expedition.

After breakfast, Jim and I went to their tent. Jim led off, saying that his principal objective was to get up the mountain and everything he had done so far was directed toward that end. To reach the summit every person on the team was important, and if he'd stepped on their toes, he apologized. Fred Stanley snapped, "Nice pep talk, but I don't believe a word you've said." I angrily interjected, "That's completely unfair." Stanley criticized the Whittakers for the way they ramrodded everything and downgraded people. As a fence-sitter, I was just as bad, and Stanley hoped I'd get a picket up my ass. His words irritated me at the time, but Stanley was right—I was a fence-sitter.

Stanley asserted that as the Whittaker brothers drove for the summit, the rest of the team, except for me, would just be bodies to carry loads. Dunham said he would continue working for the expedition because he felt he had an obligation to the people who had contributed money at his behest. I conceded to the Freds that I wanted to get to the top of K2. "That's why I came," I explained. "If I don't make it to the top, I want to leave without regrets, knowing I gave my all to get there."

I could not accept that all our problems stemmed from a clash of personalities. Granted, Jim came on a bit strong at times, Lou, too, and so did I. But I believed our real problem was a difference in motivation. Stanley insisted that he had come on the expedition to climb with Fred Dunham and me. A nice sentiment but not a suffi-

Lou Whittaker and Jim Whittaker silhouetted against Gasherbrum IV, a difficult 26,000-foot peak near K2.

cient reason to come all the way to Pakistan. In my opinion, neither man ever intended to reach the summit. I sensed that both worried about the women they had left behind. On his last expedition, Stanley had got caught in an avalanche. His wife feared that this time he might not make it back. Dunham's fiancée had lost her former partner in an avalanche, and Fred wanted to do nothing to add to her suffering. All of us missed the women we had left behind. And we could not help but notice the mornings in base camp when Jim and Dianne threw their double sleeping bag over their tent to dry.

The next day, Steve told me that portions of Rob's diary had recently appeared in the Seattle newspapers—a clear violation of our contractual obligations to National Geographic and the Sierra Club. I was infuriated to hear that Rob's girlfriend, Joanne, was giving the news media information about the expedition. Lou's wife wrote that

Joanne regularly appeared on TV reading from Rob's "love letters" and, in her most recent appearance, announced that she and Rob would marry upon his return.

Seething, I asked Manzoor to deliver the following telegram to Mary Lou:

"WE HAVE REPORTS JOANNE IS ACTING AS OFFICIAL OR UNOFFICIAL LIAISON WITH NEWS MEDIA REGARDING EXPEDITION MATTERS. SHE IS NOT AUTHORIZED TO DO SO. OUR CONTRACTUAL OBLIGATIONS TO NATIONAL GEOGRAPHIC SOCIETY AND SIERRA CLUB REQUIRE CAREFUL REVIEW BY US OF ALL INFORMATION RELEASED TO NEWS MEDIA. ALTHOUGH WE CANNOT PREVENT JOANNE FROM TALKING TO MEDIA, PLEASE ADVISE SHE FACES LEGAL ACTION IF SHE CONTINUES TO RELEASE FIRST-PERSON DIARY ACCOUNTS OR PHOTOGRAPHS TO MEDIA."

A day later, as Rob, Steve, and I ate breakfast, Fred Stanley came on the radio and demanded to know the basis of the telegram I had not yet mentioned to Rob. Pressed by Stanley, I did my best to explain and Rob nodded in understanding. Stanley charged me with stabbing Rob in the back, then attacked Jim, Lou, and me for conspiring to put ourselves alone on the summit. Rob assured me he had sent Joanne no diary entries for several weeks and promised to send no more. He promised to tell her not to circulate his photographs except as he explicitly instructed. Calmed by his assurances, I told Manzoor not to send Mary Lou my intemperate telegram. In spite of our past differences, I began warming up to Rob.

That night after dinner everyone except for the Freds came to Lou's and my tent to discuss the tensions threatening to tear apart our expedition. Rob said the Freds felt the expedition had divided into two camps: me, Lou, Jim (and by extension Dianne) in one; everyone else in the other. Galen said that ever since the approach march, he, Steve, the Freds, and to some extent, Leif, had felt ostracized. In his "K2 Marching Song," sung to the tune of "Onward Christian Soldiers," Galen captured their complaints:

Onward Wick and Louie climbing toward Camp Three
Searching for a snow-ramp that will never be.

It existed for a month in their plans and talk
But what they really saw that day were sheer walls of rock . . .

No time left for friendship while the mountain's still undone.
Everyone be positive. Aren't we having fun . . .

K2 needs a team of men who respect each other's views,
Not just prima donnas who pair off in twos.

Onward Wick and Louie reaching for K2
Ever so slowly, receding toward Skardu.

I began to regret some of my conduct but was reluctant to apologize. Too proud, I suppose.

Leif never got as demoralized as the others. He floated back and

Leif Patterson strived to unite our divided team.

forth between the factions, striving for an internal harmony the expedition never achieved. Trying once more to bring us together—the one last hope of a successful expedition—Leif diplomatically suggested that Lou and I were the principal source of the expedition's problems. Obsessed by our desire to reach the summit, we had alienated our companions. He urged us to reach out to the Freds.

Swallowing some of my pride, I dropped by their tent and asked how they were feeling. I also extended myself to Galen, using our shared interest in classical music as a bridge. We talked about my daughter's upcoming recital and discussed his mother, a well-known cello teacher and a friend of Rostropovich's. It helped to have a connection unrelated to our troubled expedition.

During the last day of the storm the team discussed the probability of failure. Reaching only twenty-two thousand feet would be a total wipeout for ours, the most ballyhooed American moun-

Lou Whittaker on K2's northwest ridge.

taineering expedition in recent years. We all knew we would eat a lot of crow. Over dinner, Jim, Lou, and I discussed our chances. So many things had gone against us: bad weather, porter troubles, illness, and unanticipated difficulties getting past the pinnacled ridge to establish a third camp, still six thousand feet below the summit. Steve and Rob had correctly assessed the route as much more difficult than I had. To make the summit we would need some big breaks: good weather, good health, and no more route problems.

Ten weeks after leaving home, Lou and I asked Leif to climb with us to the top of the first pinnacle on the northwest ridge. I led up a steep ice gully. A large rock blocked the path but I managed to pull myself over it in one swift, awkward move—hard work at twenty-two thousand feet. After stopping to belay Lou up to my position, I made a stupid error. As I tried to tie the rope to a picket I'd anchored in the snow, it slithered from my hands back down to Lou—forcing him to make the sixty-foot climb without aid of a fixed rope. When he arrived, I mumbled a sheepish apology. He merely grunted, "It's okay, it could have happened to me."

Leif joined us and led to the top of the first pinnacle. We took turns sitting on its narrow crest, astounded by what we saw: a knife-edged ridge of pinnacles draped with a dangerous blanket of hanging snow. There was no way along the pinnacles or around the sheer ridge walls. Both sides dropped thousands of feet. Even if we managed to get past these obstacles, the absence of a safe retreat back down the ridge in the event someone got sick or injured meant we must turn back. Lou and I had made a big mistake when we looked out the airplane window and concluded that a feasible route past the pinnacles existed. Our insistence that we take this impossible route had doomed our expedition from the start.

Three nights later back at base camp, cognac loosened our tongues, and for a while the team seemed friendly and relaxed . After Jim, Lou, Steve, and Fred Stanley returned to their tents, the rest of us frankly discussed what had gone wrong. Most blamed Jim and Lou (mainly the latter) for the lack of compatibility among the expedition members: by constantly putting people down, they had driven a wedge through the team's heart.

View of northwest ridge from top of the first pinnacle, 6,000 feet below the summit of K2.

I argued that had Galen and the Freds been less intimidated by the Whittakers, we would have had fewer problems, and that I thought it had been unreasonable for them to expect Jim to accept their opinions. After suggesting to Dunham that his and Stanley's illnesses were probably in part psychosomatic, I told him that I hoped the expedition had not destroyed our lifelong friendship. We had simply been moving on different tracks: I had come motivated to climb the mountain. He had not.

Resentful of what she considered unfair criticism of her husband, Dianne staunchly defended Jim. Galen surprised us both when he said Jim had changed a great deal during the expedition and for that he admired him. I never understood just how he thought Jim had changed, but Dianne seemed to appreciate the sentiment. Dianne's,

Galen's, and the Freds' criticism of Lou proved to be one of the few things they could all agree upon.

To reach the summit of K2, I realized, would require not only a strong but a harmonious team united behind a common goal. I promised myself that next time our expedition would be united, next time I would make the summit.

Before heading home, Lou and I met our wives for a brief, delightful tour of Pakistan. It was Mary Lou's first time away from the children for more than a few days and her first time abroad. When she arrived, I was taken aback by her changed appearance: she had cut short her long, dark hair. That afternoon she and Ingrid waited for Lou and me to join them in a Rawalpindi bar. A couple of high-powered British climbers were checking them out as we made our way across the room. "Who are *those* good-looking birds?" inquired one of the men. "That's my wife over there," I warned possessively.

After reaching Karachi, we headed for the seashore, where Mary Lou and I spent a romantic evening under the stars, in the midst of sea turtles making their way across the sand. After a late-night drink with the Whittakers, Ingrid and Mary Lou headed off to our respective bedrooms but stopped and laughed when they realized Lou and I were having difficulty parting from one another in the corridor. In spite of the criticism leveled against Lou, I considered him a trusted companion. With a big heart and great sense of humor, he made me laugh in a way no one else ever could. After months spent together on K2, it seemed almost unnatural to separate.

Every member of the expedition returned to the United States conscious of our failure but nonetheless surprised by the intensity of the criticism leveled against us by other mountaineers. Attending an American Alpine Club board meeting in Washington, D.C., a month after we got back, I first heard the rumor circulating among club officials that our expedition never intended to reach the summit but rather went as agents of the CIA with the sole purpose of placing a monitoring device on the saddle along the Chinese border.

Without specifying any details, the *Tacoma News Tribune* reported, "The American team of climbers that unsuccessfully attempted to climb K2 last summer left ill will behind them in Pakistan." In the same article, the president of the American Alpine Club remarked, "People who could influence the government [of Pakistan] have given us real indications of serious unhappiness with the group headed by Jim Whittaker." He went on to say that climbers must learn "to conduct themselves as members of the human race."

At the AAC's annual meeting in Seattle, the entire K2 team, with the exception of Leif Patterson, back home in British Columbia, got together and discussed the perplexing attacks on our expedition. We agreed that in spite of our many problems on the mountain, except for the currency-burning incident we had been courteous to the Pakistanis. Although the CIA had no involvement with our expedition to K2, a decade earlier some members of the team had indeed been recruited for a CIA-sponsored project. Had the government paid the bill this time, our team would not have returned home $50,000 in debt. As we began to disperse, Fred Dunham observed, "We're together on this thing in a way that never happened on the mountain. Why couldn't it have been like this before?"

Jim Whittaker confronted the AAC's president, asking him to reveal the evidence against us. All he had were two letters. A letter from Manzoor to a friend in the United States, passed along to the American Alpine Club, complained about our burning the money in front of him and the porters. An understandable grievance we conceded. The second letter came from Alex Bertulis, who alleged he had been dropped from the K2 expedition so it could be staffed by CIA agents. His letter attempted not only to discredit the team but to force my resignation from the AAC board.

Exasperated by the unrelenting criticism, I grew restless to do a climb so extraordinary it would shut the critics up. I decided to climb Mt. McKinley by a new route up the south face—alone. The prospect of relying entirely on my own wits and resources, with no chance of personalities clashing as they had on K2, appealed to me.

The night I told Mary Lou about my plans she got upset. Clearly much more worried about this climb than K2 or any previous expedition, she yielded grudgingly: "Go ahead if you insist, but you'd better make all the necessary arrangements in the event you don't return." The following morning, she retracted her reservations, saying she was 100 percent behind me. I let myself believe she supported my decision, but it was obvious she hated the idea. When I mentioned my plans to an acquaintance, Mary Schuman, she asked, "What does Mary Lou think?" I replied, "Since it's something I really want to do, and since not going would throw me into a funk, she went along." To which Mary retorted, "You're on a bloody ego trip."

The months preceding my trip to McKinley were full of reminders why I should not go. Despite the tremendous physical and psychological demands of such a climb, I did little to prepare. Each week I would write in my diary, "I need to work out at the gym" or "I need to take a practice climb up Rainier," but other than for a last-minute hike up Mt. Rainier (during which I lost my tent), I did little but practice law and fantasize about the recognition I'd receive after a solo ascent of Mt. McKinley. When Rob Schaller learned of my plan to climb alone, he urged me to reconsider, arguing that the risks were unacceptably high. I agreed that the risks of solo climbing *were* greater than with a team, but so, too, were the rewards. Even the National Park Service, while technically authorizing my plans, strongly encouraged me to change my mind.

A month before my scheduled departure, word came that another American climber, Charlie Porter, had just left to make a solo climb up McKinley's south face. Hearing that someone else might get there first, I felt as if I'd been kicked in the belly. Yet despite my disappointment, I still planned to make the climb—at least my route was different from Porter's. His objective, the Cassin Ridge, a route I'd tried but failed to climb in 1972, was supposedly the more difficult, but mine had a greater element of uncertainty. (Porter made the summit.)

The night before I left for Alaska, Mary Lou admitted to being afraid each time I left for a major climb. Afterward, I dreamed we were in some kind of prison where we were separated, except for occasional brief visits, for a period of ten years. Gradually Mary Lou began drifting away from me. I entreated her to keep loving me but she remained aloof. The pain of living without her love was almost unbearable. When I awoke to find her sleeping beside me, I felt immense relief.

I reached the base of Mt. McKinley's south face on June 6, my son Bob's eighth birthday. By my own birthday, two days later, the expedition I'd hoped would compensate for my disappointment on K2 instead became a humiliating defeat. I had grossly underestimated the difficulty of the route I had picked. The ice was so steep I could only front-point with my crampons for a few feet before hacking out a platform with my ice ax where I could rest. Without sixty pounds on my back, I might have enjoyed the climb; with it—just one long, grueling struggle.

Climbing such difficult terrain without the assistance of another climber for belays and exchanging leads frightened me, but I continued nonetheless. By late afternoon I was physically and emotionally exhausted, so I prepared to bivouac a thousand feet above the glacier. After lashing my pack to the steep slope by driving my ice ax in up to the hilt, I noticed that the snow seemed unstable. By wedging my ice hammer in the crack between two rocks, I jerry-rigged a safety belay. For dinner I tried to get some instant soups out of the bottom of my pack but couldn't reach them so I drank some grape juice and warm water and, hiccuping constantly, forced down a little beef jerky.

That night I could not sleep for fear I might tumble down the drop-off below me. I couldn't trust the ice ax holding my pack. So all night I alternately sat up or lay with my head wedged into a crack in the rocks, with my legs dangling down over the pack. Since I could not stop hiccuping, I never got comfortable. The hardest part of the night was not the cold or the fear but the realization of how stupid I'd been to come. What the hell was I trying to prove? Coming to climb McKinley solo was nothing but an ego trip. Putting my life at such great risk when I had five small children at home was incredibly irresponsible and utterly selfish.

I knew I must go down and admit defeat. But *how* would I get down? The thought of backing down a thousand feet of hard ice horrified me. Maybe I could traverse beneath the ice cliff and descend a slightly easier slope to the basin below. But if I went that way, I would have to lower myself by rope—rappelling fifty feet over the bergschrund. All night I worried about getting down. What if I lost a crampon? I had no rock pitons and only one ice screw, so rappelling was out of the question.

In the morning I determined I had no choice but to descend the ice unroped. First I slammed in my ice ax, then I set my ice hammer and descended two steps. Again and again—for three seemingly endless hours. My left leg did most of the work, front-pointing as my right foot kept balance. By the time I reached the bottom, my calf was numb from pain.

That night as I prepared to return home, I wrote in my diary,

Mary Schuman was right. Solo climbing is a denial of what's best in mountaineering: that close bond with the man on the other end of the rope. Maybe the positive thing that will come out of this expedition is a return to climbing with the best of companions. Perhaps I've gotten too wrapped up in notions of self-importance.

My failure on McKinley compounded the feelings of frustration and disappointment triggered by what had happened on K2. Uninterested in spending a weekend around a bunch of critics, I decided not to attend what was dubbed a routine board meeting of the American Alpine Club. When I didn't show, Alex Bertulis seized the opportunity to oppose our application to return to K2, and the board decided to support another team's application over ours. Infuriated by the news, I resigned.

But our K2 expedition team did not require the American Alpine Club's support to return to the mountain. We applied directly to the Pakistani government, and when they turned us down, Jim Whittaker went back to Sen. Ted Kennedy for help. Kennedy asked his old Harvard friend Prime Minister Bhutto to overrule Pakistan's minister of tourism and authorize our expedition.

Working late at the office on New Year's Eve, 1976, I received the electrifying news that we had been granted permission to return to K2 in eighteen months. Euphoric, I raced home, threw my arms around Mary Lou, and danced around the kitchen in celebration.

four

LOSS OF INNOCENCE

Three weeks before the Pakistani government granted us permission to return to K2, Leif Patterson died in an avalanche.

Leif, his twelve-year-old son Tor, and a seventeen-year-old family friend left early to climb a mountain near their home in British Columbia. It was twelve days before Christmas. Leif told his wife, Marijke, he expected to return that evening. Around noon she suddenly sensed his presence. Had something happened? The weather was clear and fairly warm, so when they failed to return that night, Marijke's fears mounted. The next morning she, her nine-year-old daughter Marjan, their German shepherd, Troll, and two local climbers hiked into the valley beneath the peak. Looking up at the mountain, Marijke felt certain Leif and the boys were dead. While the two climbers continued toward the base of the mountain, she and her daughter went to the park headquarters to arrange a search. At first, the rangers dismissed her fears as unwarranted, but eventually agreed to send a helicopter.

The pilot spotted Leif's pack in the path of an avalanche; a ground search discovered his leg sticking out of the snow, his body still roped to the boys', buried in the snow nearby. Signs of scraping across the steep scree slope above suggested that someone had slipped on the rocky debris and triggered the avalanche. Cracks in Leif's hard hat, and minor cuts on his forehead and chin, indicated he had struck rock on the way down, perhaps trying to arrest the boys' fall.

In the hours and days after Jim Whittaker relayed the terrible news, I could not stop thinking about Leif: his decency, his boyish smile, his voice with its lilt and hint of skepticism. The most fair-minded of us all, Leif Patterson was the only person on K2 who had continuously strived to unite our divided team.

Leif's death connected us as we had never been in Pakistan. The

Leif Patterson and his son, Tor.

members of the K2 expedition traveled together to the service in a van. We walked down an abandoned forest road to Leif's home where his widow stood in the doorway. Inside, we met his parents and Marjan, whose strength and poise made me think of my own three daughters. The ceremony moved me, particularly its inclusion of Leif's and Tor's favorite music. Listening to a recording of Tor playing Beethoven's "Für Elise" on the piano, I wept.

We had always expected Leif would return with us to K2. When permission to climb arrived shortly after his death, we asked another friend, Dusan Jagersky, to join the expedition. I had met Dusan in 1972, a few years after he emigrated from Czechoslovakia in the wake of the Soviet invasion.

Dusan left his job as an avalanche patrolman and mountain guide and began life in America working in a Harlem sweatshop. After he saw a poster of Washington State's Mt. Shuksan, Dusan resolved to leave New York as soon as he had saved enough money. One morning, riding the subway to work, he read a newspaper article about Mt. Rainier. Within two weeks, Dusan bought an old Volkswagen, acquired a map, drove west to the state of Washington, and became a Rainier guide and climbing instructor. Not long after he arrived, Dusan met and married Diana Chiarelli, the love of his life.

In his spare time, Dusan explored Alaska. He abandoned the cumbersome, fixed-rope tactics of previous Alaskan expeditions and forged new ways up difficult peaks with the lightest possible resources. In 1974, he and his friend Bill Sumner made the first ascent of Mt. Geist where, avoiding an easier route, they climbed a two-thousand-foot sheer ice face to the summit. But the Fairweather Range was Dusan's great passion. Located between Glacier Bay and the Pacific Ocean, these ice-covered mountains kept calling him back. Throughout the early 1970s he dominated the climbing there. He had scaled five mountains in the range, including the crown peak, Mt. Fairweather, during an expedition with me in 1973. Dusan and I first climbed together in 1972 when we scaled an exceptionally difficult route up Mt. Hood's Yocum Ridge.

*Dusan Jagersky on Mt. Quincy Adams
in the Fairweather Range.*

In Alaska and the Cascades Dusan had become one of my
favorite climbing companions and a special friend. He was among the

most warmhearted, exuberant people I knew. A short, powerfully built man, he often conveyed the impression of subdued mirth. Dusan displayed a sensitivity and thoughtfulness rarely seen in men of action. Sometimes, sitting across a dinner table from one another, we communicated entirely through glances. We looked forward to a chance to reach the summit of K2 together.

To prepare for that expedition we decided to return to Alaska's Fairweather Range. Most climbers who go there to test their abilities against the steep snow and ice meet not fair weather, but rain, sleet, whiteouts, even earthquakes. Captain Cook, who named the range, must have seen it on a rare sunny day. Its inclement conditions probably explain the dearth of expeditions to the Fairweathers, and the number of unscaled peaks still available to climb. Yet the stunning beauty of those ice mountains rising from the sea made up for all these obstacles.

Although we aspired to climb two of the range's major peaks—Mt. Salisbury and Mt. Crillon—we knew there were marvelous opportunities for first ascents on four lower, but far more difficult, peaks. They had the added attraction of being composed of hard granite, the rock most favored by climbers. One of these was Mt. Abbe. Of the remaining three, the most attractive was Peak 8440, an unnamed mountain we referred to by its altitude.

Dusan suggested we invite an exceptional rock climber, Al Givler. By training a mechanical engineer, Al had worked as an emergency paramedic for the Mountain Rescue Council and taught first aid and mountaineering at the University of Washington. Already close friends, Al and Dusan had recently gone into business together as climbing guides. Since Al had just been added to the K2 team, it made great sense for him to come. We also decided to invite cinematographer Steve Marts, my 1975 K2 teammate, to film the expedition.

During the four months preceding the trip, I did more to get in shape than before any previous expedition. I ran nearly every day, climbed stairs, and undertook a rigorous weight program to strengthen my arms and shoulder muscles. By late spring I felt mentally and physically ready for the Fairweathers, and after my disappointment on K2 and Mt. McKinley, hungry for a success.

Dusan and Steve ferried our supplies in a twelve-foot Zodiac, a motorized rubber raft. Crossing interconnecting inland water from Juneau, they reached a remote inlet of Glacier Bay where Al and I flew in by float plane and joined them. We piled into the raft and putted around, admiring the spectacular scenery. Before heading into the mountains, we donned neoprene survival suits, jumped into the frigid water, and spent the afternoon frolicking like seals. When a huge slab of ice broke away from the vertical face of Reid Glacier, we bobbed like corks on the ensuing waves.

Since we expected our expedition to last at least three weeks, we needed a lot of equipment. So we put five hundred pounds of supplies on plastic sleds and hauled them across the Brady Glacier. On the far side of the huge, fanlike glacier, a high ridge posed the one major obstacle to reaching base camp. On our third day, halfway up a 2,500-foot slope to the crest of the ridge, a storm moved in. For two days we remained trapped in our tents beneath a forty-foot ice cliff we believed would protect us from avalanches that kept thundering down. To pass the time we read, talked, and wrote in our diaries.

Early the next morning, an enormous section of the ice cliff collapsed beside us and the ground

Al Givler frolicking in Glacier Bay.

shook. I awoke with a jolt and moved instinctively into a fetal position. Peeking out the tent door, I saw several tons of debris, the closest just ten feet away. The main section of the cliff above us was still intact—but we saw ominous cracks. Badly shaken and worried more ice would fall, we moved our tents to an area directly beneath the most stable corner of the ice cliff. Even there, minor avalanches dumped snow on us. Rather than spook us, the fact we had survived such a close encounter with disaster seemed to bless our expedition with good luck.

Yet stuck in a tent and prevented from climbing by the storm, I felt discontented. Low spirits often make me introspective, and that evening, after hours of soul-searching, I made a tentative decision to stop serious climbing after returning from K2. When my son Bob turned nine the next day, I would miss his birthday for the third year in a row. Since the early 1970s I had gone on at least one expedition every year. I realized that my obsession not only distracted me from my law practice but kept me away from my children for months every year of their childhood. I needed to make more time for them, and since my business required me to travel, I knew I must cut back on climbing. I committed to be with Bob when he turned ten.

The weather improved the next morning and we climbed to the ridge crest. Dusan shoveled his way up, digging a trench in the new snow. As we followed him up the slope, I marveled at his prodigious strength. When I noticed Dusan and Al start ascending a steep, unstable stretch, I yelled, "That slope looks dangerous. Shouldn't you guys get off?" Al retorted, "Shut up!" Following their tracks, I quickly realized they had had no choice, there was no other route. I later apologized for second-guessing them. We spent the night atop the ridge, exhausted from climbing through the deep snow. From there, the walk to base camp seemed easy.

The next few days we relaxed around the campsite. Dusan delighted us with his yodeling and remarkable imitation of Louis Armstrong singing and playing blues trumpet. I could not believe how much he sounded like the real thing. Al often wandered off to a rock outcrop where, silhouetted against the sky, he played haunting music on his harmonica. To this day I think of him whenever I hear "The Streets of Laredo." Steve, who had done little if any exercise to prepare for the rigors of a three-week expedition, got sick from exhaustion and spent two days resting in the tent. I read Nabokov.

On my thirty-seventh birthday, Dusan "cooked" me a birthday cake. In the lid of one of the cooking pots he prepared a concoction of strawberry Jell-O–covered cheesecake with a border of chocolate pudding and a honey sesame cookie crust. It was delicious.

The next day, Al offered to stay with Steve so Dusan and I could attempt Mt. Abbe before we all turned our attention to Peak 8440. After two days of superb climbing, most of it on ice, and a few short stretches on exquisite granite, we stood on Abbe's summit. Knowing that we were the first ever to stand there, I felt elated. When we returned tired and filthy to base camp, Al welcomed us with a bath of melted snow heated on the camp stove. Using a foam pad, a bivouac sack, and some plastic, he had spent the previous two days constructing a full-sized tub. The only negative was putting back on my dirty underwear. (Always trying to conserve space and weight I hadn't brought any extras.)

Since the clear weather continued to hold, we decided to attempt Peak 8440 the following day. The crevasses that blocked our approach had convinced us not to climb Salisbury or Crillon, so Mt. Abbe and Peak 8440 would be it for this expedition. We knew Peak 8440, with its steep central rib, would present the most difficult climbing so far.

Steve said he felt up to tackling the mountain and got ready to film our ascent. His filming slowed us down, but we still reached a point fifteen hundred feet above the glacier by noon. Since much of the climb was on rock, Al led—with a balletic grace—as the rest of us struggled to keep up. Late in the day we came upon a narrow crest of snow. After converting it into a comfortable platform, we ate dinner and crawled into our bivouac sacks for the night.

The next morning Al led us through the last rock section. When Dusan spotted a ribbon of ice leading through a rock head-wall to the final summit slope, he whooped for joy. Instead of going directly to the top we decided to wait for cooler, safer temperatures to allow the snow to harden. After digging out platforms three hundred feet below the summit, we spent the day reading, sleeping, and catching up on our diaries.

We reached the summit near midnight just as the sky turned pink—a phenomenon of the high northern latitude. In the exquisite silence, gazing at the surrounding mountains and valleys, ocean and

Dusan Jagersky, Steve Marts, Al Givler, and Jim Wickwire on summit of Peak 8440 at midnight.

inland waters, knowing we were the first ever to climb the peak, I felt completely happy. Any thoughts I'd had of ending my climbing career evaporated. As the sun set, we lingered in the rosy twilight. "Jim, look at Fairweather over there, you can see the route we did four years ago," Dusan remarked. "That was a great climb," I responded, "but this one's better."

We all agreed that the best way to return to camp was to climb across the mountain's north face to reach a col between Peak 8440 and the next mountain to the east. From there we planned to descend a relatively easy gully to base camp. We had approached the summit roped together; on the descent we could stay roped as a foursome or break into pairs. For some time I had sensed Dusan and Al becoming a twosome, drawn together by their new business. I could tell they wanted to pair up. Feeling a bit left out, I offered to head down with Steve, who seemed depleted from his recent illness. We roped up and left Al and Dusan reveling in the view.

Although it was possible to walk along the surface in crampons, I feared if we did, one of us might accidentally punch a foot through the fragile crust and trip. So I descended diagonally, face into the slope, kicking steps for Steve and the others to follow. When I glanced up at Al and Dusan, they appeared bemused. Neither seemed to understand why I was taking this extra precaution.

After about three hundred feet, I determined it was safe to crampon across the mountain's upper north face toward the col. Steve and I had just begun our traverse when I heard a sharp, scraping sound. As I spun around, I saw Al on his stomach, sliding headfirst down a forty-degree slope. "God damn it!" I yelled, knowing I had seen the start of an uncontrolled fall. An instant later, I watched in horror as Dusan slid headfirst down the same slope, striking a rock outcrop with such force that his crampons sent up a huge shower of sparks.

Steve thought he saw Al and Dusan, still roped together, slow down before disappearing down a narrow gully. Maybe they had landed on a ledge? "We've got to descend fast if we're going to help them," I insisted. Belayed by Steve, I climbed down to a dome of snow where I could see all the way to the Gilman Glacier four thousand feet below. Shaped like a V, the steep gully had rock outcrops on the left side, snow on the right, but no ledge. No one could survive such a fall. Looking down the gully, I felt sick. "Dusan! Al!" I yelled pointlessly, knowing I would hear no answer.

Al Givler and Dusan Jagersky on summit of Peak 8440 a few minutes before their fatal accident.

I returned to Steve, who by this time was distraught. "I'll get you home to Sally," I promised. Numbed by what had just happened, I focused on getting us down safely. We traversed to the saddle, now belaying every pitch (or 150-foot rope length). Although unnecessary in a technical sense, this safeguard seemed to reassure Steve. Through the night we descended two thousand feet down an ice gully to the glacier, and then base camp. Anxious to report the accident, we did not stop to sleep but collected our equipment and supplies, zipped up Al and Dusan's gear in their tent, and headed out. All day, in my mind, I kept seeing the two of them falling, like a film clip endlessly replayed.

Leif's death had been a hard blow. But these friends died right in front of me. As Steve and I walked away from Peak 8440, I kept asking myself how this could have happened to such competent climbers. Did Al and Dusan disdain the steps I kicked for them to use? I suspected that one of them broke through the crust, triggering the fall that pitched them both down the slope. Though we saw Al fall first, neither Steve nor I could tell who actually triggered the fall. Why speculate? They were dead. Nothing could bring them back.

Steve and I camped for the night on the ridge above the slope where the ice wall had collapsed, nearly obliterating us two weeks before. All the next day I carefully belayed Steve down the avalanche-prone slope. Exhausted, we stopped at the bottom and slept. On the third day we hiked across Brady Glacier's flat expanse to the beach, where we camped for the night. At dawn we took off in the Zodiac. Steve took charge, guiding us toward the mouth of Glacier Bay and the National Park headquarters where, four days after the fall, we finally reached a telephone.

After reporting the accident to the park ranger, I called Mary Lou. "Steve and I are all right, but Al and Dusan aren't coming out." "How bad?" she asked. "They're dead," I replied. After telling her what had happened, I asked Mary Lou to go with Jim Whittaker to Dusan's wife, Diana, whom she'd seen just two nights before. Later Jim called to say that neither Diana Jagersky nor Al's wife, Linda, had yet been notified. Diana wasn't home and Linda was hiking on Mt. Rainier, so Mary Lou tracked down the women's parents, and they relayed the dreadful news.

Diana called during breakfast the following morning. As I picked up the phone, my stomach clenched. She wanted to know exactly what had happened, so I told her. Understandably, she held out some hope

Dusan had survived. She wanted to believe he had landed on a ledge where, injured, he waited for me to rescue him. Her suspicions upset me. I felt desperate to convince her I had not abandoned her injured husband. Though she admitted having lived through this many times in her nightmares, she could not believe Dusan was really gone.

Linda Givler and Dusan's friend Bill Sumner broke into the conversation. For the next hour I talked with the three of them, carefully describing the north wall of Peak 8440, the circumstances of the fall, and the impossibility of the men's survival. Bill alternately articulated the wives' concerns and apologized for being inquisitorial. Diana asked me to recover Dusan's body since "he would want to be buried near his family in Czechoslovakia." I told her that, weather permitting, we would try that afternoon. Though Diana wanted Dusan's body retrieved, she insisted we not endanger ourselves in the process. I told Linda, whom I'd not met, that though I had not known Al before the expedition, I'd come to like and admire him. I felt the inadequacy of my words. Wound up and burdened by what I'd seen, I knew my tone was impersonal, not compassionate as Mary Lou's voice would have been. But I could not let go yet—I still had to search for what was left of my companions.

When I called Jim and Lou Whittaker and asked if they would help me look for Al and Dusan's remains, they dropped what they were doing and flew directly to Alaska. As their plane landed, I felt a surge of relief; the sight of those two big men I liked so well gave me needed strength. An hour later, the three of us boarded a helicopter and flew to the Gilman Glacier. Conscious of Diana's lingering hopes, I asked the helicopter pilot to slowly move up alongside the mountain, so we could look for signs of a ledge. Starting at the base, he zigzagged his way up. But the wall was sheer, we saw nothing that could have stopped the fall.

After a couple of unsuccessful attempts, we landed in the area where we expected to find Al's and Dusan's bodies. Dumping our packs, we walked halfway up the three-hundred-foot cone of avalanche debris to an object darker than the rocks embedded in the snow around

Aerial view of Peak 8440 that shows the steep wall down which Dusan and Al fell to their deaths.

it—Al's blue parka. Around it, irrefutable evidence that he and Dusan had died in the fall: a sock, Dusan's hat, a smashed fuel bottle, Dusan's

watch, some bone fragments, and worst of all, Al's scalp—hair and all. When Jim found it, he walked toward me, tears streaming down his face. I hugged him but felt strangely detached. To accomplish an otherwise intolerable task, I had shut down my emotions.

The next morning we searched for another two hours, threatened by rocks crashing down from the mountain wall. We found Dusan's overmitten, part of his camera, a small piece from his wool shirt, some sun lotion, film, and Al's nylon ankle gaiter, along with several pieces of flesh and a small piece of skull. I found the gaiter partially buried beneath a large block of ice—untorn with a functioning zipper. Al's and Dusan's bodies probably fell into the bergschrund, but continuous rockfall prevented us from making a thorough search. They could just as easily have been buried in the avalanche cone, but we didn't know where to start digging. Based on what we found, however, we knew they had fallen with incredible force.

On our flight back to Bartlett Cove we learned that Diana, Linda, Bill Sumner, and his wife, Louise, had just arrived and were awaiting us. As I stepped down from the helicopter, Diana ran toward me and we hugged hard. She and Linda thought we'd brought their husbands' bodies with us. They'd understandably misinterpreted a radio message intended to convey to the authorities that we had found confirmation of Al's and Dusan's deaths: "We are returning with cargo." We explained that their husbands' bodies, like those of the victims of a catastrophic plane crash, could not be retrieved.

Searching for Al's and Dusan's remains by myself would have been terribly difficult; I felt grateful to Jim and Lou for coming and for their compassion. They visited with us for a couple of hours, then returned home. I accompanied the others on a flight back into the Fairweather Range for a final view of the mountain.

At dinner, over lots of wine and Scotch straight up, we shared memories both happy and sad. The next morning, Diana and I rose early and went for a long walk. Diana had been more than Dusan's wife, she had been his best friend. We talked about his past, his hopes and aspirations, the terrible wrenching of this permanent separation and the loneliness she would bear. Diana told me that on the night of the accident, she had felt Dusan come into their bed while she was half-asleep. By the time she completely awakened, he was gone. How she loved him! Her head told her he was dead, but her heart would not let him go.

*Lou and Jim Whittaker at base of Peak 8440's north face during
search for Al and Dusan's bodies. Avalanche cone at right.*

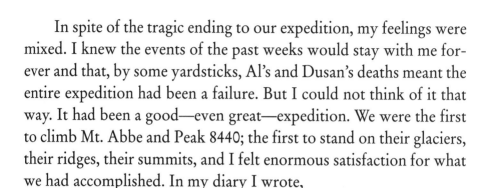

In spite of the tragic ending to our expedition, my feelings were mixed. I knew the events of the past weeks would stay with me forever and that, by some yardsticks, Al's and Dusan's deaths meant the entire expedition had been a failure. But I could not think of it that way. It had been a good—even great—expedition. We were the first to climb Mt. Abbe and Peak 8440; the first to stand on their glaciers, their ridges, their summits, and I felt enormous satisfaction for what we had accomplished. In my diary I wrote,

> *A slip on hard snow with its resulting consequences cannot erase or diminish what happened to that point. Always, there will be pain associated with this trip, but joy will be there too. The three weeks we had together will remain among my most treasured days in the mountains.*

Even though Al and Dusan had died and I had seen their horrible remains, I did not want to stop climbing. Convinced that their deaths, like Leif's, resulted from human error, I planned to avoid the mistakes they had made—to be bold yet prudent. I realized that more friends would probably die climbing, nonetheless I felt compelled to keep pushing myself to new summits and bigger challenges. By facing danger I believed I could push back my own mortality.

I did not cry for Al and Dusan for over a year. In the hospital in late 1978, recuperating from lung surgery, I suddenly burst into spasms of sobbing, and Mary Lou wrapped her arms around me as my grief for Al and Dusan finally poured out.

Nine days after we returned from Alaska, 150 friends and relatives of Al and Dusan traveled to the base of Mt. Rainier for their memorial service. At their wives' request, I related the story of our expedition, the accident, and its aftermath. Reluctant to prepare my remarks, I spoke extemporaneously. Afterward, Diana, Linda, and many others thanked me. But I felt empty, concerned I had failed to articulate what had occurred up there, how I felt about Al and especially Dusan.

We drove home from the service with Stim Bullitt, a lawyer, author, and businessman. A friend of both Al and Dusan, he had planned to climb Mt. McKinley with them later that month. A week earlier, terribly upset by the news of their deaths, Stim had gone straight to the mountains where he broke his ankle in a fall. On the ride home from the service, he seemed lost in thought for a while, then remarked, "You did a great job, Jim, successfully walking the very delicate line between over-sentiment and grisly detail on one side, and indifferent detachment on the other." His comment meant a lot to me.

The rest of the way home, we talked of nothing but climbing. When we parted, I told Mary Lou I looked forward to getting to know Stim better. Bill Sumner and I decided to honor Al's and Dusan's memory by keeping their promise to Stim—we asked him to climb Mt. McKinley with us the following spring. On that trip our friendship blossomed. We turned back short of the summit when Stim, age fifty-eight, began to stagger from exhaustion, possibly the onset of cerebral edema. As Ed Boulton had helped me down Rainier several years before, I linked arms with Stim and helped him down to camp. When Stim and I returned to McKinley two years later, he was stronger, but storms repelled us a few hundred feet from the summit. He tried again. In 1981, at age sixty-two, Stim, Bill Sumner, and a companion reached the top of Mt. McKinley.

In the months following the accident, different things triggered memories of Al and Dusan. Sometimes Dusan came to me in my dreams. Once, during a presentation of Steve's film of our expedition, I experienced a sharp tremor traveling from my head to the base of my spine at the point in the film when a large rock falls down a nearly vertical wall. Something about that moment, perhaps the sound of scraping rock, brought it all back with painful immediacy. Flying to Alaska on business, I sometimes saw the entire Fairweather Range sliding by the window. I could never see those mountains without thinking of Dusan and Al, entombed in ice and snow on the far side of Peak 8440. On one flight, air turbulence reminded me of Dusan. Was he out there shaking the elements? I missed his powerful, charismatic presence. I missed his friendship.

Twenty-one years later, I miss him still.

five

BIVOUAC ON K2

I n the months preceding our return to K2 in 1978, Alex Bertulis began circulating rumors that this expedition, supposedly like the last, was organized and funded by the CIA. Just as the *Seattle Times* prepared to break the story, Jim Whittaker retained my law partner, Chuck Goldmark, and threatened it with a libel suit. The newspaper pulled the story and the rumors stopped—for a while. Then, in Pakistan, on the day before the team began its trek, we introduced ourselves to a group of reporters.

Around we went: Jim Wickwire, lawyer; Craig Anderson, zoologist; Terry Bech, cellist and anthropologist; Cherie Bech (Terry's Australian wife), nurse; Diana Jagersky, clothing designer and art student; Skip Edmonds, Rob Schaller, and Chris Chandler, physicians; Lou Reichardt, neurobiologist; Rick Ridgeway, filmmaker and author; John Roskelley, photographer/lecturer (who would later publish several climbing books); Dianne Roberts, photographer; Jim Whittaker, president of REI and expedition leader. Then Bill Sumner described himself as a tent maker and a reporter pounced. "Are you not a nuclear physicist?" When Bill said yes, the reporter spun around to Whittaker and asked, "Are you here to plant a monitoring device

1978 K2 team arriving in Karachi, Pakistan.

on the ridge between Pakistan and China?" "No," said Jim, laughing, with a twinkle in his eye, "just a microfilm list of expedition contributors and an eagle feather." By this point, the CIA allegations, previously so upsetting, were beginning to amuse us.

Bad news cut short our amusement when word came that the British expedition preceding us up the mountain had lost a climber in a giant slab avalanche. The British abandoned the mountain at twenty-two thousand feet before anyone got the chance to attempt the summit. The climbers we saw seemed shaken and sad. Their news reminded us all of the risk we were about to take—even the best of us, even the most careful.

We returned to K2 with a larger and stronger team than we had had in 1975, but we did not avoid personality problems—

although we tried. Two years earlier Jim had decided Lou Whittaker should not return with us in '78. Despite my affection for Lou, I knew he could be a disruptive force, especially when pitted against Jim—or *with* his brother against other members of a team. Jim conceded that if both Whittakers went back to K2, their intense competition combined with an ongoing conflict between Lou and Dianne would undoubtedly harm the expedition. Lou understood and wished us well.

Lou's absence was insufficient to insure a harmonious climb. The expedition began smoothly enough; striving to avoid the dictatorial approach for which he had been criticized three years before, Jim bent over backward to solicit team members' opinions. Everyone began the climb with reason to feel like an equal participant and a valued team member. Our problems emerged slowly, but they engulfed us nonetheless.

We simply had too many competing egos ever to come together as a team. When Whittaker selected four of us to make the first assault on the summit, those denied the chance felt disappointed. They labeled us the "A" team and called themselves the "Bs": B stood for "best"; A, for "assholes." Another problem faced by the expedition—one we had not experienced in '75—was a very public lovers' triangle.

Since our last attempt, one team had reached the summit of K2: the Japanese in 1977, by the Italians' Abruzzi route. Still eager to climb the mountain by a route of our own, we set out to reach the top by way of the northeast ridge, a route that had defeated a strong team from Poland two years before.

Early on, Lou Reichardt, who joined the expedition with a reputation as a strong climber intolerant of weaker and less competent team members, commented that he, John Roskelley, Rick Ridgeway, and I appeared to be the "strong men" of the expedition. I agreed.

The northeast ridge of K2.

Reichardt's drive had so far got him to the summit of two Himalayan peaks—I hoped it would help get us to the summit of K2. Rick Ridgeway struck me as a particularly gentle, sensitive person despite his powerful build—a good man with whom to share a tent, or a rope. John Roskelley displayed an almost boundless energy.

Like me, John was highly competitive and had a wife who accepted his frequent absences as he headed off on climbs around the world. Extremely direct, he said exactly what he thought. Needless to say, this caused occasional friction within the group, but I found his manner refreshing—particularly since I seldom was the target of his barbs. Mutual respect and a shared passion to reach the summit drew us together. Although John suffered from a bronchial infection for several weeks early in the expedition, his energy hardly flagged and he never failed to fulfill his responsibilities to the team.

Our problems in 1978 had nothing to do with the 350 porters who helped us haul supplies. Unlike '75 when porter troubles plagued us from the start, this time our relationship with them stayed relatively trouble-free. Pakistan's liaison officer Mohammed Saleem Khan motivated the porters to serve our expedition with dedication, although differences of culture and language did create occasional confusion.

Other than Saleem, no one did more to help us reach base camp in the record time of thirteen and a half days than a handsome, thirty-eight-year-old ex-soldier named Sadiq Ali. When he accepted our offer to stay on as a high-altitude porter, he conveyed the impression he did not want to go. Most of us missed this nonverbal message. But Bill Sumner, who consistently made an effort to reach across our ethnic barriers and communicate with the porters, sensed he wanted to withdraw. So Bill sought him out and learned that Sadiq's wife was due to deliver their fifth child in less than a month. As much as Sadiq could have used the additional income, he felt he must return to her.

Bill and I went to visit Sadiq at the rock shelter where the porters took their tea and meals. There we said our good-byes and passed around photographs of our families. Drinking tea, eating chapatis, talking about our lives back home, I grew closer to these men who were helping me reach my goal. Bill won my admiration on this expedition. Although he stayed healthy and fit and always pulled his weight, I admired him most for his humanity. For Bill the summit was not all-important. His goal was to come away from K2 with a good climbing experience and an understanding of Pakistan and its many cultures. Watching him quietly, respectfully blend in with the porters made me realize something I could not see in '75: reaching the summit was not the only reason for someone to make this journey.

On the glacier approaching Camp 1 (which would serve as our advanced base camp during the expedition) Cherie Bech and Chris Chandler fell into a crevasse and had to be rescued. This exasperated me. Reichardt hadn't fallen in, I hadn't fallen in, Jim hadn't fallen in—what was the matter with them? Why weren't they paying attention?

Neither Cherie nor Terry Bech appeared to me to be strong. As far as I could tell, the last big climb they'd done was on Dhaulagiri (another major Himalayan peak) seven years before. No doubt Cherie had been tough then: at five months pregnant she had managed to pull Terry out of a crevasse. But why were they with us now? Jim's sole criterion for selecting team members seemed to be an individual's previous high-altitude climbing experience—regardless of *when* that experience was acquired. In my opinion, his decision to include semiretired climbers such as Cherie and Terry weakened the team.

Chris impressed me as an amusing companion who coughed a lot because of all the cigarettes he smoked, but who otherwise looked in remarkably good shape. Reichardt and Roskelley complained that he had done a poor job helping to establish Camp 2. Refusing to climb the steep ice, Chris instead stayed on the rock, causing stones to shower down upon the climbers below. "He's just plain loafed so far," they grumbled. "He takes more rest days than anyone else and carries only the lightest of loads." A couple of days later, Reichardt criticized Chris's poor performance to his face.

From the moment Chris and Cherie fell into the crevasse, we sensed a connection developing between them. Several days later, after the rest of us had descended to Camp 1 to wait out a minor storm, Chris and Cherie sent word that they intended to spend a second night together at Camp 2, whereupon Roskelley predicted, "Terry Bech is about to get hurt." Offended by their conduct, Roskelley, Ridgeway, Reichardt, and I became quite agitated. While we continued gossiping self-righteously, Bill Sumner used his time teaching the porters how to handle a rope, use a jumar, rappel, and rescue someone from a crevasse.

Jim radioed Chris and told him it would be "politically wise" to

Chris Chandler and Cherie Bech.

descend toward Camp 1 in order to kick off avalanches and make way for others to carry supplies to Camp 2. Chris agreed and started down, but then returned to Cherie. That night Jim *ordered* Chris down. "Be there in time for breakfast." The other members of the team were now so mad at Chris it seemed likely that the only person left willing to rope up with him would be—of course—Cherie.

The next morning Jim, Chris, Terry, Cherie, Dianne, Bill, and I met at Camp 1 to discuss "the situation." Jim reprimanded Chris and Cherie for hurting team morale. Team members believed they were having an illicit affair—whether or not they were—and this was a problem. They defended their decision to wait out the storm at Camp 2 and, while never denying they were lovers, complained about the paranoia running rampant through Camp 1. Throughout the entire embarrassing encounter Terry treated Chris and Cherie with affection and never raised his voice. Cherie mentioned she hadn't come down to carry supplies from Camp 1 to Camp 2 when Jim asked because she didn't think she *could*, reinforcing my belief she lacked the strength and skill necessary to make the climb.

Despite two or three sections of steep ice, we made our way toward a site for Camp 3 without difficulty. I enjoyed the opportunity to lead with Jim, who, unlike most expedition leaders, helped forge the route up the mountain. At 22,300 feet we found a protected platform beneath a huge serac. A serac is a detached, unstable section of a glacier that often collapses. Although most are dangerous to climb or camp beneath, this one we judged safe. One day standing above Camp 3, we looked down and saw a double rainbow, complete circles, one inside another. Waving our arms, we could see our refracted images inside the inner circle. The return to camp felt magical, and everyone seemed to relate a little better for a while. But that didn't last long.

Someone mentioned that Terry must be terribly hurt by Chris's and Cherie's conduct. The rest of us agreed. But not Jim and Dianne, who insisted that Terry accepted the "arrangement." Chris was Terry's good friend, Dianne explained, and Chris's relationship with Terry's wife was really none of our business.

Around this time Roskelley, Reichardt, Ridgeway, and I discussed the probability that we would be the team to make the first attempt on the summit. So far, we had been the strongest, most consistent members of the expedition, and we all shared a willingness to make the effort necessary to reach the top—even if that meant a bivouac on the way down. We acknowledged that if any one of us succumbed to altitude sickness, the configuration of the summit team would necessarily change. When Reichardt reported hearing Chris and Cherie making summit plans of their own, we scoffed at their grandiosity.

The most difficult section of the entire climb was a knife-edged ridge on the border between Pakistan and China between Camps 3 and 4. But before we could start across, a major storm moved in from the southwest, pinning us down at Camp 1 for seven days. It took considerable effort to reopen the route to Camp 3 through all the deep snow. When the weather cleared, Roskelley and Ridgeway led brilliantly on the 55-to-60 degree ice along the Chinese side of the ridge. After they had been at it two days, Bill Sumner and I joined them to finish the job.

At the far end of the ridge at 22,800 feet, we dug a flat spot for Camp 4 right upon its crest, perched above sheer drops of several thousand feet on either side. With the hardest climbing behind us, we prepared to tackle the upper mountain. We would need two more camps to get close enough to make it to the summit and back in a single day. The snow-covered upper slopes of K2 are steep—steeper and more avalanche-prone than Everest—and, in their empty bleakness, a desert devoid of life. The rapid breathing required at high altitude meant risking severe dehydration, possibly even pulmonary or cerebral edema. From now on we knew we must drink lots of water—or risk serious altitude sickness.

Once we established the route across the knife-edged ridge, we began the donkey work of ferrying enough supplies to Camp 4 to support the final effort. Each time I made this journey it became easier, more routine, until one of the ice screws suddenly popped loose and I plummeted thirty feet, where I bobbed like a bungee jumper above the dropoff, protected from a fatal fall by the remaining anchors securing me to the ridge.

Early one afternoon, we found a note Chris had pinned to his tent at Camp 4: "Cherie and Craig—there's insufficient room on this

The knife-edged ridge between Camps 3 and 4. Jim Whittaker barely visible in lower center moving along fixed ropes.

tent platform for another tent so you'll need to squeeze into the pyramid tent with me and Skip or locate another tent several hundred feet further up." In an hour's time we cleared additional platform space for two more tents and let Cherie know we thought Chris's assessment was completely wrong and a sign of bad judgment. Cherie lashed out at us for our "unfair attack." Jim snapped, "Anyone who can't build a simple tent platform certainly shouldn't be putting in a route." Chris's chances of making a summit bid were shrinking fast.

Roskelley, Ridgeway, Reichardt, and I discussed at length whether or not to use oxygen when we attempted the summit. Back in the 1930s, British climbers managed to reach 28,000 feet on Everest without using supplemental oxygen, so we knew at least *some* human beings could survive that high. Inspired by the challenge, Lou and John said they wanted to try going without. Unlike them, I had never been above twenty-two thousand feet so I did not know *how* I'd perform. I didn't want to risk blowing my one chance to make the summit. On the other hand, I had so far handled the altitude extremely well. Maybe I *should* go all the way without the aid of oxygen. I couldn't make up my mind. Rick Ridgeway doubted whether he could make it up and back the last seven hundred feet unassisted so he said he would probably take oxygen.

That night Jim announced over the radio that the four of us would indeed form the first summit team. Rob expressed concern, as a physician, about our intentions to climb without oxygen. While Diana Jagersky and Dianne Roberts demonstrated support, the others (except for Skip Edmonds, who appeared neutral) seemed sorely disappointed by the decision—having hoped to go themselves. Terry's disappointment seemed less for himself than for his wife. He didn't say we shouldn't get the chance to go, he just wished Cherie could try for the summit, too.

The day Jim announced the makeup of the summit team, heavy snowfall drove us down the mountain. Trapped for two weeks at Camp 1, the divisions between teams A and B intensified. The

Lou Reichardt on steep ice between Camps 3 and 4.

climbers who were denied a chance at the summit grumbled, "Did we come so far and endure so much to become nothing more than pack horses for the chosen few?"

That evening Bill Sumner attacked Jim's decision to abandon what Bill considered to be an orderly progression up the mountain for an oxygenless attempt, followed by one or two with oxygen. He criticized Jim for changing plans without first discussing them with the rest of the team. Bill insisted he had no quarrel with those who had been selected for the first attempt, but when he left to begin hauling our supplies up the mountain, he seemed angry.

Rob told us Bill felt he should have been invited to go for the summit. (Jim, John, Rick, Reichardt, and I had determined Bill's performance high on the mountain had not been strong enough to put him on the first team.) "Jim just lets things happen," Rob warned. "Time is running out; we need strong leadership to hold this expedition together for the final push." The griping about Jim's effectiveness as the expedition's leader continued to escalate: "He selected the first summit team too early." "He isn't handling the Cherie/Chris affair well." As far as I could tell, he seemed stuck in a no-win situation.

Jim convened the group and apologized to those he had offended. Then he made an impassioned appeal, "To climb this mountain we all have to work together." Everyone seemed genuinely moved by his remarks, but the B team wanted more than an apology. They wanted a fair chance to get to the summit but feared that once we reached it, the impetus for repeat ascents would quickly diminish.

Chris argued that Jim used the wrong criteria for selecting the first summit team. "How much route pioneering each of us did down below and the speed of our carries between camps bears no relation to how we will perform at altitude." Striving for a compromise, I suggested that Jim revoke his earlier decision and wait to select the team until Camp 5 was fully stocked, and the group agreed. The Bechs argued that the summit team should be elected by the group, but the rest of us agreed Jim should make the selection after receiving input from everyone. Finally, the B team pushed for a dual assault, Abruzzi by them, Polish by us—but we resisted.

A sudden attack of diarrhea kept me at Camp 3 while the rest of the team established Camp 5 at twenty-five thousand feet. I felt more discouraged than I had the entire trip. Perhaps I had lost my chance to reach the summit. Of the thirty-three days we had spent on the mountain so far, only seven had been clear. I feared that bad weather might defeat us. Although no longer a practicing Catholic, I wrote in my diary,

> *I hope the Almighty will grant me the opportunity to climb to the summit of K2.*

The tension dividing the expedition did not ease. On the way to establish Camp 5, Chris Chandler and John Roskelley had a heated argument about Chris's relationship with Cherie. They were roped to Rick Ridgeway and Lou Reichardt, who was leading. In the midst of the angry exchange, Reichardt suddenly broke through a snow bridge into a crevasse. Although Chris's belay kept Lou from falling any deeper, he never stopped yelling at John. Reichardt dangled while the others argued. When Rick realized what was happening, he rushed up and helped free Lou, who emerged from his predicament quite perplexed.

Back at Camp 1 during another storm-induced delay, Chris and Cherie expressed their bitterness toward the A team and maneuvered for a chance at the summit. They concealed tools for repairing oxygen regulators and began monitoring radio conversations. Reichardt and I warned Jim that if he selected a team that did not include Chris and Cherie they might head up anyway. Jim said, smiling, "Don't worry, everything's going to be okay."

The next day Jim invited me to take the microfilmed list of contributors and the eagle feather, then announced to the group that he had again selected John, Rick, Reichardt, and me as the first summit team. He expressed regret that Leif, Al, and Dusan could not be with us on the eve of what was probably our only opportunity to make the summit. Acknowledging that Rob had generously agreed to stay behind to provide support, Jim paid him a moving tribute. Listening to Jim speak, I realized, "This is it, I'm about to get the chance I've dreamed of for twenty years. God give me the strength to meet the rigorous demands of the next few days." It pleased me to learn the news on my sixteenth wedding anniversary—a good omen of sorts, I thought.

As we prepared for a final push to the summit, we considered our two choices: a direct finish on the route that had stopped the Poles in 1976 or an avalanche-prone traverse to the upper part of the Abruzzi route. We had yet to decide whether or not to climb with oxygen, so we took several bottles just in case.

Then one last crisis split our ranks. Taking advantage of some rare good weather, Jim, Dianne, Reichardt, Craig Anderson, and I climbed from Camp 1 to Camp 4 in a single day—a vertical gain of four thousand feet. But strong winds began blowing out of China, making the knife-edge ridge more arduous than usual. Jim and Dianne didn't leave Camp 3 until late afternoon. It was dark when they finally reached Camp 4, after hours of struggling against the wind, and Dianne nearly collapsed from exhaustion.

The radios between camps crackled throughout the night and early morning. Members of the B team were incensed by what they perceived as one more effort by us to gain advantage. (They had understood we would not go beyond Camp 3.) Chris's anger finally boiled over and he abandoned the expedition, heading down the mountain to join Rob at Camp 1. Cherie and Terry remained. While both continued to harbor their own ambitions, their anger quickly cooled and they seemed genuinely eager to support those of us in the first summit team. I admired them for carrying on as their own chance for the summit dwindled.

I wondered what it was about K2 that had made fourteen people leave home for three and a half months, expend so much energy, and endure so much conflict. My motivation never flagged, and though I missed Mary Lou and the kids, I did not feel guilty for leaving them to chase my dream. The chance of spending a few minutes on top of the world's second-highest mountain made it all worthwhile.

We regained Camp 5 on August 28, but before Reichardt and I finished carrying supplies to the site for Camp 6 on the Polish route, another storm forced our retreat to Camp 4. After considerable discussion with John, Rick, and the Bechs, Lou and I decided to make the traverse to the Abruzzi route. Rick and John insisted on completing the more direct—but in my opinion riskier—Polish route. Ironically, we had adopted the very plan we had rejected when proposed by the B team. Although I once aspired to do something entirely new, I now realized the important thing was reaching the summit—by whatever route would get me there.

With little time left, Reichardt, Ridgeway, Roskelley, and I returned to Camp 5 on September 2 and prepared for our ascent. About seven-thirty that evening we heard a cry for help. Reichardt and Ridgeway rushed off down the slope to find Terry at the top of the fixed rope, Cherie, below him, hypothermic and faint. They assisted Cherie up to camp where Rick stripped off her climbing harness and crampons. I pulled her into the tent and helped her out of her clothes and into Lou's sleeping bag. Then Lou crawled in to warm her with his body while Rick supplied Terry with hot drinks. For several hours, Cherie regurgitated all the liquid we gave her, but she responded well to oxygen. For an hour we gave her two liters per minute, then one liter per minute for the remainder of the night. By morning she seemed much better.

Since Reichardt and I had carried gear to the Polish route's Camp 6, we figured John and Rick could now make it on their own. They made one last plea for us to join them, but we remained committed to the Abruzzi. Despite whiteout conditions and deep snow, we decided to complete the new traverse to establish Abruzzi Camp 6. Although the Bechs had had difficulty reaching camp the previous evening, they wanted to help us carry loads. Spending the day waiting out a storm, we assumed the delay would help Cherie recuperate from her ordeal, but a hundred yards outside camp, she vomited and could not go on. We divided her load between us and she tearfully returned to Camp 5.

Traversing through deep snow, our progress was so slow that by late afternoon we gave up and returned to Cherie. The next morning, Terry, Reichardt, and I retraced our steps then broke trail to a narrow bridge across a prominent bergschrund at the base of the summit pyramid. From there, we climbed two hundred feet of steep hard snow where we found a small crevasse. Its upper lip looked as if it might provide some protection from avalanches so we established Camp 6 there at 25,800 feet, lower than we had planned. We still had 2,450 feet to go. Crammed together in a two-man tent, Terry told us that as a cellist he felt particularly worried about frostbite. Reichardt and I took this to mean he did not want to go any higher. Although Terry mentioned nothing that night, he later said that by making this assumption, we had denied him the chance to try.

Lou Reichardt and I left for the summit the next day before dawn. To protect myself against the extreme cold I wore a down vest and, at Cherie's urging, her down pants. (For some reason I had left mine at Camp 1.) A large pot of water had twice tipped over in our tent the night before, drenching my parka and half-sleeping-bag. I left them behind, now nothing but chunks of ice-encrusted fabric. Not expecting to travel at night and eager to keep my load light, I left my headlamp behind as well. To keep my water bottle from freezing, I put it under my jacket against my chest, but just as we prepared to leave camp, it slipped out and skittered down the slope. At first I did not realize what had dropped. When I did, I figured that with my stove and Reichardt's pot, we could melt snow.

Reichardt set a fast pace. Since I was having trouble getting my rhythm, I decided to turn on my oxygen set at 26,500 feet. Dismayed to discover the gauge read only two-thirds full, I knew I must conserve: only one to two liters per minute, depending on whether I followed or led. As I led us up a steep, narrow gully—now called the Bottleneck—I noticed that Reichardt's oxygen equipment seemed to be causing him problems as well.

*Lou Reichardt climbing toward Bottleneck,
the gully below K2's summit ice cliff.*

Traversing around the base of a huge ice cliff along a narrow cat-walk, we encountered snow so deep I sank up to my thighs. To make upward progress I bashed through the snow's crust with my elbow while gingerly lifting one foot, then the other, packing down the snow to make a trail. This slowed us to such a snail's pace I kept looking at my watch, wondering if there would be time to complete the climb.

At 27,250 feet, with a thousand still to go, I was puzzled to see Lou drop his pack about fifty feet below me. (It contained not only his oxygen set but our pot and a camera.) Was he turning back? He said the rubber bladder on his oxygen set got punctured somehow so he planned to climb without it. He'd left his pack in order to conserve energy. "If I begin to talk fuzzy, Wick, let me know and I'll head down." I told him that I would probably keep going if that happened. We arranged to talk every so often so I could assess his condition. For a while I continued to lead, kicking steps for him to follow. But before long Lou got fed up with the heavy snow, unroped from me, and tra-versed to the left toward a ridge crest and firmer snow.

I could see he wasn't sinking in as much, so I decided to intersect his path by taking a higher traverse. By the time I reached his steps, Reichardt had already climbed a hundred feet above me. Since we had agreed to proceed unroped, it was pointless to keep dragging one behind me. So I flopped it, uncoiled, onto a rock. Try as I might, I could not close the distance between us—and I was the one on oxygen!

Finally Reichardt began to slow and I gained ground, eventually reaching him about five hundred feet from the summit. I led up the remaining two-thirds of the mountain's final pyramid in a zonelike state, oblivious to the altitude and the steepness of the slope, calm, focused, and serene. With each step I concentrated on a different per-son—first my wife, then each of my kids, then my mom, my dad, each of my five brothers, my sister, and finally, Dusan, Al, and Leif. Stepping onto the summit ridge, I began to gasp for air—I had been moving too quickly. I crouched down on one knee and waited for Lou.

At five-fifteen I told him, "We've come this far, let's go the rest of the way together." Lou Reichardt and I walked arm in arm the last

Telephoto view of Jim and Lou Reichardt climbing in deep snow at 27,000 feet around base of summit ice cliff.

few steps up the tilted snow ramp to the summit. There, on top of the world, we watched the setting sun bathe the surrounding mountains in a soft, orange light. For a few minutes, we were the highest people on earth. As one of the first two Americans to climb K2, I'd fulfilled my childhood dream. Standing there, I thought of Charlie Houston, Bob Bates, Fritz Wiessner, Pete Schoening, and the other Americans who, but for the vagaries of storm and circumstance, would have reached it before us.

I took several photos of Reichardt holding the American and Pakistani flags, an eagle feather, and the microfilm list of four thousand expedition contributors' names; then he used my camera to take a picture of me. Elated and clearheaded, I wanted to stay awhile to take more photographs. Starved for oxygen and terribly cold,

Reichardt wanted to head down immediately. We parted with the understanding I would follow in a few minutes and join him at camp, twenty-five hundred feet below.

Lou Reichardt (left) and Jim (below) on summit of K2.

In the twenty minutes it took me to change the film in my camera, the lens iced up. So I put it away and walked twenty feet to the western edge of the summit where I looked down on the pinnacled ridge six thousand feet below that stopped us in 1975. My camera useless, I wanted to preserve the memory of this place I would never see again. So, for a few minutes, I scanned the horizon. In one direction K2's shadow stretched over the Karakoram for what seemed like a hundred miles; in the other, a sea of mountains turned orange, then purple in the setting sun.

At twilight, after burying the microfilm and a pink, plastic match case containing some friends' business cards and the gold key chain of another friend's deceased father, I prepared to descend. I could see Reichardt making rapid progress about a thousand feet below and realized there wasn't enough daylight left for him to reach camp without using his headlamp. I had brought no headlamp, so rather than risk falling in the dark, I stopped at 27,750 feet. From the beginning, I had known it might be necessary to risk a bivouac to reach the summit.

On an exposed, open slope with nothing but a thin nylon bivouac sack to protect me from the cold, I spent the longest night of my life. After digging a small platform in the snow, I crawled inside my bivouac sack as darkness fell and the temperature dropped. During the previous thirteen hours, I had consumed a couple of candy bars and a sip from Lou's water bottle. Without food or a pot in which to melt snow, I hovered over my stove, desperately trying to keep warm. The stove's fuel quickly ran out, so I unscrewed the old gas canister and tried screwing on a fresh one. When I did, most of the gas hissed away. Knowing that if I lit the stove now, it would explode, I tossed it aside in disgust. Then, with dawn still hours away, my oxygen ran out.

No one had ever survived a solo bivouac above twenty-seven thousand feet. Without water, down parka, sleeping bag, usable stove, or supplemental oxygen, I realized I faced the real possibility of developing cerebral edema or pulmonary edema—excess fluid in the brain or lungs—which, at so high an altitude, could kill me. Frostbite was almost inevitable. When a body encounters extreme cold, it will cut off circulation to the extremities, sacrificing toes and fingers, in order to survive. I worried most about the mind-numbing effects of hypothermia. Combating it on Mt. Rainier seven years earlier, I had required Ed Boulton's assistance to descend. This time, with no one to rely on but myself, I would have to stay awake and focused or I would never make it back to camp.

The cold became almost unbearable. (That night Jim and Dianne recorded a temperature of twenty degrees below zero at twenty-two thousand feet and estimated the temperature where I was to be thirty-five below, or colder.) Shivering so much I could barely control my limbs, I forced myself to flex my hands and feet, fingers and toes, hoping to forestall frostbite and hypothermia.

Writing from the cold, I slowly slipped over the edge of the platform, down the slope. Still in the bivouac sack, I instinctively dug in my boot heels and stopped. The wind kept buffeting the nylon, so I braced myself and did not slide for a while. Closed up inside the bag, I did not realize my peril. Shivering violently, I began sliding again. Again I dug in my heels and stopped. Three more times I slid before finally forcing myself to look out of my bivouac sack. I hated to let in the freezing wind, but knew I must. The white of the snow against the night sky let me make out the terrain.

To my dismay, just a few feet below me the slope steepened abruptly. Though I could not see beyond the curve, I knew one more slide and I would have fallen ten thousand feet to the glacier below. Badly shaken, I climbed out of the sack and with my teeth chattering from the excruciating cold, crawled thirty feet back up to the platform. There I pinned the bottom corners of the bivouac sack into the snow with my ice hammer and ax to prevent myself from sliding down again. Then, trying not to tear the nylon, I eased myself back into the bag. Warmed by the exertion, my shivering subsided, only to return full force a few minutes later.

For the remainder of the night I concentrated my mind on survival. I realized my violent shivers meant I was in the early stages of hypothermia. Though I could no longer feel my toes, I tried wiggling them anyway: tensing, relaxing, tensing, relaxing. "Move, move, move—keep the circulation going." I had survived miserable bivouacs before, on Mt. Rainier and Mt. McKinley. I knew that morning would eventually come. When the sun rose, I would not be so cold. I just needed to make it for a few more hours.

By morning my mind was heavy and confused. "Oh, look, that's the summit up there. How nice! Maybe I'll just stay here. No, if I want to get home to my family, I must go down!" I ordered myself to put on my crampons. "Okay, crampon, there you go on the boot. Now lace the strap through the eye here, then it goes over the boot and crosses to this loop, then back again. Now buckle it down and make sure it's fastened. Okay. One crampon on. Wait a minute,

Wickwire, look at your boot. The crampon is loose." The sight struck me as funny so I began to giggle. "If it comes off, you'll be in for a long fall. Who needs crampons anyway. You can go down later. Just lie back and relax."

Looking around, I realized I had bivouacked close to a cornice. A few feet farther and I might have fallen through onto the south face, far below. I *had* to move. As a last resort, I focused on my wife and children—using their images as motivation to begin my descent. "Think of Mary Lou, Annie, Susie, Cathy, Bob, and David at home in Seattle. You cannot die. You must survive for them. You must return to them."

I fastened the first crampon on tight, then put on the other. After placing the bivouac sack in my pack, I steadied myself and prepared to walk down the windswept slope. In my foggy state I may have left the empty oxygen bottle there or tossed it over the cornice onto the south face below. I never figured out what I did with it. Every step I took meant instructing my leg to lift up, then come down. Moving like a character in a slow-motion movie, staggering from cold and oxygen depletion, I followed what remained of our tracks. At twenty-seven thousand feet I saw John Roskelley and Rick Ridgeway coming toward me through the mist and blowing snow.

Turned back by deep snow and avalanches, they had abandoned the Polish route the day before and traversed to our Camp 6 for another chance at the summit. Lou Reichardt had returned alone several hours after dark. Disoriented from a lack of oxygen, he overshot the camp and did not perceive where he was until he saw John's and Rick's headlamps flashing on the roof of our tent. Seeing the icicles hanging from Lou's beard and recognizing some early signs of hypothermia, John and Rick had doubted I could survive the night.

At the moment they first saw me through the frozen mist, I was standing rigid like a scarecrow, my arm fixed in a wave. At first glance they thought I had frozen to death. "I'm okay," I assured them. "I can make it back to camp alone. Keep going for the summit." As I passed by Roskelley, he patted me gently on the head.

Rick Ridgeway on summit of K2 with Karakoram peaks on horizon.

When I rejoined Reichardt at Camp 6, I helped him clear snow off our tent and retrieve his ice ax from a shallow crevasse where it had fallen. Then I consumed several quarts of water—my first real drink in thirty hours. That evening, back from their successful climb to the summit (remarkably without oxygen), Ridgeway collapsed on his sleeping bag while Roskelley prepared to make hot drinks. One of their two stoves was about to go out, so John exchanged its depleted fuel canister for a new one. When the stove's flame touched the gas released from the old canister, it exploded and the tent burst into flames. Seconds later Reichardt and I watched as Ridgeway's burning sleeping bag tumbled down the slope.

It took a few moments for our predicament to sink in. "Oh, do you guys really want to get in with us? Yes, I suppose you'll have to come in with us." In they came, and we spent the night packed like sardines in the small, two-person tent. John Roskelley and I squeezed our legs into my half-bag—damn uncomfortable, but after the bivouac, heavenly warm. Huddled in Roskelley's sleeping bag, Rick gasped for air all night long.

Leaving camp at noon the next day, we walked like zombies. As we crossed the last small rise into Camp 5, Rick dropped to the ground and crawled on his hands and knees, desperate for oxygen. We gave him what little remained. After another difficult night we continued our descent. Fearful but determined, we crossed the knife-edged ridge between Camps 4 and 3. Storms kept us at the lower camp for forty-eight hours. After welcoming us warmly, Cherie and Terry provided us with plenty of hot drinks and meals. It took me a while to notice, but on the wall of the tent Dianne Roberts had scrawled the heartening message "Victory is sweetest to those who have known defeat."

Honar Baig, a Hunza high-altitude porter, assisting Jim as he arrives at Camp 1 after his bivouac.

The pain in my chest got steadily worse, but Rick seemed weaker. So when the storm let up and we finally reached Rob Schaller just above Camp 1, I suggested he attend to Ridgeway while I continued into camp for a cup of tea. Rob determined Rick had some minor frostbite, but his lungs would be okay. Examining me, Rob explained I had developed pneumonia and pleurisy and immediately began administering antibiotics, morphine, and intravenous fluids. Though my fingers were discolored, they were not seriously frostbitten.

When I took off my boots, however, we noticed two of my toes were black. I knew that eventually I would probably lose the tips. My lungs posed a more serious and immediate problem.

The energy that had got me down the mountain drained away. The pain in my chest worsened. Throughout the night Dianne Roberts and Diana Jagersky remained at my side: fetching water, whispering encouragement, wiping the sweat from my face. The next day I managed to make it to base camp under my own power, but grew so weak that some of the porters had to carry me in a makeshift stretcher partway down the Baltoro Glacier. The jostling became so uncomfortable I decided to walk the rest of the way with the help of Honar Baig and Ghohar Shah, the strongest of the high-altitude porters. When I started coughing up globs of blood, Rob explained that I had developed pulmonary emboli—blood clots in my lungs— another painful legacy of my bivouac beneath the summit.

When I turned back to look at K2 for the last time, I felt nothing. Hungry, weak, and breathless, my pace slowed. I seemed to be in my own private world. Ten steps, fifty, then a hundred, a rock to rest on, then repeat. At night, I coughed incessantly, the pain in my chest cutting through me like a razor. Rob said he thought I had suffered cardiac arrest several times—I was never convinced. But who was I to make medical judgments? As Rob's concerns for my safety mounted, he urged Jim to radio for a helicopter. "Wickwire needs to get to a hospital. Now!"

My last night on the glacier the porters performed the most innovative music I had ever heard. Not their usual monotonous shouts and rhythms but a pulsating, rocklike music. The following morning they gave Rob and me a touching farewell. Since I had nearly lost my voice, I asked Saleem to convey the message: "Thank you for carrying me that first day from base camp on the litter. I regret I can't go with you through your villages. Thank you for your music— it meant a lot." After presenting Rob and me with hand-spun woolen caps, the sixty porters sang prayers for my recovery in unison. Later that day, a helicopter came and took us away.

Jim suffering from pneumonia, pleurisy, frostbite, and pulmonary emboli during walk out from K2.
(left)

Jim thanking Balti porters for assistance before helicopter evacuation.
(below)

I had reached the summit of my dreams but felt no euphoria, only weariness. As I emerged from the airplane in Seattle, shriveled, sick, and slumped in a wheelchair, I saw Mary Lou and our five children standing amid a forest of television lights and cameras. Stunned by my appearance, relieved I was alive, they warmed me with their hugs and kisses. We were oblivious to the crowd around us.

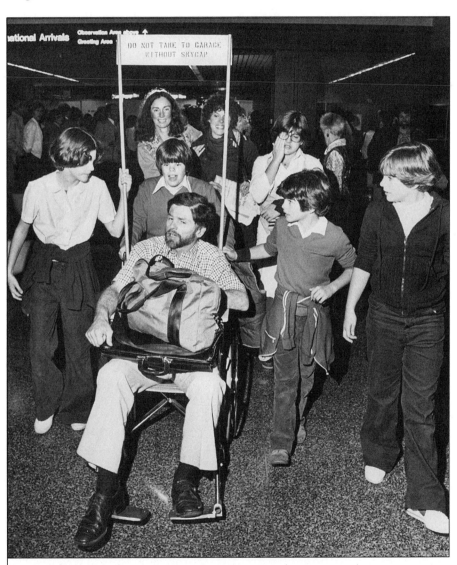

Jim arriving at Sea-Tac Airport. Mary Lou partly obscured by wheelchair; all five children surrounding him.

*Jim describing the K2 climb
soon after his return.*

A few weeks later I underwent lung surgery to remove the tissue compressing my left lung. The pain was excruciating, and for a couple of months, nerve damage to my left larynx and diaphragm reduced my voice to a whisper. The partial amputation of my two frostbitten toes some time later seemed minor by comparison. In the aftermath of my surgeries I once again considered quitting serious climbing. But as my strength and health returned to normal, that resolve diminished.

In any event, I had a point to prove. My doctors advised me I could probably never climb again at high altitude. Unwilling to accept their verdict without a test, I returned to the mountains. A few months after surgery, Chuck Goldmark and I climbed Mt. Baker, a ten-thousand-foot ice-clad volcano near Seattle. Taking my first steps onto Baker's Coleman Glacier, I immediately noted its similarity to the Baltoro Glacier on K2. Although vastly different in size, the ice was just the same—and the familiar sensations as I crunched across the icy surface filled me with joy.

To really test my lungs, however, I needed to go much higher. Mt. McKinley seemed ideal for this purpose, and I returned there with Stim Bullitt in the summer of 1980. Although prevented from reaching the summit by severe storms, we managed to get close. For me, any disappointment at turning back at nineteen thousand feet was entirely offset by how well I had handled the altitude. My lungs felt fine.

Lou Whittaker happened to be on McKinley at the same time, so before flying home to Seattle, we got together for dinner. With a gleam in his eye, Lou announced he had just received permission from the Chinese to lead an '82 expedition up Mt. Everest. "Would you come with us, Wick?" he inquired.

Most climbers who summit Everest do it by the South Col route that Hillary and Tenzing first climbed in 1953. Since I had little interest in climbing by so well traveled a path, Everest from the Nepal side had never interested me. Beyond that, I considered the Khumbu Icefall a death trap. But Tibet had always fascinated me, so I was intrigued by Lou's proposition. "I'm interested in going—it would be terrific to team up with you again, but first I need to talk with Mary Lou."

Back home with the family, they seemed happy to see that my spirits, dampened by my ordeal on K2 and the ensuing surgery, had completely rebounded. When I raised the subject of Everest a few days later, they said, "Go for it!"

Confident that my doctors were wrong in their assessment of my lungs, I figured it would be just a matter of acclimatizing over a longer time once I got to Everest—that and plenty of training in advance. In 1981, I returned to McKinley with Chris Kerrebrock, the strong, young climber who had first encouraged Lou to lead the upcoming expedition. Three weeks together on McKinley would help prepare us to team up on Everest the next year. To test ourselves we set out to do a new route up the mountain's huge Wickersham Wall.

We never got there.

six

GOOD TIMES

When I arrived home from Mt. McKinley in the wake of Chris Kerrebrock's death, I told Mary Lou I planned to withdraw from the Everest expedition. Knowing me well, she cautioned, "Don't make a decision while you're in so much pain; wait until some time has passed. Get some distance from Chris's death and then decide. Whatever your decision, I will support you." And she did, though looking into her eyes, I could see she hoped I would not go.

Still racked with guilt about Chris, I neither accepted nor rejected Lou Whittaker's invitation to go to Everest, even after he said I could remain at base camp and need never venture high on the mountain. I did, however, agree to travel with him to China to make arrangements for the '82 expedition.

In Hong Kong I met an eighty-year-old retired British military officer who, in our short acquaintance, helped persuade me to make the climb. Though I am slow to bond with people outside the mountains, something about Peter Goodwin broke through my defenses. In one afternoon, over a bottle of sherry, we shared our life stories. He told me about growing up in India, of seeing his father mauled to death by a tiger, of losing his wife and children in the London Blitz, of meeting the Dalai Lama as a little boy, and about the devastating pedestrian accident that left him crippled. In spite of all his tragedies, Peter exuded a love of life—a serenity—that revived in me something crushed by Chris's death. Talking with him, I felt infused with an eagerness to embrace life and climb again. I never directly asked Mary Lou, my law partners, or anyone else whether I should climb Mt. Everest, but I asked Peter, and he said I should. "There is a monastery at the foot of the mountain," he explained. "Touch the wall as you pass by and think of me."

Aconcagua.

To get myself in shape for Everest, I formed a small expedition to climb Aconcagua in Argentina, at 22,840 feet the highest mountain in the Western Hemisphere. I asked Rainier Mountaineering guides

George (Geo) Dunn and Marty Hoey (RMI's first female guide) to help me lead three less experienced climbers, Frank Wells, Dick Bass, and my friend and law partner, Chuck Goldmark. We all were preparing for the upcoming Everest expedition, except Chuck, who came for the fun of it.

Dick Bass and Frank Wells were both over fifty, high-powered, and ready for a big, new challenge. Bass was a talkative, charismatic oilman from Texas who owned Snowbird, the Utah ski resort. His friend Frank Wells, the tall, handsome president of Warner

Frank Wells and Dick Bass.

Brothers, would later become president of Disney. They had set their sights on the Seven Summits: the highest mountain on each of the world's continents. Though neither possessed much climbing experience, they figured they could achieve their goal with the same hard work and perseverance that made them successful businessmen.

Ultimately Dick would reach the summits of all seven peaks; Frank, all but Everest. Their book, *Seven Summits,* would be a great success. But in the winter of 1982, success seemed less than certain. Both men needed more high-altitude experience if they hoped to succeed in their ambitious quest. The previous spring, Marty Hoey had led Bass to the summit of McKinley, giving him the first of his seven summits. Later that year he reached the top of Mt. Elbrus, the highest peak in Europe. Frank had yet to make one of the summits. He was not in great shape, and Aconcagua, while no Everest, would present him with a variety of physical challenges.

Marty Hoey's reputation for winning men's hearts and leaving behind a path of discarded lovers once biased me against her. According to Lou Whittaker, every guide at Rainier Mountaineering fell in love with Marty. Each summer she would select a boyfriend and go with him for about a year. Then the next summer she would pick someone new. Lou insisted that her former lovers never seemed to get jealous or morose, something hard for me to fathom.

First in Alaska following Chris Kerrebrock's death, then in Argentina, she showed I was wrong about her. Just as I prepared to board a helicopter to fly to Anchorage after my two-week ordeal on McKinley, Marty arrived to lead a team up the mountain. Chris and Marty had worked together as guides on Mt. Rainier for several summers. The moment she heard he had died during our climb, she ran across the airfield and hugged me hard. I told her what had happened and she consoled me; I don't remember her words but I will never forget her unexpected compassion and sensitivity.

In those few minutes, my feelings about her changed. Eight months later, climbing together on Aconcagua, my admiration for her grew. In Marty I gradually discovered not just a superb mountain climber, but a woman who seemed as much like me in her basic drives and values as anyone I had climbed with before. Most of all, I admired her sense of fairness.

Geo Dunn, Marty's tall, laid-back tentmate, did much to make our expedition a success. Strong, even-tempered, and reliable, he was the kind of climber who adds value to any team. From the beginning, I watched Geo and Marty and wondered which, if either, would make the best partner for me on Everest. Since, as expedition leader, Lou Whittaker probably wouldn't climb to the summit, Geo and Marty seemed the most likely prospects.

I shared a tent with Chuck Goldmark. Although not a particularly experienced climber, Chuck was strong and as driven as I.

*Marty Hoey at 14,000 feet on Mt. McKinley
the summer before the Aconcagua expedition.*

Chuck grew up on a ranch in eastern Washington before heading off to Reed College, Yale Law School, and an army tour at the Pentagon. For the ten years we had practiced law together, I had marveled at his uncommon brilliance, biting wit, and fierce integrity perfectly reflected in the piercing eyes of his hawklike face. Passionate about classical music, Chuck introduced me to Bach's Goldberg Variations. Whenever I hear them, I think of him. Our conversations during the climb would challenge, amuse, and exhilarate me, adding yet another pleasure to a marvelous expedition.

Going to Aconcagua meant spending three weeks away from Mary

Chuck Goldmark.

Lou and the kids, only to leave them again five weeks later for a three-month expedition. I justified the Argentina trip as necessary preparation for a safe, successful climb up Everest. But Aconcagua turned out to be more than good preparation for Everest. My lungs continued to function well at high altitude as I'd hoped they would, and my will to reach the summit, tested by tragedy the previous May, got me there with energy to spare. Throughout the expedition, I felt healthy, optimistic, and strong. With none of the pressures present on a dangerous expedition such as K2 or McKinley's Wickersham Wall, we could relax and enjoy ourselves.

Leaving for Argentina I felt none of the trepidation I had experienced leaving for McKinley the previous May. Aside from problems of altitude, I expected a relatively easy climb, traveling up Aconcagua's Polish Glacier along a route first climbed in 1934. Before starting to climb, we gathered information about the Polish route and learned that the bodies of two young Americans who died on the upper Polish glacier two years before had never been retrieved. We asked the Argentine military officers who monitored access to Aconcagua whether we should bring the bodies down to an elevation where they could be helicoptered off the mountain. They said since the dead men's families had never asked for the bodies, we should leave them.

From the beginning, our expedition seemed blessed: clear weather, comfortable campsites, and camaraderie with other climbers that transcended language barriers. Yugoslav and Spanish teams climbed near us during most of the expedition. Although Dick spoke a little Spanish and a woman on the Yugoslav team spoke English, it was an uncompetitive atmosphere, a common purpose, and plenty of alcohol that caused us to get along so well. Once when we found milky water near the camp, Frank and I descended to draw clearer water at the mouth of a narrow gully. There we found Albino Quinteiro, leader of the Spanish team, who offered us his cup so we might fill our water bag from the tiny rivulet of clear water. Later in the expedition, we offered the Spaniards ledges to sleep on near our own. Excellent cooperation among the climbing teams typified this expedition.

Preparing for this trip I ran stairs, and worked out at the gym—constantly testing my damaged lungs. On the mountain I felt the benefits. Geo, Marty, and I each carried fifty-pound loads, our three less experienced companions, between thirty and forty. Frank, Chuck, and Dick held up well during the first few first days of the climb. In fact, Frank stayed out in front a good part of the first day. But to do well up high he would need to pace himself.

Though Aconcagua is in the Andes, walking toward it I sometimes felt back in the Braldu valley hiking toward K2. On the bank of the Rio de Vacas—the major river on the mountain's east side—Chuck observed, "Any brush that once existed in this area has long since been grazed off." During the trek in we saw several guanacos, elegant, graceful creatures not unlike llamas. As we stopped for lunch one day, a guanaco traveled around us in a semicircle, then disappeared with a memorable whinnying cry.

The next morning we reached the point where the smaller Relinchos River flowed into the Vacas. A mule driver named Raoul came toward us with several mules and, without ever really speaking, convinced us to cross. The scruffy but handsome young man led us down to the riverbank, where he carried Marty and her pack across, causing her to extol his attractiveness many times during the remainder of the trip. I figured it must have been the combination of his flashing eyes and expert horsemanship. Marty certainly had an exuberant appreciation of members of the opposite sex.

One evening Geo and I sat on a rock outcrop a few hundred feet above camp and talked about Marty's strength and her tendency to push. Wiry and angular—she ate hard-

George (Geo) Dunn.

ly anything—I wondered where she got her power. I thought her failure to pace herself might make her run out of steam up high and told Geo he appeared to me the stronger of the two. Amused, Geo suggested I wait and see.

We reached the 13,400-foot base camp without incident. We planned to carry loads to the next campsite, return to base camp to sleep, then climb to Camp 2 to stay. By repeating this process two more times we hoped to be positioned to attempt the summit within a week. After his strong start on the hike to base camp, Frank began moving more slowly, keeping up with us only with great difficulty. Chuck had some trouble force-breathing—blowing off excess carbon dioxide in an attempt to adapt to the altitude—so at the base of one long scree slope I took a duffel bag off his pack. Although I could stay ahead of the others, carrying twenty extra pounds on my back proved grueling. At the top of the first rise, Marty took Frank's duffel bag and Geo relieved me of Chuck's.

Surprised by Marty's drive and climbing aptitude, I found myself competing with her. Loaded down with our heavy packs, we raced each other to camp. While waiting for our companions to arrive, we leveled two tent platforms and built a wind-protected grotto in which to cook. The camp offered no view of the upper mountain, but I nonetheless felt terrific—satisfied not so much by the challenge of the climb, but by being with such fine companions. Days filled with vigorous exercise, spectacular views, and high spirits, followed by evenings of conviviality, assisted by Chuck's special concoction of hot buttered rum (made extra potent by the altitude), remain among my happiest memories.

Midway through the expedition, several members of the team were briefly stricken with illness: Geo, a 101-degree temperature and pain in both his ears; Dick and Chuck, bouts of diarrhea and headaches—Chuck's persisting for several days. Dick got rid of one twelve-hour headache through force-breathing. Fortunately, I remained healthy, ingesting enormous quantities of food and drink to maintain my strength. With as yet no adverse reactions to the altitude, I continued to sleep easily, and the resilience of my damaged lungs made me optimistic about Everest.

At Camp 2 we could see the upper Polish route to the summit. A sharp peak rose off to the northwest framed by two other massive peaks. Chuck wanted to keep pushing up the mountain, but Marty, Geo, and I agreed we should rest for a couple of days. To go high too fast increased the risk of someone's getting pulmonary edema. Since Chuck himself had been troubled by the altitude, I felt a bit peeved when he questioned my decision to select a campsite at 18,700 feet, instead of going higher. Frank and Dick seemed happy to rest a day at Camp 2 before moving up, although neither wanted to be the reason for doing so. Given the composition of this party, I believed we were where we should be.

The next day Geo and I set off with a load of supplies for our final campsite at 20,300 feet. So close to the summit, I felt tempted to take my bivouac sack and attempt it alone. With my last three trips to McKinley all unsuccessful, my ambition to reach a high summit gnawed at me. But this was a six-person team, and I didn't want my personal ambitions screwing up the chemistry as it had on K2 in 1975. We needed to stick together—at least for the time being.

On the way to our highest camp, Geo and I saw an object we thought must be one of the dead American climbers. (We later learned he was Argentine.) Dressed in a light blue, down parka and blue windbreaker, he had his arms stretched out before him like a priest's. Walking closer, we saw his face, blackened by the sun, and the remnants of his eyes. On the ring finger of his desiccated right hand, he wore a gold ring; over his left hand, a nylon bootie. Only inner boots covered his feet—no outer boots in sight. His midriff was bare but strangely unaffected by the sun; his feet were tied together with red nylon cord—perhaps the result of a halfhearted attempt to retrieve him.

I took a couple of photographs so someone might identify his body. We spotted the dead man's companion several hundred feet above us but did not try to reach him. It upset me to see the corpses of these young men exposed to the elements. Did their parents know? I wasn't repulsed by what I saw—just sad that two more young men had had to die.

After an uneventful descent to the outskirts of camp, we encountered Frank, Dick, and two Spaniards, one of whom had collapsed on the trail. With great effort we managed to move the nearly comatose man to his tent. Higher on the mountain he had coughed up blood. I tried to get him to breathe as much as possible. Cerebral edema? Perhaps an embolism? An hour later he revived some, and though he could barely stand, three members of his team assisted him down to Camp 1. Watching him, I doubted he would survive. But he did.

The beautiful weather we had enjoyed the previous two weeks disappeared the day we planned our first summit attempt. Amid a hailstorm, we questioned the prudence of trying. Geo and Marty brought snow from nearby patches, and I spent several hours melting it for water bottles and hot drinks. If the storm continued, we might run out of the fuel necessary to keep us hydrated. Our food, though dwindling, could be stretched for several days. The group met to discuss strategy. Still undecided whether to climb in three ropes of two or two ropes of three, we knew we must maintain the necessary manpower to get someone down in case of trouble. Besides Geo, Marty, and me, the ranking of the others in strength, stamina, and adaptation to altitude were Bass, Goldmark, then Wells. So how should we rope up? If we used only two ropes, I suggested Dunn, Wells, and me on one; Hoey, Bass, and Goldmark on the other. If three pairs: Dunn and Wells, Hoey and Bass, Wickwire and Goldmark.

Confined to my tent by the storm, I grew impatient to finish the expedition. I wanted to get home. Time would be short before leaving for Everest, and I wanted it all to count—not because I wouldn't make it back, but because I wanted to spend more time with the children. They were growing so fast, soon they'd be off raising families of their own. For a moment, I felt like rushing back to be their dad before it was too late. I thought about my selfishness, how I kept aspiring after the next big summit. Again I considered ending my climbing career—perhaps after Everest. The young man whose weather-charred body lay a few hundred feet below me must have harbored greater ambitions than to climb the south face of Aconcagua and end up facing the sky, slowly rotting. I wanted to climb Everest, but not enough to die there.

Impressed by Marty's competence, sensitivity, and strength, I found myself liking her more and more. A few nights earlier I had told her everything about the accident on Mt. McKinley. Her insights into Chris and various members of the Everest team struck me as both perceptive and intriguing. She wondered how Lou Whittaker, her boss at Rainier Mountaineering, would perform as leader without the helping hand of his wife, Ingrid. (Intent on avoiding the problems caused by Dianne Roberts's presence on K2 in '75, Lou planned to travel to Everest without his wife.) To my surprise, Marty expressed concern whether any of the Everest team members would want to climb with her. This puzzled me since Marty was easily the most competent woman climber I had ever known. Upon later reflection, I realized she must have been sizing me up as a potential climbing companion.

Around midnight the following day, I looked up at the southern sky thick with bright stars and thought about the brief, outright flop of a summit attempt we had just made. We had risen early, knowing Frank would be slow. But it wasn't simply his slowness that caused us to abort the Polish Glacier about five hundred feet above camp. Though not steep, its frequent patches of hard ice confounded him. With his lack of rope-handling experience, I worried Frank might trigger an uncontrollable fall like Al and Dusan's. While the others rested, I went out in search of an alternative route up the mountain. I returned disappointed by what I'd seen and told the group, "The gully isn't feasible, it's a cul-de-sac." I suggested we descend to Camp 3 where we could reconsider our options while Frank and Chuck, both suffering from the altitude, recuperated.

Reluctant to give up quite yet, Marty inquired, "Geo, do you want to go for a little walk?" He replied, "Sure." As Geo and Marty headed off on what I assumed was another reconnaissance mission, I shepherded the others down to Camp 3, feeling like a nursemaid. All afternoon I stewed. I grew so frustrated that I contemplated a solo climb the next day. When they returned to camp at six, Geo's face revealed nothing, but Marty had a wild look in her eyes, as though she had just pushed herself to the extreme. Their "little walk" had led them to the summit and back. I was dumbstruck. Geo freely admitted that it was Marty's driving willpower that had made the summit possible. How did she do it?

If my ambitions for the summit had smoldered all afternoon while we awaited Marty and Geo's return, they burned with a white heat when I learned my impulsive companions had reached the top.

Altitude had knocked Chuck and Frank out of the running, but Dick still seemed strong and raring to go. His drive and concentration suggested that—weather permitting—he could make the summit. So I called from the door of my tent, "Marty, do you think Dick

Dick Bass on climb to summit of Aconcagua.

can make it?" "Bass can go, he can make it," she replied. "Bass, you want to climb this thing?" And off we went the next morning for one of the great climbing days of my life.

Dick nudged me awake at four-fifteen, but we didn't leave camp until seven. We made our way directly across the slick glacier to the foot of the Piedra Bandera, a prominent rock buttress where the slope abruptly steepened. I led us past a section that dropped thousands of feet to the massive ice cliff on the edge of the Polish Glacier. We carried less equipment than I had ever taken on a major summit climb: a 120-foot eight-millimeter rope, an ice ax, an ice hammer, and a small day pack containing some candy bars and three plastic bottles of Gatorade. Anticipating mild weather, we dressed in windbreakers and left our down parkas and bivouac sacks behind.

From the foot of the rock buttress, I front-pointed, belaying Dick up each of four 120-foot rope lengths. We angled right hoping to eliminate some of the long ridge between the top of the Piedra Bandera and the first of a series of dips and crests leading to the summit. We made rapid progress at a fairly steady pace. Occasionally Dick asked for a brief rest, but never more than a minute or two. I felt remarkably strong and eagerly anticipated standing on top of another of the world's great mountains. A large bergschrund bisecting the ridge and summit ice cap forced us to cut left to the ridge crest. Afraid of hidden crevasses, I started probing every step. We discovered one quite near the ridge where a small bridge provided a crossing. As Dick followed me across, he broke through but I quickly pulled him out. From there we encountered a series of gentle rises that seemed to go on forever. Late-afternoon clouds swirled around us so thick at moments we saw nothing but white. Then a hump of snow in the distance broke into view. The summit?

I stopped and called to Dick, "Come on up, we'll walk there together." As we did, I thought of Chris, Al, Dusan, and my other friends who could not be there or ever again feel the joy of standing on top of a high mountain. Dick expressed delight at reaching the third of his seven summits. But we were wrong. The summit remained hidden somewhere above in the swirling mists. We had strayed too far left. As the mist lifted, we saw steep rock cliffs slightly above us on the upper south face. We worked our way across a tilted platform of rock and snow to the real summit, arriving just as a storm rolled in. Drained by our earlier emotion, we felt little standing there on the actual mountaintop.

I feared if we descended the glacier in the blowing snow, we would get entangled in seracs, crevasses, and ice cliffs, so we walked along the ridgecrest. From the top of the Piedra Bandera we angled down to a steep face where, with the rope doubled, and using an ice hammer and a carabiner—an aluminum snap link—as an anchor, I belayed Dick down as he front-pointed. Each time Dick reached the end of the rope, he chopped a small platform where he would wait while, unbelayed, I free-climbed down to join him. With darkness fast approaching, we needed to move fast. As we reached the base of the slope, we heard a friendly shout.

A few hundred feet from the base, we saw Geo coming across the glacier toward us. "Yahoo," he yelled, and we all embraced. He and the others had feared we might have been caught in the storm. Although I had broken my right crampon, I managed to stay upright crossing the icy sections. By coming out to help us those last few hundred feet to camp, Geo gave me a tremendous boost. Just as we reached the edge of the glacier, about fifty feet from the tents, Dick tripped and fell headlong about fifteen feet, injuring the "monkey muscle" of one of his legs, as he had the other playing tennis three years before. That time it took a few months to recover. Would his injury prevent him from going to Everest? Worried, Dick vigorously rubbed his aching calf most of the night.

Since I couldn't sleep either, we whispered to each other about the climb and other matters until nearly dawn. This strong-willed, independent Texan impressed me, not only for the climbs he had done since turning fifty, but for the splendid force of his personality. By morning he could walk, albeit slowly and with considerable pain. On the way back to Camp 3 we stopped to cover the head and upper torso of the dead climber with an old bivouac sack—providing him some protection from the elements and passing climbers on the Polish glacier.

Back at base camp, reunited with the rest of the team, we had an uproarious evening, greatly aided by a bottle of fine red wine and more of Chuck's hot buttered rum. The rest of the night my mind raced—as it usually does after descending from a high mountain. When I finally drifted off to sleep, I had a dream that flabbergasted me: as Marty and I stood together by the window of a large luxury hotel room, we discussed whether I should leave Mary Lou and go off with her. I awoke with a start, feeling quite perplexed. Marty and I had had no romantic contact. I had felt nothing more than a gradual, almost grudging admiration and could recall nothing from the previous evening that might have prompted such a dream.

Chuck Goldmark, Frank Wells, Jim, Dick Bass, Marty Hoey, and Geo Dunn celebrating at base camp.

The next morning Frank and Chuck left for the hike out. Their mission: go light and fast and send back sufficient mules for our group gear and, despite his objections, our injured companion, Bass. Shortly before noon, after burning the trash and packing the duffels for the mule pickup, Geo, Marty, and I started down, walking at a pace Bass could tolerate. With the aid of two ski poles and an occasional hit of codeine-laced aspirin, Dick descended without complaint.

Our slow pace allowed us to appreciate the retreating mass of Aconcagua much more acutely than we ever could have on a swift descent. The clouds clustered around it and several smaller peaks provided a beautiful counterpoint to the landscape's delicate hues of brown, yellow, red, and gray, evocative of eastern Washington but on a grander scale. Marveling at the fantastic rock faces, ridges, and outcrops in a desert landscape, and thrilled at having reached the summit, I felt euphoric.

The walk provided an opportunity for a relaxed conversation with Marty, clearly a far more complex and interesting person than I ever expected. Unwilling to give up working winters at Snowbird and summers at Mt. Rainier, she had never married. No man would stand for that bifurcated existence, and she indicated her current relationship with a man at Snowbird was not likely to be permanent. I described Mary Lou and the importance of our marriage. Slowly Marty and I found ways past one another's masks, and the more we talked, the more I liked her.

About midday, approaching Plaza de Argentinas, where we had seen mule carcasses on the way in, we noticed a military encampment. Recalling that the Argentine army supposedly liked foreign visitors—especially Americans—we walked right in. The mule-powered unit conducted maneuvers in the mountainous area around Aconcagua. Three officers, one of whom spoke a bit of English, stepped forward as we made our initial introductions. The most senior, a tall, striking man resembling Omar Sharif, introduced himself as Alessandro de Oro. The moment I experienced his strong, direct expression and firm handshake, I knew I had met a new friend. His chief lieutenant, Carlos Pesarillo, and third officer, Jacinto Debali, a fair-skinned veterinarian suffering from the sun, impressed me as well.

Despite Dick's willingness to make the entire journey on foot, I told the officers about his leg injury and asked them for their assistance. De Oro immediately offered to transport Dick twenty miles from the military encampment at the confluence of the Vacas and Relinchos Rivers to Punta de Vacas. As we talked with the officers, I watched Marty wander over to several young guanacos tethered nearby. A moment later I left the others and joined her, taking some

Marty Hoey with guanaco.

splendid photographs. Beautiful creatures but, of course, there only to provide fresh meat for the soldiers.

Marty and I walked down toward the confluence of the rivers ahead of Geo. Just as we began discussing the possibility of climbing together on Mt. Everest, a young soldier on a mule appeared out of nowhere with two saddled mules in tow. He motioned for us to get on and pointed northeast across the Vacas River to where we could see the military encampment. Not having ridden for many years, I rode awkwardly, in contrast to Marty, a horse trainer while in her teens, who demonstrated grace and expertise from the moment she mounted the mule. A half hour later we watched Geo and Dick bouncing comically toward us across the braided channels of the Vacas. The sight made us laugh until we nearly cried.

Geo, Marty, and I pitched one of our tents behind a stone hut built into the back of a large conglomerate rock. Inside the unlit hut we introduced the officers to the last remnants of the hot buttered rum as the light outside the door gradually softened, then faded to dark. They served us a simple meal of indescribably delicious guanaco meat, bread, and white wine served out of a five-gallon gasoline drum.

During dinner and the drinking that followed, the spirit of friendship with the Argentine officers grew ever stronger. At first Dick translated, but after a few drinks we all communicated easily. Though the chances of seeing the officers again were slim, I hoped I would. Before leaving we gave them our two tents and they reciprocated with a gift to Marty of an old pair of spurs they pulled down from the ceiling. Inspired by the camaraderie, I went out to my pack, retrieved my red down parka, and gave it to de Oro. He seemed overwhelmed.

Dick and Geo staggered to the tent, while Marty, the officers, and I sandwiched ourselves on the floor of the tiny room. Marty began to overwhelm my thoughts, and for the second night in a row, I barely slept. In the cramped hut, the soldiers and I lay side by side. Marty lay perpendicular to the rest of us, her head by de Oro's feet, *her* feet next to mine. Throughout the night—through the layers of our sleeping bags—our feet touched.

*Marty Hoey and Alessandro de Oro
before the hike out from Aconcagua.*

In the morning, Marty, Geo, and I left early to meet the mules at the river crossing halfway to Punta de Vacas. Freed of our packs by our generous hosts, we took off in running shoes. Before leaving the military encampment I kidded Marty about her hangover. That led directly to a competitive high-speed hike out. I had never been impressed by the physical prowess of women, but Marty proved me wrong. With her in the lead, Geo and I adjusted ourselves to several hours of machine-gun-rapid hiking. Head down, concentrating on our feet, careful not to break an ankle, we reached the river crossing, where we waited for the others.

When they arrived two hours later, we watched as the colorful Bass milled around on his mule among the drab mix of animals and uniformed military, looking like Lawrence of Arabia. As Bass rode across the swirling brown torrent, the mule of one of the officers assisting him overturned. I thought the rider had surely broken his leg or worse. But the man escaped unhurt, and after several minutes of whipping and prodding, the mule made it ashore as well. According to de Oro, water in the animal's ears probably upset its balance to the point it could not right itself. All of this infused us on the riverbank with dread, but we crossed safely: first Marty and me behind one young rider, then Geo behind another. De Oro waved a warm good-bye.

Declining lunch with Bass and the soldiers, we left the mules and continued our rapid hike out. The hills slowed me down, but Marty raced to the top without the slightest diminution of speed. Only near the end could I extract my revenge: charging up a couple of long hills—though I nearly passed out from oxygen deficiency.

We reached Punta de Vacas in the late afternoon, an hour ahead of the mule train. The three of us lay on a patch of dusty grass, waiting for Dick to arrive. I prayed Geo would leave so I could talk to Marty alone. A few minutes later, answering my silent plea, he wandered off. As we lay side by side never touching, we told each other how we felt. We spoke not of our obvious sexual chemistry, but of mutual respect and admiration. Marty admitted she had seen this coming for a long time; I'd been taken entirely by surprise. My feelings had developed gradually, unconsciously, finally springing forth the night of my dream and during our marvelous walk together the day before. As we lay there brushed by the warm wind, watching the clouds flit by, I realized I was in love.

After the mule train arrived, we rejoined Frank and Chuck and celebrated our success for the second time before heading to the airport. I left Aconcagua feeling mentally and physically prepared to climb Mt. Everest. Having traveled from near sea level to the summit of Aconcagua in thirteen days, with no trace of pulmonary edema or any other form of high-altitude sickness, I now *knew* my lungs could sustain me at high altitude. My arms, sore for many months after the accident on Mt. McKinley, were now completely free of pain. To go on an expedition with people I did not know well (other than Chuck) and for all of us to emerge good friends at the end was a wonderful contrast to my experience on K2. I knew I had been a much better companion on this climb than on many earlier expeditions, and that felt good.

As we boarded the plane, I told Marty I wanted to talk to her. Sitting together, with Geo in the seat behind us, we discussed what would become of us. My marriage to a woman I loved deeply—and whom Marty would not act to hurt—must remain intact. Considering how Marty and I felt about each other, how could we possibly go to Everest with a clear conscience? On that long flight we agreed we could never be lovers. At the Los Angeles airport, we hugged good-bye and I headed off to Seattle, she to Salt Lake. I did not want to part.

In the weeks between Aconcagua and our departure for Everest, thoughts of Marty consumed me. I wrote her letters and called her several times. Although I understood our relationship must never be consummated, I felt sorely tempted to abandon caution. Not so, Marty. Although at times she expressed love as intense as mine, she never lost sight of what mattered most to me: the preservation of my marriage and my family. Marty's resolve meant we would never make love.

In the midst of our romantic struggle, Marty and I entered a separate, parallel dialogue. Should we be climbing partners on Everest? I admired Marty's competence, drive, and endurance. My only concern was her tendency to go all out, from bottom to top. I believed that to make it to the summit safely and back home again, she must pace herself more carefully. Sometimes she seemed like a candle burning so bright she couldn't last.

We shared a similar energy, stoicism, and drive that led us to believe that, together, we could make the summit. If we did, Marty would be the first American woman to get there.

seven

MARTY

We spent much of our thirty-six-hour train ride across China drinking Chuck Goldmark's hot buttered rum. He had given it to us with instructions, "Have fun on your way to Mt. Everest and a raucous celebration when you come down," and fun we had—too much. We grew wild with drink. One member of the expedition became so angry he punched his fist through the door to his compartment, infuriating the Chinese and embarrassing Lou Whittaker, who felt responsible. I grew maudlin. Lying on my upper bunk across from Marty Hoey, I fumed. Since Aconcagua she had not once written me, though I had sent her several letters. Although we had agreed not to be lovers, I resented our decision, so, vulnerable and hurt, I lashed out in a handwritten note:

I still harbor the suspicion that I am one of a succession of attachments, a long line of men—that I am not unique to you. You are a woman of many men and I would never expect you to be otherwise. All I ask is that you level with me and not play games (I'm not suggesting you have). This is probably a turnoff because the challenge is gone, now that you've caught me.

What you are for me, on the eve of Everest, is the woman I wish I could have met in another time, another place. I think, I believe, that we would have made—could possibly still make—an incredibly good pair. You may wonder, "Who the hell is this Wickwire?" He's someone who cares about you in a way few others have, and who would love you for all the days to come. . . . This may be my last chance to talk with you for a while, but I feel the need to do so. You are so precious to me. I'm not like the others. I just want to know where you stand.

An hour later Marty walked by my bunk and flung down her reply:

Please quit assuming and/or comparing this situation to any others you might *imagine* that I have. No matter how I feel, you are correct, I will *not* risk what you have spent in years and toils-of-the-heart for your wife and family. They deserve your finest for supporting and standing by you, through so much of your glorious, notorious history. To risk what you have intricately, intimately designed would be foolish. So many would be hurt: all of us!

In many quixotic musings I have found us in that magical Brigadoon, without its pasts or presents, where we submerge into our dreams . . . but then, the nightmare of awakening once again.

Well, I'm not one to live by fatuous hope. This brings me to bumping heads with the demon you have borne in me. I cannot be true to myself; that is, to my passion for you. In a sense I must live a lie for the sake of our integrity. What a joke on us! The irony, the tragic flaw of man's morality. So I must say that you must not risk *anything;* that there will *always* be a restriction on our relationship. Yes, I will say that . . . and faithfully live a lie. So, there, I have leveled with you! We will be the best of buddies. And you will be my knight in shining armor, persistently visiting my dreams, by my side, in my heart—keeping my love alive . . . always.

When we reached Lhasa, the fabled capital of Tibet, we went for a long walk on which I apologized for my note, and we recommitted to be friends and climbing partners, but not lovers. This time I accepted the decision.

Since the Chinese prevented us from hiring Tibetan porters to help carry loads up the glacier, we arrived at Mt. Everest with seventeen climbers, most of whom worked for Lou's guide service on Mt. Rainier. The result was a harmonious, effective team with few of the personality problems present on K2.

1982 Everest team in Lhasa.

Other members of the expedition included a doctor, a school-teacher, and three men in their fifties, all on their first Himalayan climb. Dave Mahre had been among my first climbing companions. The father of nine (including twins, Phil and Steve, who would win Olympic medals skiing for the United States in 1984), he waited to begin expedition climbing until after his children were grown. Had he begun earlier, I believe he would have been one of the greats. Businessmen Dick Bass and Frank Wells, my companions on Aconcagua, provided financial support that helped make the expedition possible.

I had always thought of Mt. Everest as a formless mass, its only distinction its great height. But when we crossed over the seventeen-thousand-foot pass on the way to base camp and saw Everest, across a sea of mountains and valleys, it rivaled K2 as a classic mountain

Mt. Everest with snow plume.

pyramid. Though still miles away we could already pick out our intended route, a new way up the North Face—almost a straight line to the summit, where a cloud plume blew off toward the east.

Chris Kerrebrock haunted me. Had he not died, we would have been partners, and I felt duty-bound to get his trumpet mouthpiece to the summit. In his absence, I had come to see Marty as Chris's logical successor. I sensed she would be strong, resourceful, careful, and, like me, driven to reach the top. She never proclaimed, as some had over their beers, "I would die to climb Everest." I didn't want a person on the other end of the rope willing to die to get there.

Recalling the havoc caused by Chris Chandler and Cherie Bech on K2, I worried others would criticize me for teaming with her.

I mused to my diary,

> Sure we have a special relationship, but it's nothing like Chris' and Cherie's. And, most important, we make a hell of a strong climbing pair.

But during the first few weeks of the expedition, our interaction, far from signaling a special intimacy, rarely rose above the usual banter of friendly acquaintances.

From our arrival in base camp in late March—thirteen miles from Everest itself—we made excellent progress up an unclimbed route on the nine-thousand-foot-high North Face. As Marty and I carried loads to Camp 1, our conversation gradually became more personal. She confided that her father, present at her birth, disappeared when she was two and did not reappear for twenty years. Her mother, who never remarried, raised Marty, a brother, and a sister alone. When one of Marty's siblings died of a mysterious illness, then the other in an accident, she became an only child.

Having put thoughts of a romance behind us, Marty spoke frankly of her desire for a permanent relationship. I felt both flattered and saddened to hear her remark, "If I could only find someone like you." I began caring about Marty, not merely how she related to and affected me, but hoping she would get the chance to experience a happy marriage. That afternoon, I felt almost serene as I listened to my favorite classical guitar music, Rodrigo's "Fantasía para un gentilhombre," and watched Marty cut team members' hair.

A few days later, as we returned from our ninth carry to Camp 1, we discussed how hard it was to connect the summit with the endless load-carrying going on thousands of feet below—essential yes, but awfully boring and repetitious. By doing it we acclimatized and built the strength and stamina we would need high on the mountain. All day Marty felt sick from too much hot buttered rum the night before, but she carried anyway—stubborn as they come.

That evening I received letters from Mary Lou in which her love came through so strong I could almost touch it.

> You missed a great party last night at the McShanes. Would you believe I didn't get home until 5 this morning? I wasn't carousing—just talking all night—mostly about you and the expedition. Mary outdid herself in decorations, food, and entertainment. . . . Sherry Sheehan (who leads singing at the 11:30 Mass) sang an aria from *Madame Butterfly* (gorgeous). Then she led everybody in singing Irish songs—"Molly Malone," "I'll Take You Home Again Kathleen" and many more. She brought tears to my eyes with her rendition of "Danny Boy."

I heard the end of Rachmaninoff's Paganini variations this afternoon on the Boston Pops program—made me think of seeing and hearing it with you at the last Youth Symphony concert. . . .

Four kids and I just went to see *On Golden Pond*. (Anne stayed home to write up her biology report—she was looking at bacteria through Cathy's microscope.) I think we all thought the movie was great. I bawled in a few spots—it was a heartwarming story. I had to think the love they had as an old couple is something like what we'll have in thirty to forty years. Hope you get a chance to see it sometime or rather we could see it together.

Reading Mary Lou's words, I realized how much I treasured the life we shared. I wrote her the following letter:

Your first three letters arrived yesterday. I can't tell you what a tremendous lift they gave me even though the news was nearly four weeks old. I love you for taking the time to write from what sounds like your usual hectic schedule. You have a way of evoking an emotional response from me—just by reporting what is happening in all your lives. Your comment about spending another thirty to forty years together really reached me. That is what I want more than anything. For us to be together for a long, long time.

My focus turned to the summit. Could I get there and back without a bivouac? Without getting sick as I had in 1978? Would Marty be my summit companion? If she ran out of gas halfway up, would I continue solo? What would it mean to have climbed both K2 and Everest? Consumed with personal ambition, I wrote in my diary,

I am here to climb the mountain with my full energies—mind, body and spirit.

The higher I got, the better I performed. In spite of pain in what remained of my two frostbitten toes, I felt intensely alive, as powerful as a bull. So, Marty surprised me by announcing she had been having persistent headaches and planned to stay behind to consult with the team's doctor, Ed Hixson, as the rest of us prepared to leave Camp 2 for advanced base camp, where we could recuperate from the effects of altitude.

Despite her headaches, Marty remained strong and showed no signs of weakening. While committed to pairing up high on the mountain, we still had to resolve the issue of bivouacs. Marty adamantly opposed them because she thought it unsportsmanlike not to return to camp the same day. I considered bivouacs a likely part of any summit push on an eight-thousand-meter peak, and after my ordeal on K2, I intended to take precautions. High on the mountain, *my* pack would contain two full, unfrozen water bottles to protect me from extreme dehydration. And if I had to bivouac, no way would I lie all night in a fetal position as I had the last time, cutting off the circulation to my leg, triggering an embolism. I planned to walk off *this* mountain healthy.

On April 26, Marty and I began tenting together. Sometimes she kept me awake making plans for our summit attempt or obsessing about whether she should write a fan letter to Robert De Niro, one of her favorite actors. "Do you think I should?" "Sure, go ahead." "Do you think he'll think I'm weird?" "No, he'll be flattered—I bet it'll be the only fan letter he's ever received from Mt. Everest." So she wrote him a charming letter and sent it off with a bundle of others intended for the people back home. A relay of climbers carried the letters to a jeep kept by the Chinese at base camp. From there the letters went to the closest village post office, where they were sent and a bag of incoming mail collected.

Marty's altitude headaches diminished, now troubling her only at rest. Occasionally she took the drug Diamox for relief, but an awkward side effect of the drug—frequent urination—hardly made it worthwhile. Leaving the warmth of the tent three or four times a night to squat in the freezing wind was no fun.

When a storm confined us to our tent, Marty and I passed the time discussing summit strategies with Larry Nielson, a schoolteacher and one of the expedition's strongest climbers. Who should compose the first summit team? Should there be four climbers or two? Who would provide support? Since we felt Lou should wait until the last possible moment before deciding on a summit team, we agreed to keep our recommendations to ourselves until Camp 5 or higher, by which time the mountain would have narrowed the list of contenders.

The next day Lou told me he'd been contemplating a "crazy" summit team composed of Marty and me. Eager for Marty to become the first American woman to reach the top, Lou figured my experience high on K2 and "proven ability to get the job done" could get her there. But before formalizing the plan he wanted my frank assessment. I replied that while not as fast as Larry or me, Marty was nonetheless strong and reliable: "She possesses excellent mountain judgment and would probably keep me from doing something careless or extreme up high. We've become such close friends I would rather summit with her than with anyone else. But consider adding Larry Nielson to the team. Though three might be a trifle slower than two, Larry is so strong, he'd greatly improve our chances of success."

After dinner Lou Whittaker announced, "Weather permitting, Larry, Marty, and Wick will try for the summit immediately. Dave Mahre will go to provide support." Though I saw disappointment in Dave's eyes, he took the news with grace, expressing deep satisfaction at being part of the expedition. He committed to do anything to see us succeed, "But don't forget me when you're back home. Remember that I was a part of this."

Delighted at the opportunity to try for another great summit, I returned to Advanced Base Camp to recharge my batteries. In my diary I wrote,

Oh the joy of being where the air is warm and thick with oxygen! Sprawled out in my tent with the sun's warmth filtering through the tent walls and the open door, listening to Beethoven's Symphony No. 3, all my worries, my sore throat, and my sinusitis are fading away.

Never had I seen such a large group of climbers work so well together. I believed our expedition *deserved* success.

When Lou unexpectedly announced the composition of the summit team over the radio, nearly all the members of the expedition, scattered among the various camps, responded with enthusiasm.

Marty remained at Camp 1 nursing a head cold. Since a cold could become serious enough to scuttle our plans for going together to the summit, I disagreed with her decision to stay so high. I thought she should descend seven hundred feet to advanced base camp where, less affected by the altitude, she could more easily recuperate. But Marty preferred Camp 1 because it had lots of potable water and more open terrain, so there she stayed.

Summit or not, I suspected this would be my last big expedition. Perhaps someday I would lead my own expedition, but for the moment my goal was simple: to reach the top of the world's highest mountain without a tragedy. If that could happen, I resolved to dedicate my energies to my family and to some new, good purpose back home.

My confidence in Larry Nielson's capacity to reach the summit grew as my confidence in Marty wavered. Not only was her cold getting worse, but when Phil Ershler began maneuvering to get to the summit ahead of us, she sided with him. I considered Marty's willingness to put her friendship with a fellow Rainier Mountaineering guide ahead of her self-interest noble but irritating. I thought, despite her cold, that she, Larry, and I still had a better chance of summiting than Phil and his partner, Dan Boyd. With the monsoon season on its way, I worried we might lose *our* chance altogether if they preceded us. Since I had promised to get Marty to the summit as far back as Aconcagua, I felt she owed me her primary loyalty.

The five of us talked things over, and Phil and Dan agreed not to supplant our team.

Afterward, as Marty and I hashed out our differences and realigned our goals, we grew closer. She recited to me, from memory, A. A. Milne's poem "Us Too" from *Now We Are Six:* "Wherever I am, there's always Pooh, I'm never afraid with you . . ." Over the next several days she repeated the poem, and whenever she did, we promised to keep each other safe.

Through the middle of May the expedition proceeded without incident, pioneering a new route up Everest's massive North Face. Three camps, one at the base of the steep face, one at 23,700 feet, and another at nearly 25,000, put us in position for a summit push. Before us lay the danger of climbing at high altitude. The thin air could trigger an array of physical and mental problems that would doom our chances no matter how well we'd prepared or performed in the past. I noted in my diary,

> *We must be constantly on guard to avoid mental errors that could mean the difference between returning safely and not.*

Since everyone seemed to adapt to the altitude reasonably well, our biggest concern remained the weather. To push for the summit we needed a three-day respite from the high winds raking the face.

Above twenty-four thousand feet the altitude began slowing me down. To reach Camp 5, I had to stop several times and rest. A storm raged all that night, but when the sky cleared in the morning, I felt revived. With the storm blown out, we made plans to take off early the next morning to establish Camp 6, positioning ourselves for a summit attempt the following day. Dave still wanted to go for the summit, but Marty, Larry, and I needed him to provide support. Always a team player, Dave agreed.

On May 15, Marty, Larry, Dave, and I began climbing a prominent forty-five-degree ice gully known as the Great Couloir. After several hours we reached a small rock outcrop at about twenty-six thousand feet. I decided to wait while Larry and Dave went higher to look for a place to pitch our tents. As the wind picked up and mist gathered above and below me, I could hear snatches of Dave and Larry's conversation but could no longer see them. I removed my pack but not my waist harness, which I kept attached by a jumar to the fixed rope for protection on the steep slope. Marty arrived a few minutes later, keeping her jumar attached the same way. She planned to head up soon, so she kept on her pack. After I placed two pickets in it for her to use up above, we sat side by side on top of my pack.

The North Face of Mt. Everest.

For forty minutes we chatted about nothing very important. With us so near our goal, our spirits were high; at some point, I kissed her cheek and she kissed mine. I can't remember what we said. Above eight thousand meters, in the death zone, memory falters.

Suddenly Dave shouted, "Rope! We need rope now!" Startled, we stood up. Had Larry fallen into a crevasse? Rushing to untangle the fixed rope, Marty fumbled at the knots and kinks while I began cutting away sections, tying them together to make one continuous line. After several frantic minutes we unraveled and reassembled enough rope to justify taking it up.

I asked Marty if she wanted to take the rope to Dave and Larry. "No, you do it, you'll be faster," she replied, so I attached the coil to the back of my pack. As I bent over to pick it up, Marty said, "Let me get out of your way." In the midst of lifting my pack I heard a sudden pinging sound and turned my head to see Marty pitching backward, head-down the icy slope.

I yelled, "Grab the rope!" Though she rolled onto her side and reached out, she missed the fixed rope, sliding past it just as it curved away toward the edge of the Great Couloir. I watched in shock and disbelief as she slid at an ever increasing speed, disappearing into a tunnel of mist, over a huge ice cliff, and onto the glacier six thousand feet below. Not once did she cry out.

When I looked back at the fixed rope, I saw Marty's jumar still attached to the fixed rope with her waist harness hanging open. At first I could not understand what had happened. Only later did I realize that by failing to thread the end of her belt back through the buckle (the only way to assure it would not come loose), Marty had made an inexplicable, fatal error. Peering up through the mist, I shouted, "Marty's dead! Marty's dead! Marty's dead!"

Larry and Dave rushed down, and after I explained to them what had happened we agreed we should abandon our summit attempt and return to Camp 5. Then, without a word, I began walking straight down the forty-five-degree slope searching for some sign of Marty. Several hundred feet down the couloir I found the two pickets I had placed in Marty's pack and below them, traces of blood on the hard snow. Close to Camp 5, I found one of her crampons with its straps still in place. In my shock I had walked the entire distance unroped, completely oblivious to Larry and Dave, who descended parallel to me, attached to the fixed rope.

As soon as they heard the news, Lou and other members of the team set out from Camp 2 to search the base of the North Face for

Marty Hoey climbing the slope down which she would later fall. (left)

Marty nearing rock outcrop from which she fell to her death. (below)

Marty's waist harness still attached to fixed rope after fatal accident. (below left)

Marty's body. Finding no sign of her on the glacier, they assumed she had landed in the bergschrund. Concerned about rockfall and the threat of an avalanche, they didn't search inside the huge crevasse.

That night I could neither eat nor drink. Larry wanted me to continue up the mountain, but the idea repulsed me. In view of what had happened, getting to the summit of Mt. Everest now seemed monumentally irrelevant. Marty's death, as yet the most unexpected and unanticipated in my life, shocked me to the core. Al and Dusan had fallen while moving across a high mountain face. Marty and I were at rest, secure. I felt little of the guilt or sense of failure I had about Chris—rather a deep, aching grief.

I punished myself with thoughts of what I might have done differently. When Larry and Dave called for more rope, Marty and I should not have hurried. It turned out there was no emergency—Dave and Larry had simply run out of fixed rope and needed some more. And the loose buckle—if I had noticed it, could I have saved her? A couple of weeks before, Marty had cut off the leg loops of her waist harness, explaining, "These aren't doing any good because I can't tighten them around my thighs." At the time her decision seemed insignificant, but had the leg loops remained intact, they would have delayed Marty's fall long enough for me to catch her, or for her to grab the fixed rope. Climbing with so experienced and competent a companion, I had never worried about her safety—despite our promises to keep each other safe.

Until five-thirty on May 15, the moment Marty fell, I thought I would reach the summit. But when Lou asked me immediately after the accident if I wanted to continue, I answered, "No," without reservation. Throughout the night I spent at Camp 5, I awoke repeatedly, each time seized with the dreadful realization "She is gone." Since no one on the expedition knew how close we had been, I figured they must wonder why I was taking her death so hard. But Marty was never my exclusive friend; she had won the affection of the entire team, and I soon realized we were all bereaved. The accident replayed over and over in my mind. I did not understand how one instant Marty could be warm and vital and the next instant be dead. Later, her death would call to mind a passage from Plato: "Once you shone among the living as the Morning Star; Among the dead you shine now, as the Evening Star."

Although I felt as strong and healthy as I had on any previous expedition, I lost my will to go back up. But Lou had run a fabulous expedition and I wanted the team to succeed. Larry and two companions continued moving toward Camp 6. If the weather stayed good, maybe they would reach the summit the following day. Then it would all be over and I could return home.

When I walked into Camp 2, Lou, Phil Ershler, and some other members of the team rushed up and hugged me. Frank and Dick seemed devastated by the news. Dick mentioned that when he'd mentioned to Marty that his wife had visited a psychic who predicted a member of our expedition would die, she had remarked, "You know, Bass, I may not come back from Everest." Ershler commented, "Marty never believed she would live to be very old. If it didn't happen two days ago, I think it would have happened sometime soon." Lou reported that Marty used to say, "Lou, I'm just never going to live beyond thirty."

She never told me she was going to die.

I wanted this expedition to be a good one, a successful effort with no tragedy to wind up more than twenty years of active mountaineering. But there had been a terrible tragedy and the party's success remained much in doubt. Once again I contemplated calling it quits:

> *It is high time to start repaying my wife, family, and society for the years I've spent pursuing this almost entirely self-serving activity. I must seek the "newer world" I promised to find a year ago alone on Mt. McKinley.*

In spite of Marty's death I did not expect to look back on the expedition with negative feelings. There had been such a united effort, such camaraderie. Successful or not, we had given it all we had. Most of all I appreciated the time I spent with Marty. She taught me much about truth, loyalty, commitment, and honor. Because of her I would strive to be a better man, a better husband.

On what would have been Marty's thirty-first birthday I felt compelled to tell somebody how I felt about her, so I sought out Ed Hixson and told him, and he understood. That afternoon, while dozing barefoot, flat on my back, I felt someone touch my left foot. I tried saying, "It's okay," but couldn't get the words out. Looking up, I saw nothing but an empty tent. That evening I went around asking people if they had come to see me, but no one had. Was it simply my imagination? Or was it Marty?

Lou ran into difficulties arranging to telegraph word of Marty's death back home. Sensing something had gone awry, he was furious but not entirely surprised when word came that Marty's mother had learned the news from a neighbor who had heard it on the radio. Someone at the Chinese telegraph office had leaked the news to the international press before the telegram was ever sent.

After Larry Nielson's companions turned back a few hundred feet above Camp 6, he continued alone, but he did not reach the summit. Exhausted and frostbitten, Larry turned back at 27,500 feet. The next morning eleven members of the expedition met in the cook tent and decided to make one last attempt. Remembering Marty's drive, I convinced myself she would want me to go. Since my summit ambitions had revived, Lou designated me climbing leader, instructing me to select a team for a final push. The lethargy I had felt since the accident evaporated, and my summit ambitions returned. If the wind and storms stayed away, I believed we would reach the summit.

At Camp 3, I shared a tent with Larry the night before he was evacuated from the mountain. Attending to his needs, I hardly slept.

Unable to use his arms, hands, or legs, Larry endured all manner of indignities. In addition to feeding him pills and pouring drinks into his mouth, I actually unzipped his trousers and helped him pee. Later he directed me to a pocket of his pack where I located Chris Kerrebrock's trumpet mouthpiece—I had given it to him as he set off for the summit. I retrieved it with a promise to do my best to get it there.

Dave Mahre, Geo Dunn, and I began our summit attempt under a clear sky, but before long snow socked in the upper mountain. The higher we went, the worse conditions became. At 24,400 feet, slowed by heavy snow and fierce winds, unable to see beyond our own feet, we called Lou on the radio and discussed the pros and cons of giving up. The accumulation of heavy snow might trigger avalanches in the Great Couloir, threatening our ascent. But we had come so far. In the end we all agreed the risks were too great, so, heavyhearted, we turned around.

Jim on radio to Lou Whittaker announcing decision to give up final attempt to reach summit.

Back at Advanced Base Camp the sixteen remaining members of our team drank the last of Chuck's hot buttered rum, not in celebration as he had intended, but in grief. Talking about Marty, most of us wept, and the bond between us seemed especially strong. That night I dreamed of Marty falling down the

Great Couloir. Moments later she appeared in a church. After recovering from my surprise at seeing her alive, we embraced. As we did, she grew faint and collapsed. Holding her limp in my arms, I sensed she was dying of a massive stroke.

The next morning at base camp we gathered around a cairn we'd built for Marty on a rise near memorials for three Chinese climbers killed some years before. Lou carved "Marty Hoey 1982" in a large piece of flat slate, and around it we piled smooth granite stones. Lou, who had just received word of his father's death, spoke first: "Marty will always be remembered as a beautiful young person. All of us will age and sicken, but she will remain in our minds as she was on this climb." In the future when we thought of Everest, he predicted we would always think of her. Though Lou solicited comments from Marty's old guide-service friends, none could bring themselves to talk. Frank Wells spoke of her many small kindnesses to him during this and previous expeditions, as did Dick Bass who concluded with a reference to Frank Desprez's "Lasca," which he had modified for the occasion:

> And I wonder why I do not care
> For the summits that are like the summits that were.
> Does half my climbing heart lie forever afar
> By Everest North Face, below the Great Couloir.

Then we all joined hands in silent prayer.

Standing beside Marty's memorial, I felt strangely detached until I read one of her favorite poems aloud, "The House Dog's Grave" by Robinson Jeffers: "Deep love endures to the end and far past the end. I am not lonely. I am not afraid. I am still yours."

Riding away from Mt. Everest, I could no longer hold back my tears. The three-day bus ride to Lhasa seemed to take forever. In the

Memorial to Marty Hoey at Mt. Everest base camp.

two towns where we stopped to stretch our legs, I kept thinking I saw Marty in the crowd. Once Lou turned around in his seat to look at me, and I saw Marty in his eyes.

Disembarking in Seattle after a nonstop flight from China, we were besieged. A throng of reporters and television cameras hovered around us. So before departing with the families we had not seen for nearly three months, we held a press conference. Lou officiated, handing me the microphone when reporters asked details about Marty's accident. Later that evening I joined the rest of my family for Bob's eighth-grade graduation. (I had missed Anne's high school graduation the week before.) Afterwards, back home at last, I collapsed exhausted into our familiar bed.

Before I went upstairs I left my diary about Marty and Mt. Everest on a table in the hall. In the past, Mary Lou had expressed no interest in reading my expedition diaries. But I had sensed since Aconcagua that she worried something was developing between Marty and me. Although I wished I had conducted myself more honorably, I felt Mary Lou deserved to know what had happened—and what had not. I fell asleep nervous about how she would react. A few hours later I awakened briefly when she crawled into bed. Hugging me, she said, "I've read the diary, Jim. Everything's okay."

"What was Marty wearing when she died?" inquired Pat Blakey, our law firm's bookkeeper. When I replied, "A red parka like everybody else," she looked startled and walked away. Later she returned and explained. At the moment Marty slipped from her waist harness, Pat heard me yell and saw something red streak past in her mirror. Standing alone in her home, she felt certain something dreadful had just happened on Mt. Everest.

It had.

eight

UEMURA

One February evening, as I sat in my study making plans to return to Everest the following August, Doug Geeting called. Since long before my ill-fated expedition with Chris Kerrebrock, I had always recommended Doug to climbers heading for Mt. McKinley, and he'd recently flown in my Japanese friend Naomi Uemura. Uemura had set out to reach the summit alone. He had already made it solo once before, in 1970, but that was in August. To scale the mountain this time of year would mean the first successful solo ascent of McKinley in winter.

On February 12, 1984, his forty-third birthday, Uemura reached the summit and earned the record. But two days later he still hadn't yet returned to base camp. With obvious concern, Geeting explained that "flying over, I spotted him by a snow cave on the crest of the buttress, but forty-mile winds kept me from getting close. Uemura waved at me, indicating he was okay, but I'm worried. It's forty below up there; I think you should come up."

I quickly gathered together my gear, wrapped things up at the office, and headed north, uncertain whether I was going to celebrate a victory or launch a search. Doug met me in Anchorage and we flew to his log cabin near Mt. McKinley. Sitting by the fire, listening to him play folk songs on his guitar, I tried my best to relax as we waited for the weather to clear.

I considered Naomi Uemura the world's greatest adventurer. The first person to scale the highest peaks on five continents, all except Everest solo, he was more than just a mountain climber. Once he floated 3,700 miles down the Amazon alone in a homemade raft, and once he traveled 7,500 miles by dogsled from Greenland to

Naomi Uemura.

Alaska. On that eighteen-month journey he lived with Eskimos, learned their language and adopted many of their customs.

I met Uemura in 1977 when he came to Seattle to buy supplies for an unprecedented solo expedition to the North Pole. When our mutual friend Griffith Way introduced us, Uemura greeted me with a smile like a shaft of winter sunlight. Slightly plump and unimposing, Uemura seemed not so much powerful as seasoned by adventure. His expression was so open, animated, and broken by bursts of body-shaking laughter that he looked ten years my junior—though we were both thirty-seven.

Connecting quickly as kindred spirits do, we spoke of our adventures and shared our plans. At the time we met I was preparing to return to K2. Uemura wondered, half-seriously, if he would still be fit for such a climb since all his recent trips had involved "walking on the level." He amused me with a story about a polar bear, so impressed with the efficiency of Uemura's rifle that it stalked his game-laden dogsled as if trailing a traveling supermarket.

Debating whether it was better to sleep in animal skins and hides or under goose down and waterproof fabrics, Uemura insisted, "Natural is better, I think." Griff and I argued that, since Uemura would pass no Eskimo villages that could lend him support after he left Ellesmere Island for the Pole, he should take along both sorts of equipment. We then accompanied Uemura to an outdoor-equipment store where he ordered a new double sleeping bag we recommended and graciously accepted my gift of a custom-made down parka. Watching him study the sewing stitch by stitch, I reflected on this man of contradictions who embraced ancient Eskimo traditions yet planned to carry a radio transmitter so a satellite could track his journey.

A year later I wrote Uemura complimenting him on successfully reaching the Pole. Back came a letter of congratulations to me for reaching the summit of K2 and thanking me for insisting he take the double sleeping bag. He wrote, "When a polar bear attacked me, I survived by hiding in my double sleeping bag. The bear smelled me but he could not find me thanks to its thickness."

Since celebrity had made Uemura a prisoner in Japan, he enjoyed spending time in the United States where few people recognized him. Visiting Seattle in the spring of 1979, Uemura decided on the spur of the moment to help mountaineer/publisher John Pollock take a group of novice climbers up Mount St. Helens (a year before its top blew off). For the fun of it they agreed not to reveal Uemura's identity until he appeared as the "mystery speaker" at the group's final meeting following the climb. Upon reaching the glacier, the group split into teams and spent the rest of the day pulling one another out of crevasses. Uemura joined right in and, in doing so, left a lasting impression on everyone. "That young Japanese fellow worked twice as hard as any of us," one of his unsuspecting teammates mentioned to John. "And was twice as helpful."

"I watched him climb to the summit, tied to two middle-aged climbers of limited energy and experience," Pollock marveled. "There was Uemura, utterly serene. He'd even taken the trouble to bring along a bag of clothes I left in the car. He thought they had been forgotten and I might need them. I don't think I've ever known anyone so unselfish. At the top, Uemura rushed from side to side peering off, excited as a child and frisky as a puppy, while most of the others were collapsing from fatigue."

Pollock's story did not surprise me. Once, faced with a shortage of Sherpas, Uemura generously carried supplies for a pair of British climbers leading an ill-starred 1971 international assault on Everest, while its French, Italian, and Swiss members bickered rancorously over who would porter for whom.

Except for a postcard describing violent jet-stream winds that made him abort his winter expedition to Everest, my next contact with Uemura came in Seattle late in 1983 at the annual meeting of the American Alpine Club. Over dinner one evening he disclosed his plans to climb Mt. McKinley the following February—alone. I urged him to reconsider.

McKinley is one of the world's coldest mountains, thrusting high into the thin polar atmosphere. If Uemura broke a bone falling on the ice, he risked lying stranded in cold so fierce it would freeze his bare flesh in a matter of minutes. Climbing Mt. McKinley in February meant contending with just a few hours of light each day, more darkness than that experienced by previous winter climbers, all of whom went in March. And what about the crevasses? Undaunted by my warnings, Uemura said he planned to wear two bamboo poles of different lengths, "like samurai swords," to keep from falling into crevasses. He would combat McKinley's short days and harsh weather with tactics he'd learned in the Arctic.

The evening ended on a lighter note when I got pulled over for an illegal U-turn. As a police officer wrote out my traffic ticket, Uemura chortled with glee.

Early the next winter I received a call from Harold Soloman, Uemura's biographer, and Eiho Otani, a climber/cinematographer in Tokyo. They asked if I would climb McKinley with Otani and help him make a film of Uemura's solo expedition for broadcast on Japanese television. I did not know Otani, but the fact we had each bivouacked just below the summit of K2 established a bond. Though tempted by the invitation, my intention to return to Everest in less than six months meant I simply could not justify taking the time. As it turned out, no one accompanied Uemura past base camp. He insisted on traveling alone: all the way up and all the way down.

A few weeks before his expedition, Uemura asked if I would meet him on the mountain after his summit attempt. He wanted me to climb back up with him by a different, harder route. Though flattered, I thought this plan for back-to-back climbs was unlikely to happen and told him I probably could not go. After inviting him to stay with my family when he passed through Seattle, I did volunteer to pick up any equipment he required and promised to make all the necessary arrangements with Doug Geeting and the National Park Service.

After a week spent training Outward Bound students in northern Minnesota how to handle a dogsled, Uemura arrived in Seattle bubbling with ambitions to start a wilderness school of his own in Japan. He planned to start the school just as soon as he climbed Mt. McKinley, traversed solo across Antarctica, and trekked alone over the polar ice cap to the Soviet Union.

Before leaving for Alaska, Uemura asked John Pollock to find a restaurant where he could throw a surprise dinner party for his wife the following month. "I will invite all my American friends," he announced—how many became clear when they discussed Pollock's plan to publish Uemura's writings in English. Uninterested in royalties (trivial compared to what this Japanese superstar earned endorsing products back home), all Uemura wanted were free copies sent to his American friends—five hundred of them. In a few minutes he came in from the garage where he was packing his gear. "Seven hundred copies?" he asked. Pollock nodded. Moments later he returned again. "Eight hundred copies," he declared firmly. "I'll pay the difference." Then he bundled into the back of a taxi bound for the airport with the Japanese TV-film crew that would accompany him to his base camp.

The morning after I arrived in Alaska, word came that the summit had cleared. Without pausing for a cup of coffee, Doug and I dashed out of his cabin and headed for the mountain. We easily reached the vicinity of the landing site, but choppy air and intermittent clouds kept us from getting a good view of the fourteen-thousand-foot basin so we flew to 16,500. As Doug strapped on his oxygen mask, he offered one to me; confident of my ability to tolerate high elevations, I declined. Having taken no time to acclimatize, my hands, arms, and legs quickly became heavy and numb. Hyperventilating didn't help, so I took a few whiffs of oxygen, and by the time we finally landed the feeling in my limbs returned.

Awaiting me on a landing strip at 7,400 feet, Eiho Otani explained that the air search for Uemura had resumed, but violent winds and snow made a helicopter pickup too dangerous. So far the only signs of our friend were his ski pole, snowshoes, and one of his two bamboo poles at 14,300 feet, the second at 8,700—reason for concern but not despair. Uemura simply seemed too resourceful and strong not to survive.

When the storm cleared, Otani and I were helicoptered by the National Park Service to a large basin near Uemura's snowshoes. We wanted to be in position to help him if he needed help while doing nothing to diminish his achievement. With our heads aching slightly from the altitude we located a snow cave containing Uemura's diary; Otani translated the final entries: "My crampons keep coming off. The wind batters me unmercifully and croons of death. Though I am exhausted it is with a strong will I climb McKinley."

For five days, in good weather and bad, we searched our way up the mountain. Though at times I flagged, Otani seemed inexhaustible. We found a second snow cave at 16,200 feet near where Geeting had seen Uemura wave. It contained a fuel can, some food bags, and a telltale caribou bone. (As a favor to me, my Inupiat Eskimo clients had supplied Uemura with frozen meat, his main source of solid food.) Uemura spurned cooking: "Only melt ice for water," he explained. "Like Eskimo, I eat raw caribou meat. Chewing makes you warm."

Otani and I both knew that if Uemura were conscious and ambulatory, he would have made himself visible by now. We or the planes *would have seen him*. The only answer was that he could not. Loath to give up our search but convinced our friend was dead, we hugged good-bye and headed home.

Doug Geeting (pointing) and Eiho Otani at Naomi Uemura's base camp on Mt. McKinley. News photographer at left.

Eiho Otani reading Naomi Uemura's diary on Mt. McKinley. (above)

Eiho Otani with items found in Naomi Uemura's snow cave at 16,200 feet.

Two weeks later a team from the Meiji University Alpine Club made a discovery that raised more questions than it answered. A thousand feet above the second snow cave, they came upon a third containing more items of equipment, including Uemura's stove, inner sleeping bag, and snow shovel. Had Geeting been mistaken about where Uemura was when he waved? Would we have found him if we'd looked higher? Or had Uemura missed the higher cache while descending in a whiteout? Did he collapse from fatigue and freeze to death? If so, where? Did a gust of wind whip him off the mountain down into a bergschrund or crevasse? Nobody knows. But somewhere in all that ice and snow lies the body of a man I will never forget.

> *The pure white snow*
> *may freeze*
> *upon your grave*
> *Pillowed and dreaming*
> *in your long sleep . . .*
>
> —Shimazaki Toson

nine

RETURN TO EVEREST

Three months before I returned to Mt. Everest, my mother, Dorothy Wickwire, died of a massive stroke following an angiogram. I was moved when my dad asked me to take her wedding ring to the summit. I placed it in the pink, plastic match case Reinhold Messner had retrieved for me from the top of K2, along with the following message:

I dedicate this ascent of Mt. Everest from the Tibet side to the memory of my dear mother, Dorothy Marie Wickwire (December 10, 1918–May 2, 1984), who has been with me in spirit on so many mountain ascents. At her loving husband's request, I leave on the summit of Mt. Everest the ring which was a symbol of the nearly forty-five years of love and marriage they experienced. May she rest in peace.

I never reached the summit, so I carried my mother's ring back home to Dad. Along the way I caught my first glimpse of approaching middle age and, despite failure to achieve my personal goal, managed to enjoy the team's success.

Mary Lou and the kids, long accustomed to my absences, displayed little emotion when we parted at the airport. Taking this as evidence of their strength, a sign of love rather than indifference, I left without the nagging worries that plague so many climbers on long expeditions. Mary Lou would probably take walks around the neighborhood with various friends, host dinner parties, visit her family, play marathon games of bridge, go to the movies, and write me lots of letters. For six years she had belonged to a women's soccer league, but since her hysterectomy in 1981 she seldom played much. However, she would undoubtedly drive the kids to their games and root for them.

The four children still living at home would finish summer vacation hanging out with their buddies; maybe they'd travel to Portland or eastern Washington and visit their cousins. In September, Mary Lou would drive Cathy across the state to start her sophomore year at Whitman College, and the other three would return to high school, homework, and autumn sports. Aware I would miss our wedding anniversary for the third time in twenty-two years, I determined to send Mary Lou a telegram from Everest identical to the one I'd sent from K2 in '78: KEEP CHAMPAGNE ON ICE. EVERYONE FINE. LOVE JIM.

Flying toward China, I felt detached about the impending effort. Sure of my ability to perform well at extreme altitude, I wondered about the weather we'd encounter and snow conditions on the North Face. I'd climbed with most of the team already on Everest or K2, and in the case of our expedition leader, Lou Whittaker, on both. Our climbing team was composed of nine climbers, one doctor, one cinematographer, and a base camp manager. An eleven-person trekking team, led by Lou's wife, Ingrid, would travel with us to base camp. With the possible exception of three new climbers, among them Lou's son, Peter, I expected few, if any, surprises.

1984 Mt. Everest team.
Kneeling (from left):
Carolyn Gunn, Dave Mahre, Phil Ershler,
Greg Wilson, Jim, and Steve Marts.
Standing (from left): Geo Dunn, John Smolich, John Roskelley,
Lou Whittaker, Peter Whittaker, and Dr. Ed Hixson.

To pass the time on the long flight I listened to a tape prepared for me by my eighteen-year-old daughter, Cathy, which began with songs of John Gary, one of my favorite Irish tenors. This made me chuckle because the kids all hated his album. After Gary, Cathy recorded Placido Domingo and John Denver's "Perhaps Love," the *Chariots of Fire* album, and finally a new Vangelis album featuring tunes appropriate for the occasion: "China," "Himalaya," and "To the Summit." Looking out the plane window, my heart swelled at my daughter's thoughtfulness.

To add strength to the expedition I had encouraged Lou to include my old K2 teammate John Roskelley, by then America's preeminent Himalayan climber. But that first week John did little to endear himself to the team. On the way to the base of the mountain he managed to stir everybody up by announcing, after our bus driver took several hairpin turns a bit too fast, "Since this bus may be about to go over the edge, I, for one, plan to ride on the luggage rack where I can jump to safety." With the bus careening down a gravel road, John climbed through the window onto the roof. Only when the Chinese officials on board strenuously objected did he reluctantly come down.

Not long after the bus incident, John entered a spirited debate with Phil Ershler about ethics on Everest. Dick Bass happened to be on the other side of the mountain about to head up the popular South Col route. In John's view, by hiring lots of Sherpas to haul supplies, Bass was trying to buy his way to the summit. Phil didn't see a big difference between Bass and anyone else climbing the well-traveled route. John argued that Sherpas should not be required to haul loads up and down the Khumbu Icefall while expedition climbers avoided the deadly stretch as much as possible. He insisted that once a new standard was set (e.g., climbing without Sherpas), those who followed should never adopt a lower standard. Ershler ended the debate by citing Reinhold Messner's solo, oxygenless climb of Everest, putting John in a bit of a box, since none of us expected to take so great a risk.

Soon after arriving at base camp I walked north to Marty's cairn. Her memorial stone had deteriorated badly, unlike the surrounding cairns, which showed little if any wear. "I was rushed two years ago and didn't have the time to find a good piece of slate or to properly engrave the inscription," Lou explained. "I'll find a new stone and try again."

Early in the expedition I was not much of a team player. I roomed with John Roskelley in Beijing and conferred with Lou about expedition business, but otherwise I had little contact with other team members, let alone the trekkers. While still at base camp I began assessing the team. Other than Ershler, no one else, not even Roskelley, seemed driven to reach the top. With my sights set directly on Everest I decided that it would be up to me—and me alone—to make the summit. I expected to have one or more companions on the final push, but the nature of our route was such that I thought we might climb unroped, as Lou Reichardt and I had the last thousand feet of K2.

Saying farewell to the trekkers a week after we arrived in base camp made us all surprisingly sad. They were returning home; we were staying to tackle a mountain that had killed a member of our team the last time we tried. As the truck drove off with Lou's wife, Ingrid, he nearly crumpled over in tears. John and I hugged him from either side. That afternoon the group discussed the risks we faced: one slight misstep or error in judgment and, we knew, any one of us could die. We agreed that the mountain simply was not worth losing another team member; as husbands and fathers we felt a duty to make it home.

Listening to Vivaldi's lute and mandolin concertos on my Walkman, I mused about the summit. I knew I had what it would take to get up the mountain. Assuming decent weather and snow conditions high on the mountain, I needed only to stay fit, acclimatize properly, avoid all unjustified risks, and maintain the drive to succeed. I believed our expedition would get a man on the summit, but I realized that might not be me. On Everest there were no guarantees—a big part of its appeal.

* * *

Reading a book by the physicist Werner Heisenberg in which he examined the experience of men in war, I noticed a striking similarity to mountaineering:

> The young man who goes to war has thrown off the burdens of his daily cares and worries. When life or death is at stake, petty reservations, all those qualms that normally restrict our lives, are cast to the winds. We have only one aim—victory—and life seems simple and clear as never before.

Mountain climbing, with its significant degree of risk and the concrete goal of reaching some high summit, resembles war, except, of course, unlike the unfortunate draftee, we *choose* to climb.

On September 1, my father's seventieth birthday, John dreamed we *all* reached the summit. An omen? Not necessarily. That night I dreamed I was in a plane sitting beside a window with its shade stuck down. When I pried it open, I saw a huge mountain rock wall looming ahead; the pilot banked the plane hard to the right, but I could see we would not make it. I gathered a quick thought of Mary Lou and the kids, then we crashed into the wall.

Shortly before we reached Camp 3, Phil Ershler asked Lou to name him to the first summit team. This struck me as incredibly pushy. "How can anyone know at this stage about first, second, third, etc., summit teams?" I groused, oblivious to my own monumental ambitions, past and present. Recalling to John how Ershler had tried to position himself in '82, I bristled at Ershler's pretensions. I agreed with John that "somebody is going to have to sacrifice to get the mountain for the team." Despite my own desire to reach the summit, I genuinely began to want to put the team's interest first.

After that, perhaps due to a grudging recognition of our similarities, I began warming up to Ershler. Figuring we might actually attempt the summit together, I remarked, "The next time you see me in an oxygen mask we will be standing on the summit together." That night I dreamed of solemnly embracing Naomi Uemura as we parted for the last time.

Lou Whittaker in deep snow below North Col.

With the help of yaks, the team set up an advanced base camp at twenty-one thousand feet, below the North Col, a saddle between Everest and Changtse, its satellite peak to the north. Some steep ice-climbing took us to the top of the col, where we placed Camp 4 at twenty-three thousand feet. After climbing another two thousand feet up the north ridge, high winds blowing across the adjacent North Face from the west forced us to retreat to base camp to wait for better weather. Looking up at the monsoon load of snow still covering the North Face, we felt discouraged. Across the face we could see an avalanche let loose near four Australian climbers, then cascade over a retaining wall into the Great Couloir, barely missing them. This sight did nothing to ease our fears.

For the first time in my life, I felt my physical powers beginning to wane. At forty-four, no longer able to keep pace with the younger guys, I felt discouraged but believed, after this arduous intermediate phase, I'd be ready to head for the summit when the opportunity came. By the time I took my third trip up the North Col to Camp 4, my strength and confidence did indeed rebound, and as my performance improved, so did my spirits. Extreme altitude obviously still agreed with me.

Throughout the expedition, through all my moods, John Roskelley proved a superb climbing partner. Whether cooking, filming, load-carrying, or digging, he always went out of his way to do something extra. Always an easy and agreeable tentmate, he was also unintentionally hilarious at times.

On Everest the previous year, John had suffered from pulmonary edema. Confined to his tent at twenty-five thousand feet, he attempted to urinate in his pee bottle inside his sleeping bag—but missed. The sleeping bag eventually followed him down the mountain, but since he did not need the heavy bag at the lower, warmer altitudes, he did not open it again until a year later. By Camp 3 the temperature had begun to drop, so John decided he should switch to the warmer bag. When he pulled it out, a pungent, awful odor nearly bowled us over. John tried washing the soiled inner bag to no avail—upsetting to him, certainly, but funny to watch.

In late September Roskelley and I set out to establish Camp 5 at twenty-five thousand feet. We got within a hundred vertical feet of our goal when all hell broke loose: a sudden storm reduced visibility to near zero and pummeled us with five inches of snow in less than an hour. Having failed to mark our path on our way up, we descended one cornice-bounded stretch virtually blind. Once John headed directly for the edge; I yelled, "Turn left"—just in time.

The next morning in clear but windy weather, John, Ershler, and I tried again. At twenty-five thousand feet we spread out on the slope to search for a campsite. Remarkably, between the three of us we noticed two silver-colored JanSport tents, peeking out of the snow. Converging on the two tents (abandoned by an unsuccessful American expedition the previous spring), Phil and I dug while John worked to free a zipper of encrusted ice. Inside one tent, I found a sleeping bag; in the other, Phil found two oxygen bottles and ten butane-stove canisters. We placed all the equipment we had carried up in one of the tents and headed down, delighted with the day's work.

In early October, Lou announced to the team that he had selected Roskelley and me, the two most experienced Himalayan climbers, for the first summit team. Phil Ershler and Geo Dunn would be on the second. After John and I requested Lou's son, Peter, as our third man, Lou encouraged Ersh and Geo to select either John Smolich or Greg Wilson (both Rainier Mountaineering guides).

Critical of Lou's plan, Ershler presented an alternative: a four-man summit team composed of me, Roskelley, Dunn, and himself. He proposed a single movement of six (the first summit team plus two support climbers) from Camp 5 to establish Camp 6, from which the four would head for the summit. Lou opposed the idea because he didn't want to put all his apples (best climbers) in one basket and because he believed the support team should go ahead to stock Camp 6 before the summit team moved in. Dave Mahre argued that given our sorry record establishing Camp 6 in '82, we must establish Camp 6 in advance; he and Lou had already committed to provide that support.

Lou concluded the meeting with an explanation of why he personally did not need to reach the summit. Prior to 1963, he and his twin brother, Jim, had always climbed together. That year they'd planned to attempt Mt. Everest, but Lou dropped out for business reasons so Jim went without him. "It was okay," Lou explained, "because when Jim reached the summit, I felt like I'd got there, too. I didn't need to match him then—or now. All I want is to lead a successful expedition up this mountain. That was my motivation in 1982, and that is my motivation now."

A few hours later Ershler put aside his disappointment and reached out to me. He brought by some sausage he'd just received from home and offered me the use of his binoculars so I wouldn't need to lug up my heavier pair. The next day, climbing from Camp 1 to Camp 3, I reflected upon his suggestion that the first summit team accompany the support team to Camp 6 instead of following behind two days later. This made sense to me because it coordinated the effort to select a site for Camp 6 with our search for the best traverse route across the face. I planned to encourage Lou to consider switching to this approach.

On October 2, slowed by heavy loads and high winds, Roskelley, the two Whittakers, Dave Mahre, Greg Wilson, and I climbed toward Camp 5. At 24,650 feet, the cold wind, blowing through a gap in Lou's goggles, froze both of his eyes. In considerable pain and nearly blind, he decided to leave his load and return to Camp 4. After dumping the equipment they'd hauled up, Dave Mahre and Greg Wilson assisted Lou back down. John, Peter, and I continued up the snow-covered rocky slope to the tents we'd discovered at Camp 5.

As we prepared for the night, we spotted four Australians at 26,000 feet, climbing the Great Couloir. The previous evening we'd seen them near the huge ice cliff over which Marty fell in 1982. They'd had quite a day: after spending the night in a crevasse at 24,500 feet they'd climbed all day to reach their highest camp at 26,700 feet, just below the Yellow Band, a two-hundred-foot rock barrier bisecting the Great Couloir.

Lou Whittaker still suffering after freezing his eyes at 25,000 feet.

Ferocious wind all night and the following morning prevented us from establishing Camp 6, so we spent the day watching the Australians inch their way toward the summit. One of them turned back below the Yellow Band, but three continued up—all without oxygen. At twilight, they appeared close to the top but we couldn't tell if they had made it. Bitterly cold that night, we feared they would not survive and assumed that any who did would sustain serious frostbite injuries.

With us still pinned down in Camp 5 the next day, the Australian drama played out to its conclusion. We watched as first one, then a second, then two more climbers descended the Great Couloir at a painfully slow pace. As we retreated toward Camp 3, John spotted all four Australians at the base of the North Face, gathered in a circle, clasping hands.

We suspected they were celebrating success as well as survival. Two days later, Lou heard on India radio that two of the Australians had indeed reached the summit. Amazingly, the team's leader, Tim Macartney-Snape, had made the climb in cross-country ski boots after his expedition boots got lost in an avalanche. Climbing a new route on the North Face of Everest without oxygen seemed almost beyond belief. They hung it all out when it counted. Delighted for the Australian team and enormously impressed by their accomplishment, our entire team signed a letter of congratulations with a P.S. noting their "disgusting display of sheer guts."

The Australians' success inspired us to become a real team. Before they had reached the summit, ours was a team driven by each individual's goals and aspirations. Afterward we united behind the goal of getting *someone* to the summit. That, we agreed, would make our entire expedition a success: for Lou Whittaker, for Chris Kerrebrock, for Marty Hoey, for all of us. Never before had I felt this way, but after observing the Australians I realized it would be okay not to personally reach the summit. As long as someone did, I could join in the general success of the expedition without reservation.

That evening as I inserted Cathy's tape into my Walkman, I discovered a lovely note from her I had not noticed before. It began with the following quote from *Chariots of Fire:* "So where does the power come from to see the race to its end? From within." She also cited words from the sleeve of Vangelis's *China* album: "Ken–the mountains–to ascend–the solitude–the immovable." She closed with her hope I would "have a good climb and come back safely." Her combination of sincere concern and support touched me.

On October 7, Phil, Geo, and John Smolich set off to establish Camp 6 for Roskelley, Peter, and me. The plan: If all went well, they would proceed to the summit ahead of us; otherwise, they would come down and try again later. The Australians had informed Lou we'd be welcome to use their tent at 26,700 feet, so Phil, Geo, and Smolich ascended without one. They searched for the tent but couldn't find it, so when night fell they bivouacked at 26,400 feet. By morning Geo was vomiting nearly constantly, unable to keep food or liquid down. In the midst of helping Geo, Phil noticed Smolich coughing blood onto the snow. After caching one oxygen bottle by a rock outcrop near the edge of the Great Couloir and another in the middle of the couloir, just below the bivouac, the three men descended quickly to 21,000 feet.

Lou and Dave assisted Geo down to base camp where Ed Hixson, the team doctor, immediately hooked him up to an IV. His severe abdominal pain did not subside for three full days. John

Smolich followed Geo to Hixson's tent. He thought he might have suffered a pulmonary embolism, but the blood he coughed up turned out to be the result of nothing more serious than altitude-related throat irritation. Smolich should not attempt the summit, warned the doctor, but after some rest he might be able go back up to support the summit team. Not so Geo; he had to stay at base camp and recover.

Encroaching winter meant we could make just one attempt for the summit. Although Peter Whittaker had performed well throughout the expedition, this was his first Everest attempt. It was Ershler's third. Phil had lost his summit team to altitude-related illness, but he was healthy; John and I agreed he'd done too much to be denied a shot at the summit. When we told Phil we thought he should go with us, he responded, "Obviously I want to go, but I want Lou to ask me." We went to Lou, and unsolicited, he remarked, "Phil's done a lot to make this expedition a success; I think he deserves the chance to try with you. Any thoughts?" We strongly supported Lou, though we felt bad about Peter. No way could this decision have been easy for Lou to reach.

The group gathered and Lou announced that he'd selected Roskelley, Ershler, and me for the one and only summit team. I'm not sure he had warned his son this was coming. Visibly upset, Peter made a brief, halfhearted pitch for a four-member team. I gently argued that we'd need his support to get to the higher camps. Although deeply disappointed, Peter agreed to step aside.

Chatting with teammates over lunch that day, I garbled my words and my arm went numb. Walking quickly out of the tent, I wondered to myself, "What the hell is going on?" Although I recovered immediately, I felt unnerved, conscious that a recurrence would force me off the summit team. (I later concluded what I had experienced was probably a temporary shortage of blood flowing to my brain, brought on by altitude and dehydration.)

Displaying remarkable strength (perhaps induced by his keen disappointment), Peter led a team of climbers to help Roskelley, Ershler, and me establish a one-night campsite at twenty-five thousand feet. Peter, Dave Mahre, Greg Wilson, and John Smolich all relinquished their own ambitions to help position us for a summit bid. We selected a campsite out of the wind near the edge of the Great Couloir, fifty feet from the site where Marty and I had shared a tent the night before she died.

As I anticipated climbing up the Great Couloir toward our highest camp at 26,400 feet, I wondered if I would feel frightened or distraught passing the point where Marty had fallen. But when we finally got there, although full of Marty's memory, I felt neither fear nor intense grief.

Phil and I planned to use oxygen; John—the purist—would go without. When we could find only one of two bottles the other summit team had placed there ten days earlier, Phil agreed that, in light of my lung surgery, I should be the one to use it. The next day we left the tent before dawn. From the outset I had trouble getting my oxygen set rigged up, and in spite of a two-liter flow, I seemed to derive little benefit. Slowed down by thirty pounds of oxygen equipment and other gear, I could barely keep up with Phil. In back of me, John complained, "I feel incredibly sleepy and dizzy. I don't think I can go much higher." About 150 feet below the Yellow Band, at 27,200 feet, John admitted that he was on the verge of passing out. Feeling out of sorts myself, I agreed we should descend.

At the high point, we radioed Lou our decision and headed down. When he heard our report, he announced, "The expedition is over," but as we approached Camp 6 we began to reconsider. John declared he wanted to try again the next day; he *did not* want to be the reason we'd turned back. I considered our decision to turn back as much due to my reservations as his physical complaints (which, it turned out, were induced by codeine taken the previous night for pain from old frostbite injuries). I simply wasn't climbing well, even with oxygen. I wrote in my diary,

> *I have reached my limit for this kind of climbing. Face facts, Wickwire, at age forty-four you might be a wee bit over-the-hill for cramponing up the North Face of Everest in the predawn hours.*

John argued we should not descend and I agreed. Phil wasn't so sure but finally decided to stay. Although I believed John and Phil should keep going, I worried about climbing in the death zone with two people deprived of supplemental oxygen. The previous autumn several Japanese climbers had perished taking a similar risk. I remembered the promises I had made alone on McKinley and concluded the risk was too great; some sixth sense compelled me to hold back.

Phil wanted all three of us to go, me with oxygen, them without. I told him and John that I just couldn't. Since Phil seemed stronger than I was at the moment, I insisted that he should use the oxygen and go with John; I would stay behind and provide support. John listened quietly as Phil argued. After several hours of vigorous debate, Phil finally relented and agreed to go on without me.

The following morning I watched Phil and John climb past the Yellow Band, then burst into tears. Giving up my dream after four years of effort hurt. But I also felt happy for John and Phil, most of all happy for Lou. John and Phil progressed slowly in the bitter wind and cold. At twenty-eight thousand feet John turned back, fearing frostbite. Radio reports from others lower on the mountain informed me of Phil's progress toward the summit. I yearned for him to succeed and yelled up at the mountain, "Come on, Phil, come on!"

Three hours after he and John separated, Phil Ershler reached the summit of Mt. Everest. At advanced base camp, eight thousand feet below, Lou Whittaker and Dave Mahre, who had tracked Phil's progress with their binoculars, burst into hooting and applause. So did I. When John returned to Camp 6 later that afternoon, we came together in a hard embrace as he sobbed for having failed. I spent an hour with his bare feet against my stomach, warming his cold toes.

Standing on the summit of Mt. Everest, Phil pulled Chris's trumpet mouthpiece from his pack and placed it on the snow, fulfilling the promise that had weighed on me for so long. When he returned to high camp, flush with the satisfaction of having reached his goal, I embraced him, truly pleased at his success—and grateful. After dinner at Camp 3, Ershler handed me a folded piece of paper:

a note Marty had handwritten to him in which she quoted James Kavanaugh's poem: "There are men too gentle to live among wolves." He had read it aloud on the summit.

Phil Ershler descending to Camp 6 after reaching the summit.

Lou Whittaker and Dave Mahre celebrating Phil Ershler's success in reaching summit of Everest at moment he arrived there. (left)

Chris Kerrebrock's trumpet mouthpiece on the summit. (below)

Halfway to base camp Phil peeled off to visit Geo, who, remarkably, was headed up the glacier. John and I met Lou and walked with him the rest of the way. It was a beautiful day: no wind, not too cold, and such soft light. Lou mentioned how touched he'd been when John and I hugged him the morning his wife, Ingrid, and the other trekkers had left two long months before. As we walked, my mind filled with doubts: "Should I have continued on with John and Phil? Could I have made the summit?" When John described his descent, how every step he took meant risking a fatal fall, I thought of what it would have been like to come down alone. Though Phil came through with flying colors, how I would have done, I did not know. What I did know was that when it came to choosing between the summit of Everest and the certainty of returning home, I chose home. I believe I made the right decision.

Back in Seattle, I told Mary Lou, "That's it, I'm not going back to Everest again." A few days later a note arrived from Chris Kerrebrock's father, Jack:

We were pleased that Phil made it to the top. As you know, he was one of Chris' closer friends at Rainier Mountaineering, and I am sure that Chris would have been especially pleased to see him on top. I knew you wanted to make the top yourself, and we, too, were hoping that it would be you who would put the mouthpiece there. Failing that, it seems entirely appropriate that Phil did so.

This event somehow closes a period in our lives, as I suspect it does in yours. We want you to know that we deeply appreciate the concern that you have shown for us since your return from McKinley some three and a half years ago. Our pain has been easier to bear for sharing it with you . . .

I returned from Mt. Everest to the law firm I helped found ten years before. Our partnership, long a source of personal and professional satisfaction, had become a cause of great anxiety when, earlier that year, one of our partners fell in love with a new associate. Although neither was married, their relationship offended our traditional notions of what constituted a law partnership. Some partners became alarmed; others said we should recognize the inevitable effects of women entering the profession. Our managing partner, Chuck Goldmark, seemed especially troubled, foreseeing difficulty maintaining the harmonious working relationships that had been the firm's benchmark. Disagreement about how to respond to the situation split the partnership right down the middle.

On another front, Chuck privately expressed fears for his personal safety. He had taken it upon himself to investigate rumors he had heard about a local judge and other public officials allegedly engaged in a pedophile ring. A lawyer who took his responsibilities as an officer of the court *very* seriously, Chuck was indignant that these men might have abused their positions. So he looked into the allegations and shared what he uncovered with an investigative journalist already sniffing out the story. Chuck was worried that one of the men in question might retaliate.

On December 21, 1985, after months of turmoil, Mary Lou and I hosted the annual firm Christmas party. Everybody came, and for a few hours we all enjoyed a respite from the strife. After a festive evening of good food and plenty to drink, most of us ended up in the hot tub in the backyard. I sat beside Chuck's French wife, Annie, a professional translator, who had recently translated my correspondence with one of the Argentine officers I had met on Aconcagua. Possibly because of what she had read in the letters, maybe something else, she remarked, "You improve with age, Jim."

This pleased me because, despite the challenges I was facing as an aging athlete, I felt in many important ways, as a father, husband, lawyer, and man, I *had* improved and I appreciated the acknowledgment. Annie seemed particularly radiant that evening, the most beautiful woman present. It startled me to learn she had remarked to one of the other guests that she believed she was about to die.

Annie Goldmark.

ten

MURDER

very Christmas Eve our family goes to midnight mass. Every Christmas morning our children stand at the top of the stairs, and just for a moment, I gleefully bar their way to the Christmas tree. But not in 1985. That year I worked late on Christmas Eve, not leaving the office until nearly five. Chuck Goldmark and I stayed long after the others had left for the holiday, considering ways to restore harmony to our troubled firm. Standing with me in the hall outside my office, Chuck declared, "We've got to get back on track in the new year or the firm can't last." It was getting dark when we left the building, but Christmas decorations lit up the street still bustling with last-minute shoppers. As Chuck walked toward his car, he turned and said, "Merry Christmas, Jim." "Merry Christmas, Chuck. See you on the twenty-sixth."

Exhausted from recent business travel and worrying about the firm, I went upstairs to sleep until we left for mass. At about nine Mary Lou shook me awake. With eyes full of anxiety she told me that a friend of Chuck and Annie Goldmark's needed to speak to me at once; what I heard made my knees buckle. "Annie's been killed. Chuck and the boys are on their way to Harborview Hospital."

Two hours earlier someone had entered the Goldmarks' house and savagely attacked the entire family. People sometimes die suddenly in the mountains—we voluntarily take that risk. But not this. More than any climbing tragedy, the attack on the Goldmarks would test my faith, and forever change the way I lived my life.

In a frenzy of anger and fear I threw my clothes on and ran to the car. I raced through the city streets, ignoring stoplights, oblivious to all but the news I'd just received. After coming to a screeching halt outside Harborview, I dashed to the emergency room. I charged through the human chaos to the nurses' station where I insisted on learning the Goldmarks' condition. "All three have life-threatening head wounds. Their condition is extremely critical," reported a businesslike but sympathetic nurse.

Soon, other friends and colleagues converged on the hospital, where we held vigil day and night, reluctant to leave the family alone. Chuck's prominence and the magnitude of the crime made the case one of top priority to the authorities; police poured into the hospital, asking questions. Rumors spread. "Did Chuck have an enemy?" "Was there discord in the law firm?" "Who would want to kill them?" Before returning home I visited Annie at the morgue, still wrapped in her red-and-green Christmas bathrobe.

On December 26, I received a telephone call from an old law school classmate, since disbarred. He had a friend who wanted to talk to me about someone connected with the attack on Chuck's family. The police urged me to go. Waiting on the sidewalk outside the King County Courthouse, I could see plainclothes policemen blending into the crowd around me. "Jim!" called a man standing across the street—my old classmate, I assumed. Nervous to leave the protection of the police, I waited for my classmate and the man with him to come to me. The moment they arrived, police officers encircled us, asking my classmate's friend to accompany them. I followed the entourage to the police station where, sitting on a chair in the hall, I waited impatiently for someone to explain what was going on.

The man's name was Homer Brand. After the homicide detectives met with him, they invited me into a conference room where they disclosed, "A few hours ago we arrested a man named David Lewis Rice, who has confessed to attacking the Goldmarks." An unemployed steelworker caught up in the far-right survivalist movement, Rice was the man Homer Brand had wanted to discuss with me. Brand, the president of an organization he described as "rabidly constitutionalist," informed the police that when Rice tried to stay with him the previous night, he told Brand what he had done—confirming what Rice later told the police.

In his confession, Rice described how he had carried out his murderous attack on the Goldmarks. When ten-year-old Colin answered the door, Rice posed as a taxicab driver with a package to deliver for Charles Goldmark. Once Chuck appeared, Rice flashed a handgun (a toy, authentic-looking even to the trained eye) and ordered Chuck and Colin upstairs, where Annie was taking a shower. After handcuffing Chuck and Annie, and tying Colin's and his twelve-year-old brother Derek's arms behind their backs with their sweaters, he chloroformed all four. During the twenty minutes he knew they would be unconscious (he'd tested the chloroform on himself the night before), Rice searched the house for weapons, then stabbed and bludgeoned the family with a kitchen knife and a steam iron.

After switching off the lights and knocking the phone off the hook, Rice walked over a mile to a SeaFirst Bank machine where he tried withdrawing money from Chuck's personal account. When he punched in the code he had apparently extorted from Chuck, the machine blinked "Incorrect access code, please try again." The access code Chuck gave Rice was for our law firm's, *not* his own, account. By the time Rice figured out he had been fooled, a hidden video camera had recorded his face and sealed his fate.

Meanwhile, the Goldmarks' dinner guests arrived at the darkened home. When no one answered the door, they sat on the porch steps and waited for the family to arrive. After fifteen minutes they returned home and called the Goldmarks' number. When they got a

The Goldmarks' home, Christmas Day 1985.

busy signal, they went back and knocked again. This time they heard moaning through a little window in the door. With mounting concern they ran down the street to other close friends of the Goldmarks to borrow their key to the house, then raced back and let themselves in. Fearing the worst, they bolted up the stairs, where they discovered Annie sprawled on the carpet, dead from stab wounds to her neck and heart, the others beside her, ravaged but still breathing. Remembering he'd left his handcuffs behind, Rice returned to the house hoping to retrieve them from Chuck's and Annie's wrists. Instead, faced with flashing police lights and frantic neighbors, he quietly dumped Chuck's cash card in the bushes and slipped away.

When Colin died four days later the prosecutor charged Rice with two counts of aggravated first-degree murder and two counts of attempted first-degree murder. Rice informed the police who picked him up that he had attacked the Goldmarks because he thought Chuck was the regional director of the Communist Party and a Jew. Rice pointed the finger at Homer Brand (the man I had met on the street corner) as the person he had first heard connect the Goldmarks with the Communist Party. Brand told reporters he vaguely recalled mentioning the Goldmarks to Rice, but said if he had, he would not have been referring to forty-one-year-old Chuck but rather to his late father, John. Chuck was neither a Communist nor a Jew. An active Democrat, Chuck had attended the National Convention as a delegate for Gary Hart the year before. Raised in a vaguely Protestant tradition, he practiced no religion.

While preposterous and false, Rice's delusions had some foundation. Twenty-five years before, John Goldmark had lost a race for reelection as a state legislator when an eastern-Washington newspaper falsely accused him of being a Communist. Since John's wife, Sally, had briefly been a Communist in the 1930s (as had many intellectuals of that era) and his son, Chuck, had attended Reed College, where a Communist Party secretary once spoke, the paper labeled John a Communist.

Chuck grew up on a five-thousand-acre ranch and wheat farm on the Colville Indian Reservation in north-central Washington near the Canadian border. When Chuck was twelve, his father ran as a Democrat for the state legislature from the predominantly Republican district. John served six years, eventually becoming chairman of the Ways and Means Committee. But after the *Tonasket Tribune* charged him with being a Communist, John Goldmark lost his seat by a margin of three to one. He sued the newspaper for libel. The case, *Goldmark vs. Tonasket Tribune,* received a lot of attention at the time, and later, because it helped deter the far right from pursuing the McCarthy-style strategy of condemning people as traitors because they'd associated with people who had themselves once associated with Communists. John won a $40,000 verdict, but before the judgment could be entered, the U.S. Supreme Court determined that public figures must meet a higher standard of proof than private citizens, so John lost the damage award. Having been vindicated at trial, he elected not to appeal; to John Goldmark money had always mattered less than his reputation.

The attack on the Goldmarks put the lives of every member of our law firm in an uproar. I had a particular reason to be frightened. In the apartment where Rice had stayed before the murders, he outlined his plans on a sheet from a yellow legal pad:

GET KNIFE

FIND OUT WHAT KIND OF LEGAL SVCS

FIND OUT WHAT HE LOOKS LIKE
(Lines two and three were crossed out as if accomplished—the police told me Rice visited our law office.)

WHEN DOES HE LEAVE OFFICE

DOES HE DRIVE

WHAT KIND OF CAR

SET UP TIME TO BE THERE
(Crossed out.)

Then, at the very bottom of the yellow sheet:

JAMES WICKWIRE and our home address.

After the murders Rice hinted he had intended to use my name as a reference if necessary to gain admittance to the Goldmarks' home. Later, during the trial, the prosecutor told the press I was one of four Seattle lawyers Rice had targeted. As a precaution, I instructed the phone company to drop our home address from its directory.

We did not know at first whether Rice had acted alone or if the reasons he gave for attacking the Goldmarks constituted his only motive. In the forty hours preceding Rice's arrest we worried that men allegedly involved in the pedophile ring Chuck had been investigating might be behind the attack on the Goldmarks. The juxtaposition of Chuck's fears and the attack on the Goldmark family seemed too close for coincidence, especially when the judge in question called a friend of the Goldmarks and asked whether Chuck was expected to regain consciousness.

After investigating Rice's background, and the circumstances surrounding the attack, the police concluded Rice had indeed acted alone. No evidence has ever been discovered connecting the judge and David Lewis Rice. Three years after the attack on the Goldmarks, on the night before the story about the judge's involvement with several boys finally broke, he sat on the floor outside his chambers and shot himself to death.

At first we thought Chuck and Derek might survive. Of the two, Chuck appeared to improve the most and for a time managed to respond to instructions by holding up fingers upon command. If Derek survived, we knew he would be blind. Over the next several days we had moments of optimism, but our hope faded as Derek developed pneumonia and Chuck's brain function declined.

Visiting the hospital, meeting with police, I worked closely with Chuck and Annie's surviving relatives and an old family friend. We drew support from one another as we wrestled with the reality and implications of what had happened. I became so totally embroiled that the days merged into one confusing whole. Throughout the entire ordeal Mary Lou comforted me; strong, calm, and wise, she kept me from spinning out of control. When I got particularly angry or depressed, she would gently suggest alternative ways of looking at things or she would observe, "You're very tired, Jim. Get some sleep, and you will feel better tomorrow." I would make myself sleep, and just as she had predicted, the next morning I could cope a little easier.

On the evening of January 8, 1986, I received a long-distance call from one of the Goldmarks' relatives telling me he had just heard from Chuck's doctor that he would not last until morning. Since the family could not make it back in time, he asked Mary Lou and me to go in their place. We rushed to the hospital where others they had invited joined us for a final vigil. By ten-thirty Chuck's arterial blood stopped flowing to his brain, but his strong heart continued beating through the night. At nine-twenty the next morning, the doctor shut off the ventilator. Twenty-two minutes later the heart monitor went flat.

So ended a magnificent life. I will never know another like Chuck Goldmark: brilliant, at moments fierce, at times incredibly funny, and honest to the core. After he died I issued a statement on behalf of our firm: "Chuck Goldmark was one of the state's outstanding attorneys, a wise counselor, our partner, and our friend. He was the best of all of us."

Chuck met his wife, Annie, on a trip to Europe for a student conference where she served as his interpreter. When they married, it was with the understanding that their children would be raised bilingual, and indeed, both Colin and Derek spoke French as fluently as English. Although an enthusiastic mountain climber, Chuck's occasional hikes with Annie and the boys meant more to him. I doubted whether Chuck could have endured had he survived his family's murder; I doubted whether our law firm could survive without Chuck. In time we learned it could not.

At Chuck's memorial service many paid tribute to this remarkable man's adaptability: lawyer, family man, climber, citizen, ranchhand—he moved easily from one role to another. Some remarked on his love of gadgets: espresso machines, state-of-the-art stereos, and—long before they became a fact of life—computers. An old college classmate remembered how much Chuck liked the game cribbage, and how his love of classical music had resulted in one particularly idiosyncratic ritual: broadcasting E. Power Biggs's Bach organ suites on his stereo full blast Saturday and Sunday mornings. Others commented about Chuck's devotion to his children, his wife, his cats, and his community. Many recalled his raising one eyebrow with a half-smile that implied "I've just pulled your leg" or throwing his head back, slapping his thigh, and pounding the table in appreciation at some remark. Everyone remembered his deep and penetrating eyes.

Chuck Goldmark at Seven Summits celebration, Snowbird, Utah.

Near the end of the service, Stim Bullitt, an old friend of John and Sally's who'd known Chuck since he was a little boy, reflected about people dying too young:

"Where a life has been cut off before its time, to remark on that life's intensity or productivity or good fortune as somehow softening the loss fails to touch what matters most: a missed chance to tackle more life. And that goes for everyone. The only point is to suggest the likely rich future that was lost.

"Twice during our earthly sojourn—when we arrive and when we leave—life is ineluctably unjust. One injustice is the range of differences between us in the personal gifts we bring with us at birth. The other, truly life's worst, is mortality. As at birth, life at death is unequal: some are allowed an ample span, while others are cut down, like Colin, when just out of the starting gate. And it is universal: each of us, even if not notably wicked, even the most blameless of all, is condemned to capital punishment. The question is not whether, only when. One day the bell rings, telling you the party's over. You don't go home, you go outside in the dark."

Stim's grim remarks summed up how I felt.

Two weeks later Derek died. Children from his class packed the memorial service. Colin and Annie had shared a service. This one left no doubt it was a child's; afterward we went outside and released balloons into the sky. I had grown weary of funerals, worn-out by tragedy. Disgusted by the waste, worried about the impact Chuck's death would have upon the firm, I entered a terrible funk.

That spring, exactly four months after the murders, I had a most unusual dream. As I lay on my side, I heard Chuck's voice in my left ear—as though we were conversing on the phone. Startled by how real it seemed, I started trying to remember what Chuck said even as I dreamed. When I awoke, I recalled only the clarity of his bold, distinctive voice; unfortunately, no matter how hard I tried, I could not remember his words. I know our conversation began with routine matters, later turning to the philosophical, but what we said eluded me except that I asked him, "Chuck, where are you? What state are you in?" He didn't say, or if he did, I forgot, but I felt great comfort simply hearing his familiar voice.

In June I climbed Mt. Rainier with three men close to Chuck. Alone, under an impenetrable blue sky, we remembered him, his wife and sons. After reading aloud a short poem, we released the family's ashes into the strong wind blowing east. Tears streamed down my cheeks from behind my sunglasses, but something about spreading their ashes from that beautiful mountaintop was liberating.

"From dust thou art and to dust thou shalt return, dear Annie, Derek, Colin, Chuck."

Chuck and Annie Goldmark with their sons, Derek and Colin.

A year later David Rice went on trial for the murder of the Goldmark family. The jury convicted him and sentenced him to death. In 1997, twelve years after the attack, a federal district-court judge overturned Rice's conviction on the grounds of ineffective legal counsel. That ruling is on appeal. Although Rice should never be released from prison, whether he is executed remains a matter of supreme indifference to me. His death would not bring back the Goldmarks or fill the void left by their massacre.

eleven

GIVING UP

T
he pointlessness of the Goldmarks' deaths, and the evil that caused them, further eroded my belief in God and an afterlife, already diminished by a decade filled with the sudden and premature deaths of friends and companions. Of the six of us who had climbed Aconcagua, that happiest of expeditions, three died violent deaths: Marty in 1982, Chuck in 1985, and Frank Wells, who would perish in a helicopter crash in 1994 . I had lost my mother and watched four friends die right in front of me. In addition to Al, Dusan, Chris, and Marty, I'd grieved for Leif Patterson and Naomi Uemura.

At Chuck's memorial, Stim Bullitt remarked about the false comfort we sometimes take when a person we love dies doing the thing he or she enjoys. Stim's words stung, echoing my disgust at all the young, promising lives I'd seen cut short:

"Although many people care about their prospective deportment at death, few prefer their death to come while absorbed in their favorite pleasure. Some comment on a mountaineering death that the victim was 'doing what he loved,' as though this means of execution fulfilled him and thereby made death somehow less a dirty trick.

"Nonsense! For him whose life has been snuffed out, did the mountaineering that gave him such delight include being killed? Was he fulfilled by shivering, huddled on a wet log? By stumbling numb, by spinning in accelerating somersaults, by gasping for breath as his lungs gurgled, hurtling toward rocks? Or at the bottom of a crevasse, wedged in an icy cleft? When Chuck and Annie and their two little sons were beaten to death, were those of us who mourn them consoled by knowing they met their end together near their hearth on Christmas Eve?"

I agreed with Stim that all untimely deaths are hard to bear, but the Goldmarks had no choice how they died. My friends who died in the mountains did. They took a calculated risk. Why did I keep climbing, subjecting myself to such risk in the face of all those good friends dead—and for what? I had spent my life striving to make my existence, if not unique, at least above the ordinary. After losing so many friends, mountain summits seemed an absurd target for my ambitions, yet I could not break the habit.

I thought a lot about the role death played in my climbing. Was I pursuing some kind of death wish? I concluded I climbed not because I wanted to die, but because I wanted to know death, to understand it. In his compelling essay "The Mountain of Love and Death," printed in *Mountains of the Great Blue Dream*, Robert Leonard Reid wrote:

Mountaineers climb because they love the mountains, yes; but they climb too because climbing prepares them boldly and tenaciously for death, then guides them faithfully to the edge of another world, a world I now recognize as the world of the dead, and there allows them to dance, mountain after mountain, year after year, as close to death as it is possible to dance; which is to say, within a single step.

Chuck's murder ultimately resulted in the merger of our law firm with a large corporate firm, where I never belonged. Between August of 1985 and May of 1986 we lost nearly a quarter of our partners and fifty years of legal experience in a series of traumatic departures, some related to Chuck's death, others to the controversial office romance, one to a partner's family crisis. It was only a matter of time until the firm, as I had known it, would completely disappear.

Business pressures kept me from taking any time off between November 1984 when I returned from Mt. Everest and October 1987, when Mary Lou and I traveled to Europe on the first real vacation we had taken alone during our twenty-five-year marriage. The day we returned from that holiday a colleague called to alert me that our firm was about to launch merger discussions with a San Francisco law firm. Although I did not agree with those partners who believed we had to merge in order to compete in our chosen fields of practice, I felt I had little choice but to go along, having scuttled plans for a previous merger because of a client conflict. I had never done well in large organizations, which could only function with a committee structure I found stifling. Nonetheless, we merged with the larger firm, and I entered a period of profound professional discontent.

Down on myself as a lawyer and as a climber, I watched the last vestiges of youth slip away as my physical powers began their inevitable decline. Gossip within the climbing community about the bad luck I brought to those with whom I climbed—something I heard about indirectly—only added to my general disillusionment.

During my late forties I planned and abandoned several major expeditions. I had dreamed of returning to K2, to lead my own expedition, to reach the summit without oxygen and become the first man to climb the mountain twice. In a gesture of magnanimity, Cherie Bech gave me and my coleader, Doug Scott (one of Britain's best-known Himalayan climbers), the permit to K2 she and Chris Chandler had obtained from the Pakistanis.

After falling in love on K2, Chris Chandler and Cherie (who had resumed using her maiden name, Bremer-Kamp, after she and Terry divorced) married and continued climbing together. In the winter of 1985, they attempted Kanchenjunga, the world's third-highest peak, just one hundred feet lower than K2. At twenty-six thousand feet, as they prepared to push for the summit, Chris suddenly developed cerebral edema. Cherie and their lone Nepali companion made a valiant effort to assist Chris down the mountain, but he died at twenty-five thousand feet. Unable to carry his body down the steep terrain, they left him on the mountainside. When Cherie returned to the United States, she lost eight fingers, parts of both thumbs, and all her toes to frostbite. She could never again work as a critical-care nurse, nor could she ever climb K2.

Law firm business forced me to withdraw from the K2 team Doug Scott and I had organized. That bad weather prevented the team from reaching the summit helped ease my disappointment, but I always regretted losing the chance to climb with Scott. Next, I set my sights on Kanchenjunga. John Roskelley proposed to lead a small expedition there in 1988, and I threw myself into the preparations. For a variety of reasons, John canceled plans for the expedition and we shifted our attention to 23,553-foot Menlungtse, one of the world's most difficult unclimbed peaks. I had first thought of climbing Menlungtse in 1969, but not until 1987 did China first allow climbers on the mountain, located just across the border in Tibet. Our goal was to climb Menlungtse's east summit in 1989, the year after a British expedition led by Chris Bonington reached the mountain's slightly lower west summit. From the photographs he had sent to me, I knew we were in for a hard climb.

On the way to Beijing in the fall of '88 to get the permit, I stopped briefly in Hong Kong and paid a visit to Peter Goodwin at a rest home. Frailer than when Mary Lou and I had visited him in 1983 between Everest expeditions, he appeared quite ill and his voice was just a whisper. His Chinese nurse pointed to her heart and shook her head. The old man did not have long to live. Peter slowly ushered me into a small room, and we resumed the conversation where we had left off five years before.

Seven years earlier when I first met Peter Goodwin, he had encouraged me to climb Mt. Everest and to visit a Tibetan monastery at its base. After thanking him for his wise counsel I remarked, "When I touched the monastery wall, I thought of you, Peter, just as you had asked." I spent most of my visit listening to Peter recount fascinating stories about his life. One concerned his brother, Cyril, a personal bodyguard of Madame Chiang Kai-shek. Somehow, Cyril became a prisoner of the Japanese during World War II. As he was about to be beheaded, Cyril declined his executioners' offer of a hood, explaining that at the last moment of his life he wanted to see the blue sky. "How do you know this?" I asked. "We got the story from Japanese documents after the war," Peter explained. "The soldiers who witnessed my brother's courage were so impressed they wrote about it and photographed his execution."

Before returning to my hotel, I asked Peter when he had last been outside. "Not since I arrived here at the rest home." On a whim I found a wheelchair and helped Peter into the garden, where I silently pushed him up and down the narrow path between the rows of foliage. When it was time for me to go, I returned him to his room where, kneeling on the floor beside his chair, I said, "I love you, Peter." He looked at me and replied, "I love you, Jim." We both knew we would never see each other again. At the Hong Kong airport on my

Peter Goodwin in Hong Kong.

way home from China the following day, I called him for a last good-bye. "Thank you for the garden ride," Peter remarked. "It reminded me of the mountains."

Three weeks after I returned home to Seattle, a letter arrived postmarked Hong Kong. It was from a friend of Peter's telling me that he had died just nine days after our last conversation. Although we saw each other only three times, Peter Goodwin's death reminded me that in friendship, frequency of contact is not what counts.

With permit in hand I returned to the United States. But a few months later the Chinese imposed martial law in Tibet and closed the borders to foreigners. Foiled on the eve of our departure, John and I scrambled to join Lou Whittaker, already at the base of Kanchenjunga in Nepal with a large team. Although we had not participated in the planning, Lou invited us to join his expedition, and we appeared at base camp ready to go—but not really ready to go. We had to choose which of two possible routes to take up the mountain: one easier but threatened by avalanches, or a much harder, but safer, alternative. John persuaded Lou and his team to go hard but safe.

I was almost forty-nine, and other than for a few short climbs in the Cascades and regular workouts at the gym, I had not prepared for so physically demanding a climb. I quickly found myself pushed to the limits of my capacity. Neither John nor I had ever planned to join another large expedition, but there we were. At the sight of Sherpas hauling loads up a steep wall of rock and ice while climbers sat around the camp playing cards, Roskelley fumed, "I should never have come." I made his decision easier when I quit the expedition. Although a touch of pneumonia served as my official reason for leaving, in my heart I knew I was not up to the rigors of the climb. So, less than three weeks after we arrived, John and I pulled out and headed home. Lou's expedition did fine without us: six men reached the summit—a huge success by any standard.

In 1990, China reopened Tibet to foreigners, and once again, John and I geared up for Menlungtse, this time with two experienced climbers, Greg Child and Jeff Duenwald. I was delighted to undertake an expedition with just three others. This was how I had always wanted to climb. Now at last, here was the chance. I did not want to repeat my sorry performance on Kanchenjunga so I worked out hard and often at the gym.

Six months before the expedition to Menlungtse, two colleagues and I left the large, merged law firm to form a new firm more consistent with our professional values and personal goals. With this accomplished, I headed for the Himalayas confident that I would return to a more fulfilling professional life than I had had for a long time.

Mary Lou was her usual contained self at the airport, suppressing any concerns she may have had about this expedition. The family came out in force to send me on my way, and as always, their support helped me head off on my adventure without regrets. But on the plane, as I read *Macbeth* and listened to Bizet's opera *The Pearl Fishers,* negative thoughts kept creeping into my consciousness. I assured myself that having concerns about Menlungtse's dangers made good sense, but wondered why the mental side of climbing seemed to be getting so much harder as I aged.

Shortly after arriving in Tibet I got the chance to speak by telephone with Mary Lou and our son Bob. Bob and I talked about sports. He told me he'd watched the Chicago Bulls play Cleveland and that Michael Jordan had scored sixty-nine points and grabbed eighteen rebounds—probably one of the greatest performances in NBA playoff history. Mary Lou and I discussed ways she might contact me in the event of a dire emergency since, unlike K2 and Everest, there was no efficient way to get mail to or from Menlungtse.

On the hike into base camp I began to suffer from aches and pains I had never experienced before. My back hurt, so did my left big toe, and I strained my left calf muscle as a result of favoring the toe. Nonetheless my spirits were quite high. At the end of the week spent hiking on the dusty

Menlungtse from west.

Addicted to Danger

trail toward base camp, I left the others for a bath in a creek and exulted in the pleasure of washing my filthy clothes, hair, and body. Afterward I sat naked in the sun, surrounded by my towel, T-shirt, socks, and underpants spread out on rocks to dry, reveling in my solitude.

My first sight of Menlungtse took my breath away. As we came around a bend in the trail, the stark rock pyramid, capped with a crown of ice, suddenly filled the horizon. It looked impossibly steep, but I contained my fear by reassuring myself that our intended route was on the other side of the mountain. The narrow ridge we planned to climb was not nearly as steep, but it was corniced, and cornices can be dangerous.

Three weeks after leaving home I had two prescient dreams: one about climbing, one about home. I awoke one morning from a vivid dream in which I'd left the expedition without ever having had a chance to attempt the summit. In similar dreams, on K2 and Everest, I had left the mountain voluntarily, but I always felt terribly upset and made desperate efforts to get back to the mountain. Not so in this dream. Although I did not climb Menlungtse, I dreamed it did not matter and that I told Mary Lou I planned to stop serious climbing. The same week I dreamed of my parents. Though I knew Mom was dead, she appeared beautiful and full of life. "How could a son be so lucky as to lose his mother, yet find her again?" I remarked. By contrast, my dad, suffering from some unknown ailment, appeared parched and terribly thin and I warned him to take it easy.

With the help of two Sherpas, Ang Nima and Chhiri, the four of us established our base camp in an isolated grassy valley, surrounded by magnificent Himalayan peaks, visited by small herds of mountain sheep and scores of furry marmots. Gazing up at

Menlungtse team:
Greg Child, Jeff Duenwald, John Roskelley, and Jim.

Menlungtse, towering above us like an obelisk or some giant prayer stone, I thought of home. I had to take no action on this expedition that would prevent me from returning to my family.

Within a week, we established our advanced base camp at 16,900 feet: two tents on a grassy bench nestled among large granite boulders. On the way up, John and Jeff came within twenty-five feet of a snow leopard—extraordinary in broad daylight. After a brief face-off, the snow leopard bounded away, down a parallel grassy moraine and across the large frozen lake below our camp. John told me that four weeks earlier he had left his eight-year-old son, Jess, sitting on a chair with a stuffed snow leopard clutched to his chest.

My heavy pack and declining powers conspired to put me out of sync with the others. Greg, John, and Jeff waited for me at the top of the first moraine rise, but after that, they left me in the dust. The snow leopard episode allowed me to catch up, but before long I was behind again. We took three trips to haul all our supplies to advanced base camp. Since I had not brought up any of my personal gear the first day, I had to haul everything on the third. Along with basic gear I carried my usual extra items: diary, books, water purifier, extra camera and lens, electric razor, crampons, and double boots. Although my load was just forty pounds, carrying it was a struggle. In my younger days I would have carried more without thinking twice. Despite my physical limitations, I still felt optimistic thanks to good weather, beautiful scenery, and excellent companions.

Throughout the early stages of the expedition I reflected on why I had come. Again and again I determined to exercise great care. I must not make some stupid mistake and kill myself. I wrote in my diary,

If I climb Menlungtse that would be fine. If I do not, so be it.

On April 19, four weeks after leaving home, we got caught in a snowstorm. I figured we would be confined to our tents for a while so I began rereading Nabokov's *Conclusive Evidence*, the 1951 version of *Speak, Memory*. I first read it in 1977 on the expedition to the Fairweathers with Al and Dusan, then reread it during my ordeal on the Peters Glacier in 1981 after Chris died in the crevasse. Each time I read it, I discovered something new. Reading about Nabokov's childhood always provoked me to remember aspects of my own, particularly the early years when my brother Bob and I were small and Dad was away at war.

In the middle of the storm John suggested that the four of us walk up the subsidiary ridge. By then a pattern had emerged: John, Greg, and Jeff traveled uphill at the same speed; I invariably trailed behind. I was nearly fifty and though I didn't feel weak, I just could not go as fast as the others. Although I believed I had a real shot at the summit, I knew that becoming competitive would just irritate me. "March to the beat of your own drummer," I reminded myself. The Menlungtse expedition was one long mind game. Would I stay healthy? Would I maintain the necessary motivation to keep advancing day by day toward the summit? Would the ridge above twenty-one thousand feet exceed my technical capabilities? If I reached the summit, could I get down safely? These questions kept arising, usually at night. With thirty years of climbing experience I believed I could physically meet the mountain's challenges, but could I maintain the *mental* commitment? I wanted to climb Menlungtse, but not enough to risk everything.

Sitting in my tent, I thought about accidents. If one analyzed all the accidents that had killed climbers in the Himalayas, I suspected they would fall into three general categories. First were those resulting from external dangers, such as a collapsing ice cliff, an avalanche, or a blizzard. Second were those resulting from ordinary human error such as Marty's failure to secure her waist harness. The third kind involved "pushing oneself too far," allowing the desire to reach a summit to overwhelm one's judgment. I had done that on K2 in 1978 when I risked all and almost died.

By the time I reached 18,300 feet on the way to help put in a fixed rope to the crest of the east ridge, my companions had been awaiting me for more than half an hour. Back at Advanced Base Camp, we had been able to see the entire corniced ridge through our binoculars, but could not determine how dangerous it might be. Now, on the ridge crest, a sharp pinnacle at twenty-one thousand feet blocked our view of the ridge beyond so we still did not know what awaited us. That night, tucked into my warm sleeping bag and listening to the snow patter against the roof of the tent, I wondered if tomorrow I would be stronger. Probably not.

On the verge of turning fifty, I thought about Stim Bullitt still climbing at seventy, technically able but slower every year. The image haunted me. Age had begun to slow me down as it had slowed Stim before me. Now, just eight years younger than he had been when we first attempted McKinley in 1978, I was no longer the hotshot who could beat most anyone else up a mountain. Always a hare, I perceived myself becoming a tortoise.

The next day I performed better. I left the tent a few minutes ahead of the others. Though they quickly passed me, I felt satisfied to keep a steady pace behind them all the way to our cache at 18,300 feet, ascending a respectable thirteen hundred vertical feet in seventy minutes. From there, Greg and Jeff took the lead while John and I lagged behind with heavier loads, clambering through a boulder field and up the fixed rope.

The wind picked up as we worked our way up to the icy and exposed east ridge. I climbed up the fixed ropes to the point where John had left his pack anchored to an ice screw. (As the temperature dropped and the wind picked up, John realized he had forgotten his parka and returned to camp.) Perched on the steep ice, I carefully emptied the food and stove cartridges out of John's pack and into my own. Then, with the extra load, I jumared to where Jeff was belaying Greg to the base of some seracs. While Greg finished the pitch, I used my ice ax to hack out a tent platform for us to use as Camp 1. It proved hard work at 19,400 feet, and I only got two-thirds done. As the weather deteriorated we rappelled off, returning one by one to advanced base camp. Although I felt pleased with my performance, I still harbored qualms about my capacity to climb the mountain.

My soul-searching continued far into the night. I awoke from troubled sleep convinced I should not go with the others when they went for the summit. On Everest in 1984, then again on Kanchenjunga in 1989, I had suspected my days of serious Himalayan climbing might be over. I had left the last expedition because the route exceeded my physical conditioning and my mental strength. I had come to Menlungtse with high hopes but now realized I was no longer up to this kind of climbing. Unlike on Kanchenjunga, I did not want simply to walk away. Indeed I planned to do everything I could to help the expedition I had conceived.

Following a fabulous breakfast of fried eggs, Sherpa pan bread, fruit cocktail, and chocolate pudding, I joined John in our tent. When he asked, "How's it going?" I responded awkwardly, "Not so good. I'm no longer the climber I was on K2, either mentally or physically. The route up Menlungtse's east ridge is beyond me, so I've decided to drop out of the climb. I've never been a particularly good technical climber; what has gotten me up mountains has always been more will than skill. I have lost my will. It is time for me to quit."

John understood. Although initially concerned about the impact my decision might have on Greg and Jeff, he assured me that climbing as a team of three instead of four would pose no serious problems. Near the end of our discussion, I got choked up and we clasped hands. Then I walked to the small creek where Greg and Jeff were washing and told them, "I've decided to drop out—in fact I intend to stop serious climbing altogether." Like John, they seemed sympathetic and understanding.

In the hours following my announcement I felt a tremendous relief. Freed at last from the chains of my mountaineering ambition, I would wrap up thirty years of climbing with the K2 climb as my principal accomplishment. I looked forward to a new life uncomplicated by my preoccupation with climbing. I fell asleep satisfied I had made the right decision and awoke the next morning without regrets.

In 1984 I had talked about quitting during a *Climbing* magazine interview: "When I quit, it will not be because of the accidents but rather the fact that climbing no longer attracts me. When I am not physically or mentally able to respond, I'll do something else. Being able to make that inevitable transition with a modicum of grace is a most interesting proposition." That time had come.

The others were preoccupied with the demands of a summit push. To my surprise, John remarked that he might "fall off" the mountain and not come back. At one point, he said that never before

Menlungtse's east ridge. Pinnacle at 21,000 feet at top center.

had he dreamed of dying until just before this trip, when he dreamed an avalanche killed him. When John, Greg, and Jeff finally left, we all shook hands and hugged each other good-bye. A few moments later John returned to remind me he had pictures of his kids in the tent. As he walked away, tears welled in my eyes.

Although at times I got restless, I enjoyed the quiet afforded by my solitude. Tenting alone, I could spread out my gear, and I slept better without John snoring beside me. Alone with time on my hands, the tent clean and orderly for the first time since our arrival, I again contemplated my decision. Despite the fact that I would not climb Menlungtse, I felt remarkably happy and satisfied.

The days passed slowly. I spent hours reading Shakespeare's tragedies and writing in my diary. Now I knew how Lou Whittaker must have felt. As a leader of a Himalayan expedition there must be many times when there's little to do except wait for something to happen. By nature I preferred to be where the action was, but I had made my choice. Looking ahead, I wondered how I would stay fit without an expedition as a goal to spur me on. Would I work out at the gym? Run around the neighborhood? Take long walks? I knew that without some regimen, I would probably do nothing. More significant loomed the prospect of no longer regarding myself as a mountain climber, so long a part of my identity.

The notion—which I had long subscribed to—that engaging in high-risk activities such as mountain climbing somehow protected me from the more customary avenues to mortality now struck me as ridiculous. Exposing myself to sudden death in the mountains clearly had little to do with whether I would get cancer or some other fatal disease. Life resembled a crapshoot; I could tilt the odds in my favor (i.e., stop trying to climb the Menlungtses of the world), but I could never entirely eliminate risk.

On April 28, my companions returned, forced back by bad weather. They planned to try again, so I reconciled myself to several more weeks of waiting. Having taken myself out of the action, I felt estranged from the others. While John, Greg, and Jeff made their summit attempt, I proposed to circumambulate the mountain. If I went without a tent or a stove and simply relied on cold food and my trusty bivouac sack, I could go with a light pack. The more I thought about this, the more it appealed to me—a way to salvage the expedition. When I told John about my plan, he suggested I take one of the Sherpas and go just for the day. "What if you fall and break a leg?" he asked. Frankly, to go alone appealed to me more; I viewed it as a way to derive something unique from the expedition.

Weather and disagreements about climbing strategy kept the others from making their summit attempt for several days. If they didn't succeed on the next summit push, I wondered whether they would try again. I suspected that if poor weather was the sole cause of the next turn-back, John would argue for another try. As much as I wanted to return home, I felt I could adapt. It cost us $85 per day to keep a jeep and a truck waiting at the road head. I wondered how long the drivers would wait for us before returning for food and shelter. John and I had raised $40,000 from various sponsors. Would that be enough to cover the costs of the expedition or would we return to a big debt? (We were short a few thousand dollars, and I absorbed the loss.)

On May 5, a bright and breezy day, my companions left for their second attempt. Jeff, who had suffered from severe intestinal problems for the previous thirty-six hours, said if he stayed ill, he might come back. I could feel his apprehension as he walked away. Once again John seemed distressed. "If I don't come back," he instructed, "you have my letter and you know what my thoughts are about my family." Then fifty yards from camp he turned and yelled, "Wickwire, you're not old, you're young." He and Ang Nima suddenly stopped. They'd forgotten something. Ang Nima needed my ski poles. John and I ran toward one another and I handed him the poles. As we hugged once more, I said, "You are a good man, John." Then off they went.

Alone, without distractions, I began to notice various aches and pains. My shoulder hurt, my calf still hurt a little, so did my big toe.

A few hours later Jeff returned. He had decided to give it up. No longer isolated from the other three, I now belonged to a pair, albeit a sick and retired pair. We were down to one strong, two-man team. Jeff admitted that the route above twenty-one thousand feet was beyond him. "I probably would have bowed out at Camp 2 even if I hadn't been sick," he confessed. "What troubled me most was the prospect of traversing like a crab along all those steep side slopes." Assuming that he recovered from his stomach problem soon, we agreed to start circumambulating the mountain the following morning. I felt a twinge of regret not to be going alone.

Threatening weather caused us to delay our plans. So I sat in my tent and thought about the subject of will. Given my faltering willpower in the previous few years, I wondered how I had sustained the necessary drive to climb K2. Competitiveness? Pride? After the climbing community pundits denigrated our 1975 attempt and the American Alpine Club gave its endorsement to the other K2 expedition, I remembered telling myself that nothing would keep me from the summit in 1978. But since that triumph—like an aging sports star—I had followed a steadily declining curve of achievement.

After a day of heavy snow, punctuated by loud claps of thunder, John and Greg left to make their third summit attempt. We parted with little emotion. That afternoon Jeff and I concluded we should not circumambulate the mountain in such deep snow and discussed my decision to quit climbing. Jeff could not understand why I wouldn't at least continue weekend climbing. But ever since I'd stopped weekend climbing in the 1960s, all my climbs in the Cascades had been in preparation for the next expedition. Anyhow, I wanted to make a clean break. Reinhold Messner once said that one should not engage in serious Himalayan climbing past the age of forty-two. On Everest in 1982, I was forty-two and in my prime, but Marty died, and the summit slipped away. When I returned to Everest in 1984, I had already suffered a decline—albeit more mental than physical.

When John and Greg went beyond the end of the fixed ropes, I sat five thousand feet below and, through my binoculars, observed the slow progress of the high-altitude climbers at work. It was sort of like watching old cars rust or grass grow. The next day they moved even more slowly. As they approached the pinnacle that afternoon, clouds formed and blocked my view. I assumed they had found a campsite but worried about their safety nonetheless. When I awoke on the third morning, ominous black clouds hung over the Nepal border. A few clouds wafted about the pinnacle. Using my binoculars, I caught a glimpse of one figure, then a second, through a hole in the clouds. Did they plan to go higher or were they merely testing the cornices? Before I could make out what John and Greg were doing, they disappeared behind a cloud.

Their slow pace convinced me to descend to base camp where I alerted the Sherpas not to bring up the yaks to retrieve our equipment for another couple of days. The next morning, as I hiked back up the

John Roskelley leading steep ice pitch on Menlungtse's east ridge.

grassy moraine to check on the climbers' progress, John came around a corner. After a hug he announced, "The expedition's over." He explained that when he found himself on a paper-thin cornice and probed it with his ice ax, all he touched was air. He tried to maneuver his way across, but became convinced if he took another step he would plunge through. Though Greg might be able to hold him, John realized if he was seriously injured, he might never be extricated. So he yelled back to Greg, "It's too risky, I can't get safely across here." Greg agreed, it was time to go home.

I returned from Menlungtse determined to end my climbing career. After informing Mary Lou and the children, I notified my partners and my client, the Arctic Slope Regional Corporation. Then I went to my life insurance agent and asked him to remove the extra $2,500 annual "climbing" premium from my policy. "I've stopped for good," I explained.

And I really thought I had.

twelve

CHANGE OF HEART

Not once in the weeks following my return from Menlungtse did I doubt my decision to stop climbing, so when Eiho Otani called me from Fairbanks the following month, my reaction took me by surprise. Otani had just completed his first climb to the summit of Mt. McKinley—a mountain that had captured his interest when we were searching its slopes for Naomi Uemura six years before. When he said he wanted to climb with me again, I significantly failed to mention my decision to stop climbing. Stim Bullitt had called earlier the same week asking me to join him on a rock climb. As with Otani, I declined his invitation but did not say why. Although I had been open with everyone else about my decision, I simply could not bring myself to level with these two friends who still climbed mountains, and who wanted to climb with me.

In August 1990 my second Menlungtse dream came true. The news that my father had kidney cancer, which had already spread to his liver, hit me like a sledgehammer. We all quickly realized this was it—Dad was dying. When I spoke with him on the phone, his voice sounded weak, altered by weariness. But he remained focused and quite analytical, and we talked frankly about his situation. His doctors, who doubted radiation or chemotherapy would make a difference, gave him four to six months to live. Although we spoke in a low-key, businesslike manner, I managed to say as we rang off, "We all love you, Dad," to which he replied, "I know."

Over the next three months I traveled frequently to visit Dad at his home in eastern Washington. On my first visit, two of my brothers and I sat with him on the patio. "I thought I'd live a lot longer," he admitted, "but I know it will be over soon. I've had a good life with no regrets." Dad was seventy-six. I was fifty. Each time I saw him he had lost a few more pounds and his skin had grown a little grayer. Without hope, Dad focused on dying. I marveled at his courage. He never uttered the slightest complaint about his fate, only concern for his wife, Peg (whom he had married two years before).

I read to him portions of my diary from the 1977 Fairweather expedition when, stimulated by Nabokov, I had reviewed the most significant events of my early childhood, principally his absence during World War II. Somehow Dad summoned the energy to talk about those years. He would start a sentence, falter, then with great effort continue. We couldn't settle on which Christmas he had come home—1943 or 1944. He did remember that my brother Richard was conceived on that trip—so it must have been 1943. Dad mentioned an air-group commander on his aircraft carrier betting the eager young pilots that they would never see combat over Japan. Dad remarked that, by shortening the war, the atom bombs dropped on Nagasaki and Hiroshima saved him from combat.

As always, we spoke of sports; he recalled a basketball game with other naval officers (his team lost) and a game of bridge he played with a senior officer who bet one cent a point, Dad, a tenth of a cent. (The officer lost a lot of money.) Later that afternoon Richard asked him, "What was the most fun you ever had?" He paused a long time, then answered, "Watching Jimmy play football."

In early September word came that Dad's eighty-year-old brother, Parker, planned to visit, and he revived for a while. But a few nights later Dad told Peg, "I want to go tonight." The following week he appeared markedly thinner. What remained of his flesh hung loosely from his arms and legs. He slept most of the time, yet when he awoke, he was lucid. Although gradually withering away, Dad was blessedly free of pain.

On October 16, my father collapsed in the bathroom. Peg yelled, "Jim, Jim." Thinking she was calling me (rather than her husband), I rushed in to find Dad propped upright against the wall, eyes open but sightless. Peg cried, "He's gone," and moved aside. I wrapped my arm around his back and said, "Come on, Dad, come on," as I applied repeated pressure to his chest. After a few seconds his heart beat again and he began to breathe.

The next day Dad told Peg, "I died last night." When I returned the following weekend, Dad seemed different. At dinner he announced, "I've come back from the dead, you guys." For the first time in six weeks he ate some solid food. None of us could believe or comprehend the apparent reversal in both his attitude and eating habits. Yet in spite of his improved health and increased energy, he clearly wanted to die.

Before Dad's initial diagnosis, I had stopped believing in God or an afterlife. I thought the only thing awaiting us after death was nothingness. A chance reading of a newspaper article on the near-death experiences of children led me to read Melvin Morse's *Closer to the Light*. Nearly all his case studies described the experience of moving toward light—not darkness as one might expect. Further reading supported my emerging belief that some aspect of us does indeed survive, not just in "good" people, but in all human beings.

A few weeks later, Dad told Peg he wanted to speak to me and my five brothers. As I entered his room, he began talking about murder. I had no idea what he was saying, a dream perhaps. When I reminded Dad how much we all loved him, he replied, "Don't talk too much, save it for later." During this he tapped my hand with his fist to emphasize his point and said that sometime he would tell me more. For some reason this odd exchange greatly lifted my spirits.

Later that week I called the house and my sister, Mary, relayed a question from my dad: "He wants to know how your engineers are doing." Confused, I responded, "Fine," not knowing what he meant. Afterward Mary explained he was referring to the engineers at work on one of Seattle's floating bridges, which Peg had told him had partially collapsed. When Dad got on the phone, I said, "I love you," something I had never been able to say aloud to him before.

Over the next couple of days my father mentioned seeing "a trail of gold and crystal-clear water." He died December 7, 1990, and we buried him five days later. My interaction with him during his illness had been incredibly fulfilling—the gift of a slow, painless death, denied me and my siblings when our mother died.

On New Year's Day, sitting with my son Bob at the Rose Bowl watching the Washington Huskies beat Iowa, I fought back tears. Never again would I attend a sporting event with my father. Though I ached with grief I also felt uplifted by the way he had died and by the long, full, honorable life he had led.

Over the next several months I often dreamed of my father. Once I dreamed we had a conversation about his relationship with *his* father. They had never been close. He explained that though he had strived to be closer to his own children, he knew he had been pretty distant. I told him I wanted to become closer to *my* children and began to cry. A few months later as I lay in bed, on the edge of sleep, I dreamed my father spoke to me. As with my "visit" from Chuck Goldmark a few months after his death, I could not see my father, but I did hear his voice. It was soothing and replete with gentle admonitions to "take it easy" and not push too hard. Although I could not recall his words, the sound of his voice made the back of my neck tingle.

Years later, climbing in South America, I dreamed my father came to me. At first I thought he was still alive. When he reminded

Jim's dad, James Wickwire.

me he was dead, I asked him what it was like. He could tell me nothing about an afterlife except to confirm its existence. "Will I see you again, Dad?" "Possibly," he replied.

In May, Mary Lou and I attended a Mountain Summit gathering in Tokyo. As I sat on a panel, someone asked me, "Why do you climb?" I said, "For each of us there is a different answer. Sometimes it is easier to say what something is not, rather than what it is. I can tell you that climbing is not the expression of a death wish. It also is not the pursuit of a 'thrill junkie.' But it is not enough to define something by way of negatives.

"At the risk of saying what it is—as Greg Child [also on the panel] said earlier, it could simply be seeing a beautiful sunrise while bivouacked high on K2. It may be something more: an affirmation of life—a searching for what is precious in life. When we find what it is we seek, we are able to return home to our loved ones, to those we cherish. Maybe in the end climbing is about love." I never mentioned to the audience I had decided to stop.

Unexpectedly, Eiho Otani called the next morning, having just arrived home from Kathmandu. We saw him later in the day, looking very young for forty-four. He mentioned that he had a permit to climb Everest via the South Col in 1993 and asked me if I would join the expedition. I politely fended him off with the excuse "I've never been interested in that side of Everest."

A few weeks later Mary Lou and I attended David's college graduation—the last of the five to obtain a college degree. On the four-hour drive back to Seattle, I began to think about the unthinkable: going to Everest with Eiho Otani in 1993. Perhaps I could prepare by climbing Aconcagua the following January with another Japanese friend, Toshiro Matsunaga, whom I had known since we climbed together with Ed Boulton back in the late sixties. Despite a firm decision to end serious climbing—a decision communicated to nearly everyone I knew except Otani, Matsunaga, and Stim Bullitt—and an equally firm commitment never to undertake an Everest climb via the Khumbu Icefall and the South Col, I began to contemplate climbing it with Otani. Most of my past mountaineering ambitions had arisen in the euphoria accompanying a few glasses of white wine. This time I was stone sober.

I'd been a different man on Menlungtse. Absolutely certain that no afterlife existed, I had exercised excessive caution—maybe even cowardice. I had feared that if I went up on Menlungtse's east ridge I might fall to my death, and if I did, my soul would be extinguished forever. My father's near-death experience helped persuade me that we do indeed survive our own deaths. Though this revelation did not send me back to the Catholic Church, it stirred in me a spirituality that linked me to all the world's religions—and something more. This freed me from the paralyzing fear of utter extinction that had for years tormented me late at night as I dropped off to sleep.

I wanted to do a few more climbs to see if this change of attitude would affect my decision-making in the mountains. I had detested the words "I've quit climbing . . . I'm through with the big Himalayan climbs." Until my body—not my weak will—told me it was time, I wanted to continue climbing. But quietly, oh, so quietly, with absolutely no fanfare or publicity. One thing for sure, I was not ready to disclose my change of heart to Mary Lou or anyone else.

Over the next few months I secretly planned my return to Everest. I intended to watch how my mind and body functioned in the months ahead. I knew I would need to rigorously ready myself, but at fifty-two, I would still face less of a physical than a mental challenge. Despite some tendinitis in my right elbow I felt good physically and looked forward to a two-year conditioning program with a concrete goal at the far end. If Kurt Diemberger could get to the top of K2 at fifty-three without supplemental oxygen, I thought, then why couldn't I get up Everest? Once on the South Col, if weather conditions were good and I felt fit and acclimatized, I planned to climb to the summit without oxygen.

I wanted to quietly prepare for the climb without telling anyone, then slip away on a "trek to Nepal." I did not want to climb Everest as part of some prepackaged American expedition simply to get to the summit. The Otani-led Japanese expedition would work—if it actually came off. I did not *have* to go to Everest, but if the right opportunity presented itself, then I would go.

Around this time I read Everest veteran Dr. Tom Hornbein's findings in a *New England Journal of Medicine* article titled "The Cost to the Central Nervous System of Climbing to Extremely High Altitude." Hornbein and his four coauthors concluded that, to varying degrees, brain impairment *does* result. According to the study, individuals with a high ventilatory response perform the best at high altitude but will later experience the most neurobehavioral impairment. The reason postulated for this conclusion was that the high-hypoxic ventilatory response increases the oxygen delivered to those muscles being exercised while reducing the amount of oxygen going to the central nervous system. Short-term effects did not concern me, but a long-term diminution in my rational faculties would be difficult to accept.

When I participated in a 1982 study of hypoxic ventilatory response, I was told I had a high response. I wondered if this had anything to do with my difficult birth, when, blue from lack of oxygen, I struggled desperately for air. Was that experience a reason why I functioned so well at high altitude? Aware that my high ventilatory response might actually impair my rational faculties, how could I even consider a climb of Everest without supplemental oxygen? Despite what I had read, I felt if I couldn't reach the summit without using oxygen, I would rather not climb the mountain at all.

The guilt I had sometimes felt risking my life on distant mountains had largely disappeared. Although I knew my wife and children wanted to have me around for many more years, I convinced myself they would understand my need to pursue my "destiny." I knew my mountain diaries were replete with admonitions to myself to cease climbing, to seek "other Annapurnas." Well, maybe my "other Annapurna" was simply another mountain. Since my decision on

Menlungtse, I had patiently waited for a new challenge to present itself. So far nothing had turned up—until now, until Everest.

In June 1991, John Roskelley and I confided to each other that, despite our very public retirement from expedition climbing, we both were seriously tempted to return to Everest. I explained to John how my views had changed since my father's death. On Kanchenjunga and Menlungtse, I told him, I had been paralyzed by concerns for my personal survival. Now I felt ready to climb again. When I mentioned Otani's invitation to join his Everest expedition up the South Col, John responded, "I'm not interested in going up the Khumbu Icefall—it's too dangerous. What about Tibet? Can you get a permit from the Chinese?" Despite my poor performances the past few years, John flattered me by his wish to climb together again. By the end of our conversation, I had agreed to ask my China contact, Ying Dao-shui, if we could climb the North Col in 1992 or 1993. Notwithstanding the opposition I expected from Mary Lou, my kids, partners, and clients, I wanted to return.

Two weeks later, while doing business in Alaska, I received word from my office that a letter from Ying had arrived. On the flight home I wrote in my diary,

> *Ying's letter awaits me. What has he decided? I fully accept whatever is his answer. I am indifferent to the outcome for the decision has large pluses and minuses. At this stage of my life, I am prepared to respond to the path that is open—not to force open a path that is closed. If he says yes then the question is 1992 or 1993. If he says no then there is Otani's trip from the Nepal side.*

Ying came through for me. John and I could climb the North Col route in 1993 behind an Indian expedition—a good result since it meant someone else would put in the fixed rope to reach the col. Although I would be a year older in '93 than in '92, the delay would give me time to climb both Aconcagua and McKinley to see if I still had the stuff for Everest.

The road back to peak physical fitness at times proved humbling. With my plans still secret, I elected for my first excursion a trip to Mt. Rainier, where I wandered alone in the fog on the Nisqually Glacier searching for the Wilson Glacier Headwall. By the third time I walked across my own tracks, I decided to head down. Next, I climbed Mt. Hood alone for the twenty-fifth time. Thanks to excellent snow conditions I made one of my fastest ascents. By consistent, strong pressure breathing, I could keep a steady pace. I felt good about my performance, much better than I had anticipated, and it gave me great hope. A few weeks later I climbed Rainier for the twenty-eighth time by way of the Wilson Glacier Headwall, my twenty-sixth different route. I returned largely satisfied with my performance but several hours too late to make the dinner party I had promised Mary Lou I would attend. As usual, she was understanding.

Later that month, Stim Bullitt and I climbed Jabberwocky Tower in the Cascades, my first pure rock climb in twenty years. Slowed by age, Stim, seventy-two, had shifted from ice climbing to rock climbing where technical skill could help compensate for his declining strength. (He continued to perfect his technique, and by the time he turned seventy-eight, he led rock climbs 5.10 in difficulty.*) Stim led the entire two-pitch climb, and despite my lack of grace, I enjoyed myself. Afterward, we sat on a notch below the tower and I divulged my secret ambition to return to Everest.

---

* From 5.0 to 5.14 represents the spectrum of technical rock climbing requiring a rope and other forms of protection. The rating 5.9 is generally recognized as the point after which balance and technique are no longer enough. Climbs above 5.9 in difficulty require substantially more arm and finger strength. Most 5.10 climbers are between ages fifteen and forty.

Stim Bullitt rock climbing.

After my father's death I paid particular attention to the Fairweather Range as I flew by on frequent business trips to Alaska. I could not pass without thinking of Dusan and Al—once vibrant and alive—now part of the glacial ice where, but for the choice of a rope partner, I could be lying, too.

No longer so cynical about death, I now believed Al and Dusan's last moments may have been less terrifying than I had feared. I came to this conclusion after reading an unpublished translation of Reinhold Messner's *Grenzbereich Todeszone (Border Region: Death Zone)*, in which he exhaustively details accounts of climbers who fell but did not die. None reported feeling fear as they fell; in fact most felt a tremendous sense of well-being.

As Al and Dusan—and Marty—fell, maybe they felt not fear but acceptance. Perhaps Al and Dusan communicated with each other at the moment of death as they passed into a tunnel of light. When Chris and I fell into the crevasse on Mt. McKinley, I recall only thinking, "This is it," no out-of-body experience, no life review. I wondered what Chris had experienced those last hours alone before he froze to death. I hoped that, like my father, he saw a river of gold and crystal-clear water and, in the end, found peace.

In October, following a three-week vacation traveling with Mary Lou around New England, I returned home recharged in all respects. My life had settled in ways that provided me with unexpected tranquillity, both old and new.

I threw myself into my preparations for Aconcagua, still uncertain how much of my old power I had left. Would I leave Aconcagua convinced my active climbing life was over? Or would I return with my ambitions for greater things confirmed? This uncertainty made the prospect especially inviting.

The Roskelley family came to stay for what we dubbed "a football weekend." Officially, John joined me for the Huskies' and Seahawks' football games; secretly we talked of climbing Everest. Amazingly, John declined my suggestion that we add a third strong climber. He expressed interest in going as a twosome, apparently untroubled by the fact I would be fifty-three in 1993 or by my performance on Kanchenjunga and Menlungtse. John's confidence in me made me think perhaps I still had the necessary tools to climb Everest, but since my decision to go would undoubtedly upset my family, law partners, and clients, I did not want to face their disapproval until I knew for sure I had it in me to make the climb. I promised John that I would decide whether I would go to Everest after testing myself on Aconcagua.

After reading a 1962 Washington Supreme Court decision about someone denied insurance because her late husband had misrepresented his heart condition on his insurance application, I reviewed my life insurance policy and quickly concluded that my decision to resume serious climbing left me skating on thin ice. If I died on Aconcagua, Mary Lou would get nothing. So I sent my agent a letter advising him that he should go ahead and up the premium. When he called me to report that he'd added the requested $2,500 annual surcharge, he chortled, "No client has ever asked me to increase his premium before."

thirteen

TWO ON EVEREST

My plans to climb Aconcagua fell apart when Matsunaga informed me that, due to a serious heart ailment, he could not go. Scrambling for an alternative, I entertained the idea of accompanying Phil Ershler's guided expedition to sixteen thousand feet, where I planned to peel off and make a solo ascent. After a couple of months I decided to skip Aconcagua altogether and climb McKinley with John Roskelley instead. McKinley was the tougher mountain, a better test of my capacity to tackle Everest.

In early 1992 John flew over from Spokane to read from his latest book, *Last Days*, at the Elliott Bay Book Company. Mary Lou and I went to listen. Having reached the point where we could plan an expedition on the back of an envelope, John and I took fifteen minutes to agree on the supplies and equipment necessary for our trip to McKinley. Just as he moved toward the podium, John inadvertently mentioned our plans to return to Everest. Mary Lou turned to me with an expression of mock surprise and remarked, "So, that's how I find out about these things." She later conceded that from the time I announced my decision to stop climbing in 1990, she had assumed I would change my mind. "I've known you too long and too well not to be skeptical," she explained.

Mt. McKinley from air. Cassin Ridge rises in center.

Conscious of my age and limitations, I trained extra hard for McKinley. To achieve the level of physical fitness the mountain required, I knew I must push myself without injuring my muscles or

connective tissue. I needed to be bold but cautious. Curious to see whether I had any major physical problems, I signed up for several sessions of Rolfing (extra deep cross-fiber massage). Structurally, I seemed okay except for my midtorso, which twisted slightly to the left, the side I had favored since my lung surgery in 1978. During the final months of preparation I worked out daily on the StairMaster with fifty-four pounds on my back and three pounds on each of my ankles. Twice a week I carried the pack up and down a local water tower, averaging sixteen hundred feet an hour. By subjecting myself to the discomforts of Rolfing and a strenuous exercise regimen, I hoped I could increase my lung capacity.

I left for McKinley in high spirits, confident I had done all I could to prepare myself and ready to return to the site of my greatest anguish, the mountain where Chris Kerrebrock had died eleven years before. John and I planned to briefly acclimatize on the West Buttress, then drop back down to the base of the Cassin Ridge for a fast climb to the summit, but we never got the chance. Instead we quickly became embroiled in some of the worst weather and series of accidents ever recorded on the mountain.

Within hours of our arrival at the main camp at fourteen thousand feet, we learned of four separate incidents within a mile of our tent. A Park Service helicopter had retrieved two American climbers from Denali Pass: one had frostbite, the other cerebral edema. After that, several Koreans fell down the ice slope leading to the top of the West Buttress. Although most survived the fall unscathed, one climber broke his arm. The next day an American (a friend of my brother John's) slipped on the ice slope below the West Buttress and broke his ankle. Just as a big storm came in, a Frenchman abandoned his wife at 17,300 feet, without a stove or any other gear. (After rescuing the woman, the National Park Service fined her husband for his appalling breach of duty.) Anticipating more trouble, John and I introduced ourselves to three volunteer climbing rangers, Matt and Julie Culberson and Ron Johnson, and offered to assist in future rescues if they could use a hand.

A few days later as John and I settled down for a meal, Ron popped his head into our tent. "Would you guys help Matt and Julie rescue two young Koreans? They fell into a crevasse when a snow-bridge collapsed under them. Their companion just came down in search of assistance." We made our way through a driving storm to

Main camp at 14,000 feet during extremely windy, cold weather.

a yawning forty-foot-wide chasm. Peering over the edge, we spotted one of the men sixty feet down, buried in snow up to his waist. We flung him a rope to clip onto his waist harness, but he needed assistance, so John and Matt made their way down. Julie coordinated the rescue effort from the lip, while I acted as anchor, belaying the people below.

It took more than an hour to retrieve the first Korean, unhurt except for a tongue wound. He had tried to free himself with his pocket knife. When that failed, he had cut his tongue in an attempt to bleed to death, so he might die honorably. His companion lay buried beneath large chunks of ice and snow. We could not see him, but we could hear him moaning. When John and Matt pushed the debris off the man, he complained of acute back pain. (He had broken his pelvis.) They tried to rig a waist-and-shoulder harness to bring him up, but his pain was too great, so Julie radioed down to camp for a litter.

During the hour we waited for Ron to arrive with the rescue sled, I continued to anchor the men below. I stamped my feet to stay warm, but my bigger concern was resisting the tremendous urge to move my bowels. Eventually, Ron arrived with two companions, and they gingerly lowered the litter into the gully. Then they set up a Z-pulley system with jumars to act as temporary brakes to help gain slack for each successive pull. Once John and Matt got the injured Korean onto the litter, we began to pull, hard work that seemed to take forever. Meanwhile, my bowel kept going into spasms. When the litter finally cleared the lip and John and Matt climbed back onto the surface, I tore loose my waist harness and barely got my pants down before erupting—a huge relief, tarnished only by my embarrassment that Julie Culberson was around to watch.

During the chaotic days that followed, the mountain racked up additional casualties. Two Italians were blown to their deaths off the Cassin Ridge, and a Swiss guide mysteriously died in his tent while his wife prepared his breakfast. When reports of the fatalities on Cassin Ridge reached the media, John and I worried that our families would jump to the wrong conclusion since the Italians had died on our intended route. Ron Johnson kindly lent me his cell phone so I could call home and reassure Mary Lou. She informed me that friends and relatives concerned for my safety had called her from all over the country. Our son David had called her from Japan.

Before the week's end three more Korean climbers got into trouble, stranded by the storm at eighteen thousand feet on the Cassin Ridge. During a break in the weather, a Park Service helicopter plucked them off, one by one, and deposited the cold, hungry, exhausted men at our camp. While we waited with Johnson and the Culbersons for a larger helicopter to transport the Koreans to Anchorage, their frostbitten leader demanded they be flown back to eighteen thousand feet to retrieve their packs and passports. "We can't do that," Ron explained. "The helicopter is for saving lives not property." When the army helicopter finally arrived, John and I had to drag the angry climber across to the helicopter and shove him on board.

While we were on McKinley eleven climbers died, including one of the country's greatest alpinists, Mugs Stump. Mugs was bringing two clients down McKinley's South Buttress when he came upon a snow bridge. He asked his clients to wait behind him while he tested it with his weight. As Mugs stepped onto it, the bridge collapsed, entombing him in ice and snow. His astonished clients peered down into the crevasse, but all they could see amid the crumbled snow bridge was a tangle of rope far below.

When the weather finally improved, John and I abandoned our plans for the Cassin Ridge and opted for a simpler route to reach the summit. This was John's first time on the mountain, and he wanted to reach the top, one way or another. We got up the West Buttress, but ferocious winds prevented us from going farther. Most of the other climbers returned to the main camp at fourteen thousand feet; we decided to wait out the storm. It lasted three days.

As John and I were leveling our tent platform at 16,200 feet, we glanced up just as a climber blew off the West Buttress, about thirty yards away. He took a second man with him, who, in turn, yanked off a third. Just as the last member of this Korean team began to go, a young German guide with a nearby expedition ran over, grabbed him round the waist, anchored the Korean's rope, and reeled in his terrified companions. This entire sequence took a matter of seconds, but to John and me, watching from our tent, it seemed to take much longer—a horrifying, heroic, slow-motion ballet. We thought all four were done for, but this one alert guide saved them all.

John Roskelley.

When the weather cleared, John and I climbed four thousand vertical feet to the summit in a little less than seven hours. Without me in tow, John could have gone much faster; when we unroped about six hundred feet below the summit, he raced ahead. I felt the nine years' difference in our ages; the contrast in our strength and speed bothered me, particularly when I remembered my swift and easy ascent with Leif Patterson twenty years before. But self-criticism gave way to joy when I joined John on the summit, and I was glad to end our climb on a good note.

Sadly, the next year Julie Culberson was killed on Canada's Mt. Temple. She and her husband, Matt, were injured when an avalanche swept them down a gully. Julie broke her leg, Matt broke his ribs and injured his chest, and both were briefly knocked unconscious. Since Julie could not move, Matt left her and went for help, but as he started down a scree basin, he kept passing out. Two days later a party of hikers came upon him staggering through the trees. By the time a rescue team reached Julie, she had bled to death.

My performance on McKinley, while quite respectable, convinced me I was no longer a match for John Roskelley, whose strength now far exceeded mine. I had kept up with him in 1978 and 1984, but not on McKinley, Kanchenjunga, or Menlungtse. I concluded that if John really wanted to climb Everest, he should pair up with a younger man. "I've decided not to return to Everest," I explained in my letter to him a few days after we returned home. "Not only am I slower than you, I now doubt whether I could safely climb Everest without oxygen." Before mailing the letter I showed it to Mary Lou. When I asked her what she thought, she refused to be drawn into my decision-making.

When John and I spoke later that week, he took sharp issue with my position on the use of oxygen. "You have to decide whether you really want to climb Everest and not be so hung up on the use of oxygen," to which I muttered, "It's my competitive nature at work." When I mentioned I still harbored regrets for having used oxygen when I climbed K2, John retorted, "That is ludicrous!"

Roskelley sent me a letter in which he pleaded with me to reconsider. I agreed to give him a final answer within the next three weeks. I struggled to decide whether I really wanted to climb Mt. Everest—with or without oxygen. Although Mary Lou insisted the decision was entirely mine, I knew that she (and most of my relatives, friends, and partners) would prefer I not go. It would be easier not to go.

But would it? Climbing McKinley had fulfilled my ambitions for that mountain; I did not need to go back. Not so Everest. I had already invested a lot in Mt. Everest, more than I had previously realized. I knew its obstacles and its weaknesses as well as any other mountain, and I longed to see Tibet again. Its barren hills, valleys, and plateaus, so strangely beautiful, were etched indelibly in my memory.

Although I aspired to reach Everest's summit without oxygen I figured I should probably take some, just in case. Since one of us could get sick at high altitude, refusing to bring oxygen would be foolhardy. Throughout our acclimatization I planned to watch my performance. If I concluded the only way I could keep up with John was on supplementary oxygen, I could—as a last resort—take some with me to the summit.

Near the summit of Everest is a zone that marks the uppermost limits of man's ability to breathe, to function without artificial aids. That zone attracted me. I wanted to go there under my own power, to be at the very edge of my limits. How marvelous that the highest point on earth so closely approximated this limit of human endurance and function. I fully realized that to climb Everest without oxygen would add immeasurably to the risk and challenge. But the reward would be greater, too.

Of the sixty-two Americans who had so far climbed Everest, only two—Larry Nielson and Ed Viesturs (with whom John and I had climbed on Kanchenjunga)—had done it without oxygen. Of those I had accompanied to Everest in 1982 and 1984, five had already made the summit: Larry Nielson, Phil Ershler, Eric Simonson, Geo Dunn, and Greg Wilson. Instead of becoming numbers sixty-three and sixty-four to climb Mt. Everest, I wanted us to become the third and fourth Americans to do so without oxygen.

Beyond my abstract aspirations, I really did not want to don another oxygen mask. I had felt so constrained on Everest in 1984, grappling with my oxygen gear in the dark, close confines of the tent. This time I wanted to be completely free of both the constriction and the weight. By leading and kicking steps for me, John could probably equalize our respective rates of ascent. When we climbed McKinley, I experienced neither headaches nor any other altitude-related ailments. Similarly acclimatized for Everest, shouldn't I perform as well?

A few days after we returned from McKinley, I received a revised budget from my China contact, Ying Dao-shui. To keep my options open, I signed the protocol agreement and sent it back to him immediately. Within a week my doubts began to fade, and I returned to the StairMaster.

I trained diligently for Everest, but never with the ferocity I devoted to McKinley. On Everest, I knew I would build strength carrying loads up the glacial moraine during the month I spent acclimatizing. By contrast, I arrived on McKinley prepared to head straight up the mountain. Nonetheless, by the time we left for Tibet I felt in great shape. My only worry was whether I would have the necessary mental toughness.

Two years earlier, when I first contemplated going back to

Everest, I had planned to proceed without advance fanfare. But as our departure approached, the media got interested, and John and I agreed to be interviewed for feature articles in the *Los Angeles Times*, *Outside*, and *Rock + Ice*. We figured we owed it to our sponsors. Without them we could not have managed the $40,000 cost of the expedition.

During the three months before we left, I had several particularly vivid dreams about Everest that boosted my self-confidence and helped me gear up for the expedition. In all these dreams John and I climbed to the summit without oxygen. Although I seldom remembered details of the climb itself, I always awoke with a calm sense of certainty and joy, and sometimes a shiver up my spine.

The family saw me off at the airport. Mary Lou wished me "a great adventure," but when we spoke by phone a few days later, she announced, "You had better climb Everest this time because you aren't going back again." I asked her if she had reached her conclusion before I left. "Yes," she answered, "and now I am telling you." Despite her lighthearted tone I had no doubt she was serious.

John seemed to accept the fact I would not use oxygen. Nonetheless, he urged me not to treat my ambitions for an oxygenless ascent as a matter of ethics but to "keep an open mind." I told him I would wait to make a final decision but emphasized it would be my decision to make.

What I did not say was that—ludicrous as it sounds—my strong desire to reach the summit without oxygen was fundamental to my search for a fuller meaning to my life. I wanted to achieve something special. To climb without oxygen would be unusually demanding and dangerous, but I felt prepared to make the sacrifice; what mattered to me was *how* I made the ascent. I expected John would urge me to use oxygen as we approached twenty-seven thousand feet. But I planned to resist even if it meant forgoing the summit—as it had for him in '84. It was this very uncertainty about what lay ahead that made the undertaking so appealing.

John and I traveled with Ang Nima and Chhiri, the Sherpas who had accompanied us to Menlungtse. They came to cook for us until we left advanced base camp at twenty-one thousand feet to attempt the last eight thousand feet alone. They prepared simple and delicious food: potatoes cooked every conceivable way, fresh vegetables, cheese, eggs, and tea mixed with milk and sugar. I detest English-style tea at sea level, but high in the mountains it tastes great.

Our expedition, so lean and efficient, greatly appealed to me. Unlike the furious activity of the large Everest expeditions I had been on before, this was simple and serene. Although I expected I would soon start suffering from the altitude, the moment I walked into base camp I felt terrific. The accumulated debris of previous visitors cluttered our campsite. I tried to look past the broken bottles, plastic, and cardboard and think of how it must have looked to Mallory, Norton, Somervell, Irvine, and the other British climbers who camped there in the 1920s.

Soon after we arrived, I walked up to Marty's memorial. The stone Lou Whittaker had carved in 1984 showed no signs of wear or deterioration, in contrast to the 1982 stone lying behind it, on which the lettering was nearly invisible. As I placed several small stones around the memorial, I gazed up at the mountain and thought about all the lives it had taken.

In the weeks we spent acclimatizing, John and I visited and filmed some Tibetan monks at the Rongbuk monastery six miles below base camp. Afterward, we hitched a ride back up with three Chinese meteorologists in their Land Cruiser. As we arrived at camp, we spotted another jeep with a Norwegian and two other Chinese. The Norwegian explained that a Chinese glaciology professor was sick at 19,700 feet. Despite supplemental oxygen, he could neither walk on his own nor speak coherently. The Chinese asked us to join their rescue mission. John and Ang Nima volunteered to hike up immediately. Chhiri and I agreed to follow in the morning with extra food and water.

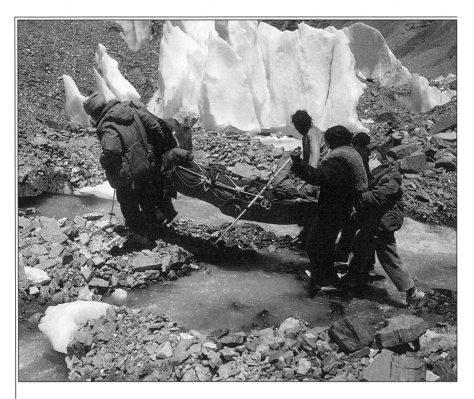

Tibetans carrying cerebral-edema-stricken Chinese professor down East Rongbuk Glacier.

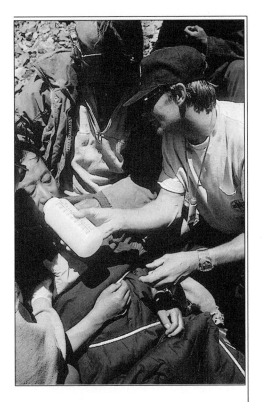

John Roskelley administering water to Professor Qian during descent from 19,700 feet.

After five hours of steady walking up the glacial moraine, Chhiri and I encountered John and several Tibetans, gingerly carrying Professor Qian down the rough terrain. He appeared nearly comatose and unable to control his muscles; his arms splayed out in odd directions. The night before, John had administered dexamethasone (a drug to treat cerebral edema) and placed the oxygen-starved man inside a Gamov bag, designed to simulate a lower altitude. But John's efforts had failed to revive him.

It took us nine hours to carry the stricken man to base camp. The Tibetans could manage just a hundred yards at a time before they had to rest and change position. The full weight of the two-hundred-pound professor fell on the lead Tibetan while three others carried his head and upper torso. Professor Qian revived a bit each time John injected some more dexamethasone, but quickly relapsed. When he started to vomit on the trail below Camp 1, John and I feared he might die by morning if we did not get him down fast.

As we walked the last stretch in the dark, I marveled at the contortions the Tibetans went through to keep the sick man's head from hitting rocks. I tried to help by advising them where to place their feet. Just as we glimpsed the taillights of the Chinese's Land Cruiser, the head of the professor's scientific group, Professor Xu Ru Wei, ran up and gave me a big hug. I pointed to John and explained, "He is the one who saved your friend's life."

We managed to stuff the sick man into the rear seat of the vehicle, and John gave him one last shot of dexamethasone. He revived for a moment and muttered a few words of Chinese. One more big hug from Professor Xu, then they dropped us off at our camp. Later we learned that the professor had survived.

A couple of days after the rescue John and I had a little tiff. John beat me to Camp 2 by fifteen minutes and then filmed my arrival. When I saw the video camera pointed at me, I gave John the finger—extended high over my head. Although I did not want my belated arrival recorded for posterity, I was not seriously annoyed; when John asked if I was mad at him, I replied, "Absolutely not." On our approach to Camp 3, I felt much stronger. Carrying almost identical weight, we ascended the sixteen hundred vertical feet in an hour and fifty minutes, and I stayed at Roskelley's heels the entire way.

The amount of garbage strewn over the moraine near advanced base camp made it resemble a city dump. Yet its setting was so magnificent, we managed to forget the ugliness and focus on the view. John and I were able to withstand the altitude at twenty-one thousand feet much earlier than I could in either 1982 or 1984. In 1982, I did not sleep that high until twenty-one days after we arrived at base camp; in 1984, sixteen days. This time we did it after twelve.

However, the quick ascent did produce some temporary reactions to the altitude. First I noticed a problem with my left eye. I could see perfectly well, but a small, grayish defect kept moving from right to left. The higher the altitude, the worse it got. Vaguely recalling a similar problem during the 1984 expedition, diagnosed as a retinal hemorrhage, I did not expect any long-term damage.

As I stepped out of the tent to urinate during the night, my legs wobbled and the base of my head began to ache. I climbed back into my sleeping bag and hyperventilated until I fell asleep. Each time I awoke after that, I made myself hyperventilate some more. In the morning, John observed that, despite my efforts to control my breathing, it became highly irregular whenever I fell asleep. In spite of this, I felt fine by midmorning.

On our first foray to twenty-one thousand feet, we limited ourselves to an exploratory probe of the slopes below the North Col. They seemed safe enough, but we were not sufficiently acclimatized to begin forging a new route to the col itself. Instead, we decided to retreat to base camp to recuperate from the altitude.

Eight days later we returned to advanced base camp and began working our way up the forty-five-degree slope to the North Col. We placed some of our own fixed rope and supplemented it with fixed rope from previous expeditions that we found buried in the snow. Digging out the rope at twenty-two thousand feet was hard work.

Everything went smoothly until the day we expected to finally reach the North Col. I was leading the first steep section using a jumar and my ice ax when John yelled up, "Why don't you just use your jumar alone? It will work better." I yelled down, "I'll do it my way." He took my remark as a heated rejection of his advice, and we yelled back and forth for several minutes. At the first anchor we talked it out. From my point of view, he was criticizing my technique. He thought I was overreacting to everything he said. "I'm not as good a climber as you are, John," I grumbled, "but I've been at this for over thirty years, and I have my own way of climbing." I did not like being in a subordinate position, although I recognized that, in many respects, I was. We eventually shook hands and, without changing our respective techniques, continued up. Meanwhile, the weather worsened.

As we reached the North Col, I spotted the top of a tent peeking out of the snow. It turned out to have been used by an Irish expedition the previous spring. After digging for half an hour we crawled inside and discovered among the discarded equipment a down sleeping bag, an insulated bivouac sack, and a lot of fixed rope that we could use to fill in the gaps on our route up to the North Col.

The storm intensified so we put our gear inside the Irish tent and headed down through the deep, soft snow, keenly aware of the instability of the slope. Avalanches crashed down from the North Col but never crossed our path. The snow conditions were the worst I'd ever seen. In certain sections I sank up to my thighs every time I stepped into John's tracks. Later, I rappelled to the glacier floor and broke through the bergschrund, where I hung upside down in the hole for several minutes before John arrived to help me out. As we headed back to camp across the final stretch of moraine, I thought I saw Ang Nima coming toward us. I yelled, "John, there's Ang Nima in the mist." "No, that's a rock, Jim." "No, it's Ang Nima." "No, it's a rock." It *was* Ang Nima bringing us hot tea—a welcome, touching act of generosity.

With all the necessary tents, food, and fuel now stocked at the North Col, we were ready to go for the summit. It was August 5.

As always, the months we spent on Everest getting acclimatized gave me opportunities for reading and reflection. My son David had given me two tapes of humanist Sam Keen narrating excerpts from his book, *Fire in the Belly*. Some of what Keen discussed made me regret, once again, my failure to be a better father when my sons were growing up. My desire to excel as a lawyer and a climber had taken time and energy away from my relationship with the boys during those years. Once again, I concluded it was not too late. In fact I knew I had already made strides toward becoming a better parent. In the three years since my father's death, my wife, some of my children, and various friends had acknowledged I was "more there for them" than I had been in the past.

Each of my children had sent birthday and Father's Day cards to me on the mountain. Touched by their affection, I recoiled when I thought about the excessive and repeated risks I had taken throughout their childhood. They could so easily have grown up fatherless. I intended to proceed with care on this expedition and return home safely.

After finishing a book on the psychological side of sports and

John Roskelley leading up snow slope to North Col.

Nabokov's *Pale Fire,* I turned to Milan Kundera's latest novel, *Immortality.* Unlike Nabokov's preoccupation with the survival of the human personality after death, Kundera's "immortality" related to the survival of a person's reputation and character. At some point in our lives, Kundera maintained, we begin to live with our own immortality by shaping our actions in ways that will enhance it. Was that what I was doing?

Unlike my optimistic dreams in the months preceding our departure, the only dream I had about the mountain *on* the mountain was a dream of defeat in which I felt bitterly disappointed, conscious I would never get another chance.

After my discouraging dream I decided, on a superstitious whim, to open a pack of tarot cards a friend had given me for the trip. I shuffled the deck and drew a single card: the Star. I turned to Tony Willis's *The Magical Tarot* for interpretation. On a moral level the card suggested spiritual rejuvenation; on a mental level, optimism, fresh faith, renewed vigor, and pumped-up courage; and on a material level, the Star indicated good luck and a promise that present gains would not be lost no matter what troubles or strictures I might be under. In spite of my natural skepticism about such matters, I chose to find encouragement in the card.

As I helped Ang Nima and John reconstruct the cook tent platform, damaged by a recent storm, I experienced another altitude-related incident. I stood up abruptly after squatting by the edge of the platform and collapsed in a heap. My shoulder smashed against a block of ice as my hips and legs dropped into an adjacent ice pond. I got up quickly, embarrassed but not seriously hurt. John mentioned that he had nearly fainted earlier in the day, and I recalled something similar happening to Dave Mahre at twenty-two thousand feet in 1982.

Although we were ready to ascend, we could not make real progress until both the weather and snow conditions improved. The waiting game had begun. When we awoke the next day to brilliant sunshine, we felt encouraged, but, still worried about the instability of the slopes above, we decided to wait a little longer. Sitting around camp all day with nothing to do threw me into a funk. John asked, "Are you mad at me, Jim?" Taken aback by the question, I responded, "How could you think that?" To which John replied, "You're so quiet." I told him he was imagining things, and to make my point, I playfully beat my head on my sleeping pad several times.

We headed up to the North Col the following morning to pull out all the fixed ropes still embedded in the snow. After a nearly sleepless night, I performed poorly. Although I had fallen asleep early, around seven, I slept for only half an hour, then try as I might, I could not get back to sleep. We took off at dawn and at first I felt okay, but then it began to hit me—the sense I had no gas left in my tank. The higher John climbed, the farther I trailed behind, testing his patience.

When I finally caught up with him, I either fainted or simply drifted off to sleep briefly (I remembered dreaming). John muttered something about "your fainting spells" and complained I was making him nervous. He suggested we head down but I assured him I would be okay. We continued up, and by the day's end we had reestablished a nearly continuous safety line from the glacier to the North Col. Assuming no new snowfall buried the ropes, we were ready, once again, to make our summit push. But all our work was wiped out by another snowstorm, and when the weather finally broke, the threat of avalanches loomed overhead. Still, if the clear weather continued and the snow stabilized, we would attempt the summit the following week.

Despite moments of hope, each time we began our summit push, a storm would arrive, covering the slope with enough new snow to make it dangerous. The defect in my eye continued to expand, and my back had started to bother me on the walk up to twenty-one thousand feet. But I took large doses of Advil, and, before long, my back felt better. We decided to head up the following day.

Knowing that I might not return, I wrote a letter to my wife and tucked it in my diary. I gave a second letter to Ang Nima with instructions to deliver it to Ed Viesturs in the event of our deaths. In the letter I described to Ed (who was about to try a solo ascent of the mountain's North Face) the location of our personal effects, which I asked him to return to our families.

All night it snowed, ruining our chances for a summit push anytime soon and destroying our cook tent. We spent the night beating the inner walls of our tent to push off the fast-accumulating snow. When we rose at six to construct a new cook shelter out of the poles of the old tent and the tarp, snow blew in our faces and clung to our clothes. After the storm finally stopped in the early afternoon, the sun beat down on us, triggering avalanches on the slopes above and turning our tent into an oven. John recorded temperatures as high as 118 degrees F.

Over the next couple of days the heavy snowpack triggered numerous avalanches on the slopes of the North Col, sweeping clean large portions of our intended route. Still we waited, just to be sure the weather had broken and the threat of avalanches had really passed.

On August 30, the mountain basked in brilliant sunshine. We should have been on our way to the North Col, but had misread the weather. We would head for the col early the next morning barring another snowstorm. My plan was to try to sleep during the day, since at so high an altitude sleeping through the night was difficult.

Another storm piled snow on our tents, our route, and our hopes, then it started to hail. Another American team was poised on the other side of the col, so there were now five of us whose hopes for climbing Everest depended on a lasting weather change. Two days later word came from the other Americans that two separate avalanches had hit their tents. The two men inside the first tent hit could not breathe until a companion jabbed an air hole into the tent wall. After their close call, the men piled into their companion's tent, which was nearly crushed by a second avalanche a few hours later.

As the storm continued to rage, my hopes for the summit waned. John, obviously discouraged, announced that we ought to hire Ngti (a Sherpa with the Korean team) to go up and retrieve our gear from the North Col so we could go home. "Are you serious?" I asked. "Yes," he said. Skeptical, I planned to wait and see.

The next morning we followed Ngti, his brother, four other Sherpas, two Koreans, and two Indians up to the North Col. As we trudged up the slope, John noted his diminishing strength: "Ten years ago I would have given Ngti a run for his money." Apparently oblivious to the danger, Ngti planned to traverse right across the main avalanche gully. After an avalanche came down, John convinced him to take our route instead. Ngti started the steep pitch but after a few feet gave way to John, who, despite his earlier complaints of weakening, led the rest of the way to the col.

On the way up, John was hit, but not smothered, by four small avalanches. Afraid the entire slope would avalanche, John detached himself from everybody else as he approached the last steep pitch before the col. Last in a long line of climbers, I watched John plow his way up the unstable snow. Once beyond the danger, he looked down on the treacherous slope and yelled at the top of his lungs, "Fuck you!"

Back at advanced base camp, I felt good about my performance climbing to the col. But I decided that, in the unlikely event we got a shot at the summit, I should plan to use oxygen. Reluctant to add the heavy bottles to my pack, I planned to look for unused canisters left by previous expeditions. If, by some remarkable turn of events, the snow conditions dramatically improved, we planned to move up to the North Col on September 3, then to Camp 5, Camp 6, and finally the summit, on September 6. But the conditions did not improve and John concluded we should give up. Reluctant to turn back, I resisted and only grudgingly relented after several hours of tense conversation. At which point, John changed his mind. "If the conditions dramatically improve in the next forty-eight hours, we should go for the summit after all."

As we prepared to make our final effort to go above the North Col, I felt pessimistic but willing to give it the old college try. Not wanting to burn myself out too early, I arrived at the col long after John. Depressed over the earlier decision to quit, I was having a hard time bouncing back. It snowed all night. My feet got so cold I had to stuff them into my down parka. John gave me hot-water bottles for my feet and chest, so I could sleep. In the middle of the night he left our tent to help one of the Indian Sherpas who was complaining of bubbles in his lungs. The Indian, vomiting and barely able to breathe, probably had developed pulmonary edema. The Indians had bottled oxygen but no oxygen regulator, so John used ours to administer oxygen to the sick man, and he quickly revived.

When I awoke the next morning, my head ached and my spirits dragged. I did not think we could really make the summit—the North Face, so laden with heavy snow, appeared untenable. We were just kidding ourselves. The weather worsened, and on September 4 we finally admitted defeat.

As I walked down Everest for the last time, I felt an acute sense of disappointment after being poised for the summit an entire month without ever getting a chance to try. Later, I found some consolation in that, had we waited for another month, we still wouldn't have made it. Bad weather blocked every single team on the Tibet side of the mountain that fall.

Waiting around for the truck to take us off the mountain, John consumed a fair amount of Wild Turkey. When our Tibetan truck driver, a thin guy dressed in a cheap gray suit and matching fedora hat, ordered us to pay him an additional $200 if we wanted to give two other Americans a lift, John lunged at the driver. Our liaison officer, Fu Lin-de, and the other team's interpreter quickly pulled the men apart. That evening Fu met with the truck driver to sort out the transportation arrangements—or so we thought.

The next morning as our truck stopped at the checkpoint near the Xegar-Tingri Road, a nonuniformed official (in his fifties or sixties) refused to let us through until we paid the truck driver for our extra passengers. John jumped out of the truck and confronted the official. As I walked around to the front of the truck, a tall, young Tibetan assistant to the official stretched a chain across the road. John rushed toward him. They shoved each other back and forth, then the Tibetan picked up a rock and threw it at John, followed by a larger one, then another—barely missing him. John ran by me, chased by the angry Tibetan hurling ever larger rocks.

By the time I caught up with them behind the truck, John had picked up a rock himself. The men edged toward one another, each clutching a rock with their arms cocked, ready to fight. Instinctively, I lunged at the Tibetan and wrestled him to the ground. Fu and Davis, our Chinese interpreter, insisted that I release the man, which I promptly did. Then, furious, the Tibetan picked up a grapefruit-sized rock and threw it at me. It whizzed past and hit Ang Nima in the stomach. Outraged by the assault on the diminutive Sherpa, I yelled, "Stop throwing rocks you son of a bitch, or I'll kill you!" All of a sudden the melee ended and the senior Tibetan official opened the gate and our truck drove through. As we drove off, Fu remarked, "This will be discussed at Xegar."

When we arrived in Xegar, we learned that the jeep we had hired had not come from Lhasa to take us to Zhangmu, the last town before the Nepal border. Fu advised us that unless we paid $200 to the Tibetan truck driver, he would not take us or our gear any farther. Infuriated, I retorted, "If that's your position, we will stay at a hotel here in Xegar until we can hire another truck—one that won't attempt to hold us up," and proceeded to pull our gear down off the truck. After about six of our bags hit the sidewalk, Fu yielded and we resumed our journey.

A rock slide had obliterated a section of road near Zhangmu, forcing us to spend the night in Nyalam. When our driver made one last attempt to extort the $200 payment, we made clear that we would not pay one cent more and were prepared to stay in Nyalam until we found another truck. A truck parked next to ours had plenty of room and no passengers, so I asked the driver to take us the rest of the way to the border. He offered to do it for $100. I said $20 and no more. He came back with fifty. I reiterated my bottom line. Eventually, the second driver said he would do it for twenty dollars. But then our original driver relented and Fu yelled, "Let's go." Further delays, resulting from several road closures caused by record monsoon weather, compounded our frustration. By the time we reached Kathmandu two days later we could not wait to board the plane.

I left Everest convinced I would never return. The great British climber Doug Scott once told me that though he had climbed Everest, K2 had repeatedly eluded him. "But I don't have to go back to K2," he explained. "I've climbed it in my dreams—dreams so vivid I feel certain I've reached the summit, perhaps in some parallel existence." I understand what he meant.

Since 1993, I have climbed Mt. Everest in my dreams, always awaking with a deep sense of satisfaction and completion, knowing I need never go back.

fourteen

LOOKING AHEAD

A few years ago I read Bill Bradley's *Life on the Run* and was struck by his observations about the special challenges faced by aging athletes. Comparing retiring athletes to the extreme elderly, Bradley wrote, "The athlete differs from the old person in that he must continue living. Behind all the years of practice and all the hours of glory waits that inexorable terror of living without the game."

My hair had turned gray and I was not as fast or strong as I once was, but the intensity that once drove me to climb K2 still burned. Only my priorities had changed. After I attempted Everest in 1993 I lost interest in returning to the Himalayas. I was no longer willing to spend the time required to climb an eight-thousand-meter peak. Instead, I came to prefer shorter expeditions to other remote destinations, in particular, South America. They left me more time for other pursuits, such as family gatherings, book collecting, various urban pleasures, and service to my community. But even though my interests had broadened, I was not yet ready to hang up my crampons.

A few months after John Roskelley and I got back from Everest, we began planning a very different expedition. Our objective:

Mt. Sarmiento.

Mt. Sarmiento, a classic double-summit peak in Tierra del Fuego, the vast, storm-swept island at the southern tip of South America. Sailing past Sarmiento in 1834, Charles Darwin described the mountain as

"a noble and even sublime spectacle" with its "steep, sun-glittered [ridges] intersecting the sky." Though hardly "sun-glittered," I found Tierra del Fuego's reputation for generally miserable weather oddly appealing. I also liked the fact that at under eight thousand feet, Sarmiento required no time for acclimatization. In over a hundred years of attempts, its twin summits were each climbed only once—by Italians in 1956 and 1986. If possible, we wanted to make second ascents of both peaks by untested routes.

John and I invited two outstanding climbers to round out our team: England's Stephen Venables and Australia's Tim Macartney-Snape. In 1988, Venables reached the summit of Everest alone after his small team completed a difficult new route up the Kangshung Face. On his descent he broke my record when he survived a solo bivouac at 28,000 feet, a few hundred feet higher than my bivouac on K2. In 1984, Macartney-Snape led the Australians' first successful ascent of Everest (which John and I observed through our binoculars). He later made a remarkable solo ascent, beginning at sea level along the Bay of Bengal, then walking across India and Nepal to reach the mountain. Neither man used oxygen to climb Mt. Everest.

To determine the best season for our climb, I contacted Charlie Porter, the American climber who had made the first successful solo ascent of McKinley's Cassin Ridge two weeks before my own ill-fated attempt in 1976. Charlie, who had moved to Chile sixteen years earlier, recommended autumn (April '95) as the most favorable time. To my surprise, he expressed interest in accompanying us to Sarmiento. His offer to take us in his fifty-foot sailboat, *Gondwana*, on a roundabout route from the Beagle Channel to the Sarmiento area sealed the deal.

For a landlubber like me, the unusual six-day excursion added greatly to the expedition's appeal—though our time on board the boat proved uneventful. Traveling against strong westerly winds most of the way, we rarely hoisted the sails. Most nights we moored in small coves, protected from blowing into the main channel by lines tied to trees along the shore and two large anchors. The trees we saw were all bent or twisted; most vegetation had been swept away. As we neared the western end of Tierra del Fuego, we saw that violent winds had stripped the terrain of nearly every sign of life. It was a relief to find a cove safe enough to moor *Gondwana* during our three-week stay on the mountain.

Although some of us began the climb as strangers, our high-powered, international team proved quite compatible. As advertised, the weather was horrible. Nearly constant rain and occasional high winds complicated our ascent. We spent the first week carrying loads through bog and forest to our first camp high above the inland water channels on Sarmiento's southwest flank. Once we reached two thousand feet, the rain turned to snow, and for two weeks clouds obscured the upper part of the mountain and prevented us from assessing the route we planned to take.

The snow slope above the first camp, while not particularly steep, was, in places, extremely icy. That, combined with sudden gusts of wind, made the climb unexpectedly treacherous. We had just established our second, and highest, camp at four thousand feet, when we finally saw a series of steep ice flutings leading to the top of Sarmiento's west peak. Excited about the prospect of making a second ascent, John and I went down ahead of the others to retrieve our gear for the summit climb.

As I stood on a crest of snow about to photograph John, descending two hundred feet below my perch, a powerful gust of wind blew me off my feet. I sailed fifteen feet before crashing onto the slope below, severely wrenching an ankle. The force of the fall propelled me downward. Just as I was about to smash into John, who was unaware of my predicament, I managed to arrest myself with my crampons and a couple of ski poles. "Why didn't you yell?" he inquired. "Too busy trying to stop," I replied. Relieved that I had survived the fall with a relatively minor injury, I hobbled back to camp, but knew I had lost my chance to make the summit.

Sorely disappointed, I waited at camp the next morning while the others headed up the mountain to finish the climb. Late that afternoon, they returned unexpectedly. In almost the same place I had been blown off the ridge, Charlie was knocked off *his* feet by another sudden gust of wind. To stop his fall, Charlie jabbed his arm into a narrow crevasse and—we thought—dislocated his right shoulder.

John Roskelley assists Charlie Porter down mountain after he broke his shoulder.

Roskelley, a licensed emergency medical technician (EMT), examined Charlie and determined his shoulder should be put back immediately, before it seized up. "We need a flat, dry place, out of the wind," John explained, so they descended to camp. Stephen and I held Charlie down on the tent floor while Tim and John made repeated attempts to rotate his arm back into position. Despite codeine sedation, Charlie was in agony. Our efforts proved futile; his shoulder had already seized up. Charlie needed to see a doctor soon, so we put his arm in a makeshift sling and made plans to take him out.

The others thought this meant they must give up their chance at the summit, but I volunteered to accompany Charlie out by boat, assisted by a young Frenchman, Minos, the ship's cook. My arms and upper body worked fine, and even though I limped, my ankle didn't hurt that much as long as I kept it confined in my boot. I urged the others to go for the summit, which they did.

Unfortunately for Charlie, neither Minos nor I was a skilled pilot. So Charlie was forced to navigate the Strait of Magellan to reach the hospital at Punta Arenas, ninety miles away. To concentrate on his all-night task, Charlie refused medication despite intense pain, and I marveled at his stoicism. The doctors determined that the field treatment we had administered had just exacerbated his problems. Charlie's shoulder had been broken—not dislocated—and required surgery.

During the time I spent rounding up a fishing boat and return-ing to the Sarmiento area, Roskelley, Macartney-Snape, and Venables took advantage of a ten-hour break from the constant wind and snowfall and completed a new route up Sarmiento's west peak. There was not time to tackle its eastern twin. Although my injury prevent-ed me from making the summit myself, my initial disappointment soon gave way to delight at our expedition's success.

When I got home from South America, my approach to climbing continued to shift, due more to chance than design. After climbing Sarmiento, John became involved in local politics and ran successfully for a position as Spokane County commissioner. During his campaign, he emphasized (in addition to his position on a variety of local issues) his experience organizing Himalayan mountaineering expeditions. But I think what got him elected was his reputation for honesty and straight talk.

Tim Macartney-Snape approaches the summit of Mt. Sarmiento's west peak. Slightly higher east peak behind.

With John no longer available as an expedition partner, I soon found myself in the unfamiliar role of a guide, helping others to realize their ambitions. A few weeks after the 1996 disaster on Mt. Everest that claimed the lives of several climbers including Scott Fischer and Rob Hall, two particularly strong and experienced Himalayan guides, I spoke with professional climbing guide Greg Wilson, a teammate of mine on Everest in 1984. He invited me to tag along as an unpaid, "unofficial" guide on an expedition to Bolivia's 21,300-foot Mt. Illimani, and I readily agreed.

Together we assembled a team that included, among others, a federal judge from South Dakota, a psychiatrist from Texas, two young Seattle rock climbers, and one of my former law partners. Before we left on the trip, I resolved to be especially careful after what had just happened on Everest. On the hike to the base of the mountain, I observed four climbers six thousand feet above us, descending a snow slope near the summit. Although the slope appeared easy, I noticed that an uncontrolled fall from that spot would send the climbers thousands of feet over a steep drop-off, tucked inconspicuously less than a hundred yards away.

When our eight-man team reached that point on our way to the summit, one of our clients announced he could go no higher. Greg offered to descend with him to camp if guide Bill Vanderbilt and I would take the other four to the top. Reluctant to assume responsibility for the group, I suggested we descend a couple of hundred feet to where the slope eased, so we could talk things over.

Moments after we turned around, the climber next to me suddenly fell. He made no effort to self-arrest, but I managed to stop his fall by slamming my ice ax into the hard snow. When a third climber began having difficulty, Greg made the command decision to give up the climb. Though what remained between us and the summit looked like a fairly easy stroll, we were on a tight schedule and had no time to make a second try.

On the long flight home I reflected on the sharp contrast between mountain climbing with my peers and those with less ability and experience. I could not imagine what it must be like to guide someone to the summit of Mt. Everest. After all, I hadn't managed to get myself there in three attempts.

Most of my guiding experiences have been on Mt. Rainier—and never for money. Once, as a donation to a fund-raising auction, I volunteered to take a father and his two sons up the mountain. One of the boys, the thirteen-year-old, pooped out at 11,400 feet. When I suggested we all turn back, the father insisted he had paid a lot of money to get his family to the summit so I should at least take up his nineteen-year-old while he waited behind with the younger boy.

I hacked out a large platform on the snow slope and instructed them to stay put until we returned. It took six hours to get to the summit and back. Afraid that the father might become impatient and leave, perhaps falling into a nearby crevasse, I agonized the entire time. But when we returned, father and son were sitting just where we had left them. Although no one got hurt, the experience left me reluctant to guide other inexperienced climbers.

Despite my reservations, I later changed my mind. Chatting with a couple I met at a dinner party, I learned that the wife, aged sixty-one, had dreamed of climbing Mt. Rainier for more than forty years. After climbing several lower peaks as preparation, she had tried twice with the mountain's guide service. But, she explained, "I was too slow to make it on the schedule they set. I need ten hours to get there." Convinced she had the will and physical fitness to reach the top, I offered to escort her. The next summer, slow but steady, we reached the summit, and she wept for joy. Her achievement delighted me. Moments later, I was astonished to see a couple approaching the summit with a four-year-old boy and a six-year-old girl!

At a recent dinner party with climbers Bill Sumner, Stim Bullitt, and Tom Hornbein, we addressed the subject of risk in relation to guided expeditions. We agreed that, in most situations, a guide has an obligation to get clients to the summit and back down safely—with safety being of foremost concern. But what about on a mountain such as Everest, where clients each pay as much as $65,000 for the once-in-a-lifetime chance to reach the top? Does the high price change the guide's duty? What if clients insist on proceeding to the summit too late in the day, after the weather turns, or when they begin to display signs of altitude sickness?

Is it the guide's obligation to accommodate the client's wishes or keep the client safe? What about the guide's obligation to children back home or to other clients on the climb? How far should a guide risk his or her own life for clients who otherwise appear certain to die? We concluded that on a mountain such as Everest, ill or injured clients cannot depend on guides to get them down the mountain. There is a point on those high mountains where climbers are on their own, a point beyond which no one can safely carry or belay another. In the end, we could not agree on just where to draw the line. Since situations will vary, guides must balance each client's goals and welfare—and their own.

One aspect of my climbing career that I particularly treasure has been getting the chance to know some of the century's most notable mountaineers, such as Tom Hornbein, and his late climbing partner Willi Unsoeld. As a twenty-three-year-old climber, I'd marveled at their achievement in making the first traverse of Mt. Everest. After climbing a new route up a steep gully on the mountain's North Face—now known as the Hornbein Couloir—they descended toward the South Col in darkness. When they caught up with two teammates who had taken the traditional route, all four survived an open bivouac at twenty-eight thousand feet. What struck me most was Unsoeld's selflessness in keeping Hornbein's toes warm on his chest through the night. Hornbein emerged from the ordeal unscathed, but Unsoeld lost all his toes. What they did inspired me to risk a bivouac in order to reach the summit of K2. I believed that since they had survived, I could, too.

In 1993, several other climbing luminaries gathered in San Francisco at an American Himalayan Foundation dinner to honor Sir Edmund Hillary, Maurice Herzog, Reinhold Messner, Chris

Bonington, and Junko Tabei, the first woman to climb Mt. Everest. When I saw Ed Hillary standing in the lobby of my hotel, I walked up to him and introduced myself. A tall, impressive, and energetic man in his midseventies, Hillary differs from most other great climbers I have met in that he has devoted most of his life to service, working hard to improve the Sherpas' living conditions since climbing Everest in 1953. After recounting my father's journey to Hillary's homeland, New Zealand, I told him how much I admired his work on behalf of the Sherpas.

My service to community has been modest by comparison. Among other things, I'm a member of the Henry M. Jackson Foundation Board, a cochair with Mary Lou of a major capital campaign for our daughters' old high school, and chair of the American Alpine Club's David A. Sowles Memorial Award Committee, which honors significant mountain rescues. I am conscious of how much more Hillary has done with his life, and he serves as an inspiration. As my dedication to climbing declines, I hope to increase the time I devote to community service.

A few hours before encountering Hillary, I met Maurice Herzog whose book, *Annapurna*, first stirred in me the desire to climb mountains. To meet one of my earliest heroes thrilled me, and standing beside him, I felt as awestruck as a teenaged boy. Slightly under six feet, Herzog still cut a striking figure with his smart mustache, red check-patterned suit, pink shirt, and matching tie. Since frostbite had cost him nearly all his fingers, he held his glass with both hands. As I began to introduce myself, I looked down at those hands and wondered whether I should extend mine. While I hesitated, he set aside his drink and extended his.

Riding up in the elevator to dinner, I stood beside Reinhold Messner, the climber I most admired. We discussed his efforts to organize the Sherpas so they could earn more money for their work on expeditions. At the reception before dinner, I chatted briefly with Chris Bonington, with whom I felt self-conscious about my failure on Menlungtse.

Each honoree gave a talk. Messner plugged hard for human rights in Tibet. Hillary remarked that his work with the Sherpas meant more to him than making the first ascent of Mt. Everest. Bonington remarked, "It doesn't matter how you get there [to the summit of Everest], only that you got there." In 1982, Bonington lost two companions on a four-man expedition to Everest. When he spoke to me shortly after that incident, Bonington had questioned the wisdom of tackling the mountain with so small a team. I'm sure his comment at the banquet (effectively endorsing large expeditions and supplemental oxygen) was affected by that experience. I disagreed with Bonington's opinion—no doubt due to my own decision to attempt Everest without oxygen, and with but a single companion, in 1993. I think that *how* one makes the summit matters a lot—but then I never made it.

Another pleasure I have derived from climbing has been the chance to accompany various friends and relatives into the mountains. When my son David disclosed his desire to climb Rainier, I recommended we start with a practice climb up Oregon's Mt. Hood. When we took off at six in the morning, the weather was warm and clear. After a long, slow slog, we neared the summit where the slope steepens. Suddenly, a cascade of rocks and ice chunks rained down on us. We dodged most of them, but one discus-sized ice blade tore into my foot and hurt like hell. I asked David if he wanted to keep going. He responded, "Sure, Dad, if you think it'll be okay." Cautiously, we resumed our ascent. David handled the upper section well, so I asked him to lead the last hundred feet to the top. We hugged when we got there. My son's toughness and perseverance impressed and pleased me. Though he said it was the hardest thing he'd ever done, we went on to climb Rainier as planned. My pride increased with that climb, which we made in particularly poor conditions. Despite the fact we ascended the last three thousand feet in a whiteout with snow encrusting our faces and wind blowing hard against our bodies, David never complained.

Looking back at my climbing career, I realize my ambitions always exceeded my achievements, from my botched solo attempt of a new route up McKinley's south face in 1976 to my goal to be the first American to climb both K2 and Everest—a feat accomplished by Lou Reichardt in '83. Only in reaching the summit of K2 in 1978 did I achieve the distinction I had continuously sought. I only achieved that lifelong dream because of a concerted act of will, far exceeding that generated for any peak before or since. But it was in the mountains I discovered I could overcome my fears, survive in the face of adversity, and sometimes—as on K2—rise above my many limitations and accomplish a great objective.

I regret that by trying to balance my roles as climber, lawyer, father, and husband, I excelled at none. I now recognize that my greatest accomplishments—if I can claim them as such—were achieved not as the result of my climbing, but rather in spite of it: a successful thirty-six-year marriage and five remarkable children.

Though I spent much of their childhood away on business and expeditions, as adults my children have been generous with their companionship. I deeply regret the cost my absence imposed on them when they were young. Some weathered my time away more easily than others; Anne, our oldest, suffered the most.

During high school Anne cut herself off from the family, deadened her feelings, and risked her safety in ways rebellious teenagers often do. At eighteen, she abruptly left home and moved across the country. When she finally returned four years later and finished college, I learned the role I had played in driving her away. She explained that my frequent absences left her feeling abandoned, while Mary Lou, busy caring for the younger kids, lacked the time to focus on what Anne needed. She and I finally forged a close relationship when she reached her late twenties.

Anne admits that certain aspects of her childhood, though dif-

ficult at the time, now seem valuable. For example, Mary Lou's insistence that the children had nothing to fear when I left on expeditions sometimes bothered her as a child. When people asked her, "Aren't you scared that your dad won't come home?" Anne always

*The entire Wickwire family at
Susie and Karl's wedding.
From left: Melissa, David, Cathy, Karl, Susie, Jim,
Mary Lou holding Emma, Bob, Anne, and Victor holding Ana.*

felt obliged to say no. Now, Anne realizes Mary Lou's strategy actually worked quite well. When I was gone, Anne missed me, but she never really worried about my safety. Like her mom, she felt confident I would come home. Fortunately, I always did.

Each of my kids was affected to some extent by my climbing, but all are quick to emphasize the benefits: the exposure to foreign cultures, the interesting houseguests, the trips they got to make while I was gone, the chance to spend a summer on the water, house-sitting for the Whittakers. They recall the time I took each child out for a special evening before I left for K2: dinner and a movie or a sporting event, just the two of us. These occasions were rare. I now realize how much I missed, how much we all missed.

After helping me prepare for many expeditions, all of our children have become highly organized themselves. As adults they are independent, resourceful, and self-sufficient. All are discerning and critical listeners—unlike their father. Their mother instilled the children with a strong sense of responsibility, to see the job that needs doing and do it. They seem to find it difficult to fail—perhaps inevitable with parents so exacting of themselves. Each has worked hard and achieved a lot.

A concierge at an upscale hotel, Anne lives in Seattle with her husband, Victor, a Peruvian businessman, and their twin daughters, Ana and Emma. Cathy, an architectural historian, also lives in Seattle, as do all our kids except for Susie, a foreign affairs officer with the State Department. Susie and her husband, Karl, a linguist from Ukraine, live in Washington, D.C., but her work on global climate issues takes her all over the world. David, who just graduated from the University of Texas law school, has returned to Seattle to work for a large law firm. His wife, Melissa, is studying to be a naturopathic physician. After stints with two major sports franchises, Bob works as an editor on Starwave's NBA Web site.

I am proud of what our children have accomplished and admire them for their intelligence, their sense of humor, and the way they interact. I'm awed by their sense of fairness and the sensitivity they show toward others. Most of all, I enjoy their company. The time I spend with my family now means more to me than anything else in my life.

Anne and Victor's twin daughters have proven to be a source of unexpected delight for me. Walking to a recent Huskies football game, my son Bob remarked, "Dad, since Ana and Emma were born, you've been a lot more laid-back and relaxed." He's right—although laid-back I'll probably never be.

My relationship with Mary Lou, once so patriarchal and traditional, has evolved into a different, more equal partnership. We continue to enthusiastically pursue our shared interests in opera, theater, book readings, and the symphony. In the past six years we have traveled together more than we did during the previous thirty. In addition to trips to the East Coast, England, and Ireland, we traveled to Peru with our three daughters and Victor. After visiting Victor's family in Lima we explored the Inca ruins at Machu Picchu and drove into the Cordillera Blanca, the main range of the Andes. From our rented villa we could see Huascarán, the second highest peak in South America. As I studied the mountain the first morning, Mary Lou remarked, "I suppose you're checking out your next climb."

Though Mary Lou downplays the impact my climbing has had on her, I know it has taken a toll. Observing that there was no point in complaining to me about my climbing, she explains, "If I had, you would have done it anyway." Mary Lou now concedes that certain aspects of my climbing bothered her: my preoccupation with an expedition months in advance and the intense relationships I had with certain climbing companions. She even admits being bored by my slide shows. Sometimes she felt like the wife of a baseball player, required to listen while he rehashed in excruciating detail every play of a game.

The time I spent away on expeditions forced Mary Lou to bear more than her fair share of responsibility for child rearing, and the risks I took required her to steel herself to the prospect of an early widowhood. Perhaps most of all, the self-centered and controlling aspects of my personality that led me to climb mountains inevitably

Mary Lou in Ireland.

trickled over into our home life and the way I treated her. But time has softened my edges and made me a little easier to live with.

I have always had faith in Mary Lou's character and devotion. That she continues to display a similar faith in me says more about her fidelity than my virtues, but makes me proud nonetheless. In retrospect I realize that Mary Lou was already grown-up when we met. She loved me in spite of my immaturity and stuck by me while I caught up.

I am still catching up.

GLOSSARY

avalanche cone: an accumulation of snow at the bottom of a mountain slope caused by frequent avalanches.

belay: a technique used to safeguard climbers who are roped together. The belaying climber, usually anchored to an ice screw, snow picket, piton, rock horn, or tree, belays his/her moving partner by paying out or taking in slack, ready to hold fast if the other slips.

bergschrund: a deep crevasse or series of crevasses at the head of a glacier where it meets a steeper slope above made of rock or ice. The upper lip of a bergschrund may be many feet above the lower lip depending on the steepness of the slope.

bivouac sack: an uninsulated nylon sack large enough for one or two climbers to crawl inside for protection from the wind. It is normally used in the event of an emergency when the climber is forced to spend a night away from a camp with tents.

buttress: a broad, steep mountain wall near the lower end of a ridge usually with rock exposed.

cache: a hiding place for goods, provisions, and other gear.

carabiner: an aluminum snap-link used to attach two other items to each other: rope, anchor, climber's harness, sling, etc.

central rib: a steep ridge that rises up a mountainside toward the summit.

cerebral edema: an altitude-induced accumulation of fluid in the brain, which can be fatal to a climber unless he or she descends quickly. Certain drugs help prevent the onset of cerebral edema or reduce or eliminate the condition once it occurs.

cornice: an overhang of snow along the crest of a ridge formed by wind.

couloir: a steep gully on a mountainside.

crampons: steel spikes fixed on a frame that is attached to the climber's boots to prevent slipping on ice or hard snow. Crampons have ten to twelve points usually, with two slanted forward.

crevasse: a split in the surface of glacier ice caused by the changing direction of the glacier or a change in the angle of the slope over which the ice stream flows. The most dangerous crevasses are those concealed by a thin crust of snow on the glacier surface.

force-breathing: a breathing method believed to help climbers adapt to high altitude as they climb up. Inhalation is normal, but exhalation is forced to blow off excess carbon dioxide.

front points: the two points on a crampon that are slanted forward. When kicked into steep ice, they hold the climber's foot to the slope.

gaiter: a zippered sheath of insulated cloth that covers the ankles and lower legs of a climber so that snow will not get in over the top of boots.

hypothermia: the condition of having a body temperature substantially below normal, which can be caused by exposure to extreme cold or moisture. Unless warming occurs promptly, hypothermia can be fatal.

ice ax: a tool for cutting and scraping steps in hard snow or ice and for supporting the climber as a slope or glacier is ascended or descended. It consists of a steel blade and pick in one piece mounted on one end of an aluminum shaft with a sharp pick at the other end.

ice cliff: a steep or overhanging wall of ice formed when ice accumulates above a steep slope that cannot support its weight.

ice hammer: a specialized tool for steep ice climbing—shorter than an ice ax—that provides additional support for the climber.

ice screw: tubular metal device with a sharp end that is twisted into ice to provide an anchor.

jug-handle hold: a colloquial name for large rock-climbing holds of all descriptions.

jumars: a pair of mechanical devices that when attached to a fixed rope (itself attached to an anchor or another climber) allow the climber to ascend—or descend—the rope while standing in nylon slings. A third sling from the climber's waist to one of the jumars provides added support.

lead: the rope length between a belaying climber (below) and the climber being belayed (above), usually 150 feet.

picket: an aluminum stake two to three feet long that is used as an anchor when driven into snow.

pinnacle: a slender tower of rock tapering at the top.

pitch: a short segment of climbing, usually one rope length in distance.

piton: a spike driven into a crack in rock. A ring at the outer end permits a rope to be attached for protection.

pulmonary edema: an altitude-induced accumulation of fluid in the lungs, which can be fatal to a climber unless he or she descends quickly. Certain drugs help prevent the onset of pulmonary edema or reduce or eliminate the condition once it occurs.

rappel: a method of descending over steep rocks, snow, or ice by sliding down a fixed single or doubled rope. Traditionally, the rope is passed under one leg, across the body, and over the opposite shoulder. Most climbers now use a variety of mechanical devices enabling the climber to slow down or stop his/her downward movement.

rock headwall: a steep cliff usually at the top of a gully or mountain face.

scree: an accumulation of stones or rocky debris lying on a slope or at the base of a mountain or in a gully.

serac: a detached section of a glacier that often collapses. The instability of these small towers makes them dangerous to climb beneath.

sling: nylon loop in which the climber can stand while ascending or descending a rope attached to an anchor.

wand: a thin stick, often bamboo, with a slip of colored paper at one end. Used to mark a trail in the snow.

CHRONOLOGY

Date	Event	Chapter
1940	Jim Wickwire born, Wenatchee, Washington.	2
1960	Starts climbing.	2
1962	Marries Mary Lou.	2
1963	Minnehaha rock climb.	2
1964	Anne Wickwire born.	2
1965	Cathy Wickwire born.	2
1967	Graduates from law school.	2
	Susie Wickwire born.	
	Starts working for Sen. Henry M. Jackson.	
1968	Bob Wickwire born.	2
	Family moves to Seattle.	
	Starts work for Davis Wright.	

1969	David Wickwire born.	2
1971	Mt. Rainier's Willis Wall with Ed Boulton.	2
1972	First expedition to Mt. McKinley. Team: Rob Schaller, Leif Patterson, Alex Bertulis, Charlie Raymond, and Tom Stewart.	2
1975	First K2 expedition. Leader: Jim Whittaker. Team members: Lou Whittaker, Dianne Roberts, Fred Dunham, Fred Stanley, Rob Schaller, Steve Marts, Galen Rowell, and Leif Patterson.	3
1976	Establishes law firm with Yale Lewis, Chuck Goldmark, John Dystel, and Jon Schorr.	2
	Solo attempt of Mt. McKinley.	3
	Leif Patterson and son Tor climb in British Columbia.	4
1977	Fairweather Range expedition with Dusan Jagersky, Al Givler, and Steve Marts.	4
1978	Mt. McKinley attempt with Stim Bullitt and Bill Sumner.	4
	Second K2 expedition. Leader: Jim Whittaker. Team: John Roskelley, Rick Ridgeway, Lou Reichardt, Cherie Bech, Terry Bech, Chris Chandler, Diana Jagersky, Skip Edmonds, Rob Schaller, Bill Sumner, Craig Anderson, and Dianne Roberts.	5
1980	Mt. McKinley attempt with Stim Bullitt.	5

LIST OF ILLUSTRATIONS AND CREDITS

All photographs by Jim Wickwire (or in his collection with control of rights) unless otherwise indicated.

Chapter 1   Crevasse

Chapter 2   First Steps

Chapter 3   Discord on K2

Chapter 6 Good Times

Chapter 7 Marty

Chapter 13 Two on Everest

Chapter 14 Looking Ahead

ACKNOWLEDGMENTS

everal of our friends and relatives were exceptionally generous with their time, energy, and expertise in providing us
with a careful and rigorous review of various draft chapters,
and in several instances, the entire manuscript. Their contri-
butions ranged from valuable observations about the book's
structure to precise line-by-line editing. For this counsel, encouragement, and assistance we are deeply grateful to Susie Nix,
Nancy Antonelli, Tom Orton, Kay Bullitt, Jim Hailey, Fred
Nemo, Karin Welch, Charles Seluzicki, Conrad Wesselhoeft,
Judith Pierce, Bob Bowen, Tom Brewer, Larry Piersol, Ros Ghan,
Curt Ghan, Mike Wickwire, Bagley Wright, Mark Wessel, Signa
Treat, Cindy Weilminster, and Amber Schlag. We also thank
Amber for her logistical support throughout the entire process.

This book is graced with the work of several exceptional
photographers, most of whom were expedition teammates, and
who were generous in allowing the use of their photographs.
They include Dianne Roberts, John Roskelley, Galen Rowell,
Rob Schaller, Stephen Venables, Phil Ershler, Carolyn Gunn,
Craig Anderson, Dick Bass, Greg Child, Jeff Haley, Misty Haley,

and Chris Maier. Thanks also to Joe Blackburn for his consultation on photography issues and to Diana Jagersky Crist for the dust-jacket use of the stunning photograph her late husband, Dusan Jagersky, took on Mt. Hood's Yocum Ridge.

Finally, we want to thank our agent, Jane Dystel, and our Pocket Books editor, Mitchell Ivers, for their faith in our book and their excellent advice. They, along with Jane's colleague Miriam Goderich, our copy editor, Steve Boldt, and our composition and layout designer, Robert Engle, made publishing a great experience.

Seattle, 1998
Jim Wickwire
Dorothy Bullitt

INDEX

ABOUT THE AUTHORS

Jim Wickwire is a partner in the law firm of
Wickwire, Greene, Crosby, Brewer & Seward.
He lives in Seattle with his wife,
and has five children and twin granddaughters.

Dorothy Bullitt is the author of
FILLING THE VOID: Six Steps from Loss to Fulfillment.
She lives with her husband in Seattle.